Twayne's United States Authors Series

Sylvia E. Bowman, *Editor*

INDIANA UNIVERSITY

William Dean Howells

WILLIAM DEAN HOWELLS

by CLARA M. KIRK

and

RUDOLF KIRK

Rutgers University

(TUSAS) 16

Twayne Publishers, Inc.   ::   New York

813

TO
SUE AND DONALD
WITH LOVE

Preface

WILLIAM DEAN HOWELLS, Mark Twain, and Henry James form a triangle, the base of which shifts from decade to decade according to the taste of the period. Does Mark Twain's *Huckleberry Finn* stand at the very foundation of our contemporary taste for the natural and the native? Is Henry James the creator of the symbolic impressionism of a later day? Certainly, in his own generation hardly a reader in this country or abroad would have hesitated to say that the writing of William Dean Howells established the line which directed the important post-Civil War writing in this country and that he—in a deeper sense than either of his contemporaries—helped form the taste of the rapidly expanding nation between 1865 and 1900.

Mark Twain was our first important writer to be born west of the Mississippi; Henry James, of Albany, New York, spent most of his youth in Europe; Howells, growing up neither in a frontier settlement nor in an eastern city, achieved a remarkably literary education in the various Ohio towns to which his father, as country editor and printer, moved the family.

A few years younger than Twain and a few years older than James, Howells welcomed both of them in the office of the *Atlantic Monthly,* where he was an editor, while both of these men were relatively unknown. Author of several popular books of travels and novels as well as innumerable sketches, Howells was the sensitive and generous critic who recognized with uncanny immediacy the signs of true genius and unhesitatingly gave his support to these two gifted writers. Moreover, he became the lifelong friend of both Twain and James (neither of whom could endure the writing of the other), and he outlived them both. At the death of Twain in 1910, Howells wrote *My Mark Twain,* a critical appraisal which has never been surpassed; at the time of his own death in 1920 he was working on an essay about Henry James, which, though never finished, was a fitting conclusion to the many essays and reviews of the books of his younger friend that he had published during the preceding fifty years.

Both Twain and James would have agreed that Howells guided their development as writers, though they themselves differed so widely from each other. Twain, in his stories, explored the unlimited territory of frontier experience while James, in his novels, treated the equally unlimited area of European-American relationships. Howells, in his "fictioning," looked in both directions, toward the West and toward the East; but he maintained, meanwhile, his central position—that of recorder of "commonplace" American life.

The Howells' "shelf," containing over forty carefully-wrought narratives, is, then, a monumental record of life as it was in this country between 1870 and 1920. Though an editor during his entire career, first associated with the *Atlantic* and later with *Harper's,* Howells not only turned out an unceasing stream of novels, but also a flood of plays, critical essays, poetry, travel books, editorial comment, and sketches, all of a remarkably high literary standard. Howells was far more attuned to the thoughts and feelings of the wide circle of the American middle class and to the growing population of magazine readers extending from coast to coast than either of his famous contemporaries. As Henry Adams once remarked, were all our reminders of the 1870's lost to us, we could reconstruct the age from the novels of Howells. To grasp the intent and meaning of Howells' novels, one must also consider his expression as a poet, dramatist, and critic, for they are all subtly interrelated.

In the following chapters we shall attempt to study Howells in the *time* and *place* in which he was writing, hoping thus to recapture something of the originality, ironic humor, and poetic sensitivity of this writer whose voice, listened to and heeded by thousands in his own generation, has sometimes failed to carry over the tumult of two world wars. Howells' writing, perhaps more than that of most novelists, reflects the events and circumstances of his own life, not infrequently "remembered in tranquility" years later. We shall consider, then, the various "problems" discussed by critics today—Howells' social philosophy, his attitude toward sex, his religious allegiance, the meaning he gave to the term *realism,* his attack on the British novel, his relationship to Twain and James—relying not so much on the Howells scholarship that has appeared in the last two decades as on Howells' own discussions of these questions in his voluminous writing, not only as a novelist, but also as a critic, editor, dramatist, poet, and letter writer. Only by considering his writing in relation to his own life can we hope to avoid a stereotype analysis of the thought of another generation in terms of our own.

To discover Howells the novelist, we must turn to his work in many fields. As the editor of the "Easy Chair" observed in one of his last contributions to *Harper's Monthly,* "Every author tells himself in his work if his work is inventive"; this novelist "tells himself " in his "work" which extends to well over a hundred volumes. Because of the very extent of Howells' writing, all we can attempt in the following book is to study again the massive bulk of his writing, and to "place" him as a novelist in the matrix of his extensive literary production.

Though this study is based on a rereading of Howells' writing, both published and unpublished, we realize that our views over the last twenty years have been widened and clarified by the books and articles of scores of Howells scholars. To these men and women we are deeply indebted; since we cannot express our sense of obligation individually, we thank them now collectively. Howells' novels are constantly appearing on book lists, edited by such astute scholars as George Arms, William M. Gibson, Edwin Cady, and Howard Mumford Jones. Comment by Richard Chase in *The American Novel and Its Tradition* (1957), and Lionel Trilling in "W. D. Howells and The Roots of Modern Taste" (*Partisan Review,* XVII, Sept.-Oct. 1951) direct our thoughts to new aspects of Howells. Critical biographies by Everett Carter, Edwin Cady, Olov W. Fryckstedt, and Van Wyck Brooks cast light on the extraordinarily complex life of one of our central literary figures.

We wish here to express our special appreciation to several persons and institutions that have aided us by criticism and material help. First of all, the Rutgers Research Council has encouraged our studies by substantial grants for summer trips to important collections. The Rutgers University Library has given us every service, including the use of a choice "study" overlooking the Raritan River, which Howells himself would have appreciated. The Harvard College Library, the Princeton University Library, the New York Public Library, and the Library of Congress have allowed us to use their enormous resources. Mrs. Elizabeth R. Martin of The Ohio Archaelogical and Historical Society, Columbus, Ohio, and Mr. W. P. Marchman, of the Hayes Memorial Library, Fremont, Ohio, went out of their way to help us. To all of these individuals and institutions we give our thanks. Professor W. W. Howells has kindly given us permission to quote from the letters and published works of his grandfather, and to him we are most grateful.

CLARA M. KIRK
RUDOLF KIRK

Rutgers University
July 27, 1961

Contents

Chronology

1837   March 1, Howells born, Martin's Ferry, Belmont County, Ohio.

1846   Howells already setting type on his father's paper.

1851   Became compositor on *Ohio State Journal*.

1852   Howells' father moved his family to Ashtabula in order to take editorship of *Sentinel*; moved a few months later to Jefferson, where *Sentinel* remains to this day. Howells contributed to family paper for many years.

1855   Howells contributing to *Sentinel, Ohio Farmer, Ohio State Journal, National Era,* and other papers.

1857   Lived in Columbus and became correspondent for Cincinnati *Gazette*.

1858   Reporter, news editor, and editorial writer for *Ohio State Journal*.

1860   Contributed to *Atlantic Monthly, Saturday Press,* and Cincinnati *Dial*. Published (with J. J. Piatt) first book, *Poems of Two Friends*. Wrote campaign *Life of Lincoln*.

1861   Appointed consul to Venice.

1862   Married in Paris to Elinor Gertrude Mead, of Brattleboro, Vermont.

1863   Published letters in Boston *Advertiser*.

1864   Began contributing to *North American Review*.

1865   Returned to United States; began writing for New York *Times, Round Table,* and *Nation*.

1866   Assistant editor of *Atlantic Monthly*. *Venetian Life* published.

1867   *Italian Journeys*. Harvard gave Howells M.A.

1869   *No Love Lost: A Romance of Travel*. University Lecturer at Harvard, 1869-1871.

1871   Editor-in-chief of *Atlantic Monthly*. *Suburban Sketches*.

1872   *Their Wedding Journey.*

1873   *A Chance Acquaintance; Poems.*

1875   *A Foregone Conclusion.*

1876   *The Parlor Car.*

1877   *Out of the Question; A Counterfeit Presentment.*

1879   *The Lady of the Aroostook.*

1880   *The Undiscovered Country.*

1881   Resigned editorship of *Atlantic. Doctor Breen's Practice; A Fearful Responsibility and Other Stories.*

1882   Trip to Europe. Offered professorship at The Johns Hopkins University. *A Modern Instance.*

1883   Returned from Europe. *A Woman's Reason.*

1884   *Three Villages; Niagara Revisited.*

1885   *The Rise of Silas Lapham.*

1886   Began "Editor's Study" in *Harper's.* Refused Smith professorship at Harvard. *Indian Summer; Tuscan Cities.*

1887   Letter to New York *Tribune* asking clemency for the Chicago Anarchists. *The Minister's Charge; Modern Italian Poets.* Began contributing to *Harper's Weekly.*

1888   Moved to New York. *April Hopes.*

1889   Death of Winifred Howells. *Annie Kilburn.* Moved back to Boston.

1890   *A Hazard of New Fortunes; The Shadow of a Dream; A Boy's Town.*

1891   *Criticism and Fiction.* Returned to New York.

1892   Resigned from "Editor's Study." Co-editor of *Cosmopolitan* for four months. *An Imperative Duty; The Quality of Mercy.*

1893   *The World of Chance; The Coast of Bohemia.*

1894   *A Traveler from Altruria.*

1895   *My Literary Passions; Stops of Various Quills.* Began regular contributions to *Harper's Weekly.*

1897   *The Landlord at Lion's Head.*

1898   Contributing to *Literature,* a Harper publication. *The Story of a Play.*

1899 *Their Silver Wedding Journey.*

1900 Began "Editor's Easy Chair" for *Harper's. Literary Friends and Acquaintance.*

1901 Received Litt. D. from Yale. *Heroines of Fiction.*

1902 *The Kentons.*

1904 Received Litt. D. from Oxford. *The Son of Royal Langbrith.*

1905 Received Litt. D. from Columbia. *Miss Bellard's Inspiration.*

1906 *Certain Delightful English Towns; London Films.*

1907 *Through the Eye of the Needle.*

1908 Elected first president of the American Academy of Arts and Letters. *Roman Holidays and Others.*

1910 Mrs. Howells died. *My Mark Twain. Imaginary Interviews.*

1911 Library Edition of the Writings of W. D. Howells. *Parting Friends.*

1912 Received L. H. D. from Princeton. Seventy-fifth Birthday Dinner.

1913 *New Leaf Mills.*

1915 Awarded gold medal for fiction by Academy of Arts and Letters.

1916 *The Leatherwood God; Years of My Youth.*

1920 May 11, died in New York City. *The Vacation of the Kelwyns.*

CHAPTER 1

From Ohio to Venice

I *Village Limits*

A VISITOR TO Jefferson, Ohio, is able to recapture even today something of a sense of the leisurely county seat to which William Cooper Howells, as co-owner and editor of the Ashtabula *Sentinel,* moved his family in 1852. One can, in fact, drive through tree-lined streets to the printing office, built by the elder Howells, where his two sons, Joseph and William Dean, helped set type and edit the paper for many years thereafter. With the proceeds of this family business the Howellses were able to build and maintain their own home not many blocks from the printing office, and this, too, one may visit and re-imagine, if one can, the life of the family over a hundred years ago. This home, the only one actually owned by the Howellses—except for the two-room brick structure in Martin's Ferry where William Dean was born March 1, 1837—remained the family center long after the second son had achieved fame in his own country and abroad. Howells was fifteen when his hard-working family moved to Jefferson, and here he shared its fortunes for the next five years until he was ready to launch himself independently as correspondent for the Cincinnati *Gazette.*

By the time the Howellses settled in Jefferson, the two older sons had already for many years helped their father in the struggle and anxiety of "the long adversity" of his efforts as a printer, reporter, and editor in various Ohio towns. Though Joseph, four years older than William Dean, had assumed the heavier load, his younger brother had from the age of seven set the type and delivered the papers edited by his father. The boys, when they reached Jefferson, shared two ideals: one, to live in a village rather than in the country or in a city; the other, to renounce "the printing-business in every form" for all time, for they had been asked to give too much of their youth to toilsome labor. Village life they achieved in such rich abundance that neither ever after lost its imprint; neither of the brothers, however, succeeded in escaping the printing business, though Joseph attempted for a time to fulfill his ambition to become a river pilot and William Dean actually achieved his literary ideals and became for most of his countrymen their "foremost American writer." He remained, however, acutely aware of the "printing business" all of his life.

How demanding these literary aspirations were for the small, barefoot son of the village printer is made movingly clear in an autobiographical account of these years, *My Literary Passions* (1895), written when "the boy" was nearly sixty years old and an established leader in the literary world of New York and London. As a child in Ohio, he wrote (147) "literature, not life, was my aim, and to reproduce it was my joy and my pride." However, several earlier acounts of these Ohio days make it quite evident that "life," too, was fervently felt by the second of the five Howells boys who enjoyed fishing, ice skating, and swimming with the villagers in spite of a persistent tendency to conceal himself in the apple tree with a book. In *A Boy's Town* (1890), for example, Howells pictures the daily round in the small southwestern Ohio town of Hamilton before the Civil War as truly as Mark Twain describes the life in Hannibal, Missouri.

William Cooper Howells had moved his family to Hamilton when William was three years old; and there the father became editor of the *Intelligencer,* a Whig paper which he controlled until 1849, when he bought the Dayton *Transcript* and brought to a close the happiest period of his son's boyhood. The move to Dayton also ended Howells' formal education; school, however, had never been so important to him as the education he received in the large, warm kitchen at home. There the father read aloud from Irving's *Conquest of Granada* or from the poetry of Scott and Moore, while the mother, also a lover of poetry, sat by the table with her sewing basket, and the children lay on the floor. "I was always reading when I was not playing," wrote Howells, looking back at this period in *Years of My Youth* (1916). His education was also furthered by his industrious setting of type for his father—"The Country Printer" whom he later described in an essay of that title written for *Scribner's* (May, 1893)—and by his association with a wide assortment of typesetters, editors, and printer's devils who called their small fellow worker "the old man."

When the Dayton enterprise failed, William Cooper in 1850 established the family in a log cabin by a little stream and near Xenia, Greene County, where, with his brothers, he hoped in time to retrieve his fortunes by rebuilding an old paper mill. This enterprise also failed after a brief trial; but Howells' account of it in *My Year in a Log Cabin* (1893)—later incorporated into *Years of my Youth*—makes one realize that his gifted, unsuccessful father redeemed the harshness of a winter in a primeval forest by reading aloud before the roaring fire, not only from the literary classics but also from the religious writings of Swedenborg, *The Heavenly Arcana* and *The Book of Worship*. Snow drifted softly through the roof of the loft where the boys slept, but discomforts were forgotten when William discovered a barrel of old books—among them was Longfellow's *Spanish Student*, which inspired him to attack again the old Spanish grammar the father had brought from a soldier of the Mexican War.

By the end of the year, the elder Howells had become clerk of the House of the Ohio Legislature at ten dollars a week, and had installed his family in a small, rented house in Columbus for which he paid ten dollars a month. With the help of the three dollars a week earned by Joseph and with the contribution of four dollars weekly from William, now a compositor on the *Ohio State Journal*, the family managed to survive until the father obtained a more lucrative position as editor of the Ashtabula *Sentinel* in 1852. After six months in bustling, commercial Ashtabula, the office of the *Sentinel* was moved to Jefferson, where the long odyssey of the Howells family ended. For here William Cooper was at last successful in establishing a home and business, and here the family remained long after the father's death in 1896.

Howells, in a way characteristic of him as a writer, brought together in 1916 the chapters or parts of chapters from his varied autobiographical studies and turned them into a composite picture of the formative years which produced the man of letters. Although Howells was seventy-nine when he composed *Years of My Youth*, his memory was still stirred by visions of life "In an Old-time State Capital." Under this title he wrote a series of essays for *Harper's Monthly* in 1914, and he then used them to form chapters of this final picture of his youth. So rich to the ageing novelist was this process of remembering that two novels, *New Leaf Mills* (1913) and *The Leatherwood God* (1916), flowed from his pen in this decade; both of them give us pictures of the simple—and sometimes primitive—life in the remote areas of Ohio, when the state still retained many characteristics of the frontier.

Howells himself, then, in his autobiographical studies from *A Boy's Town* to *Years of My Youth* presents copious material on the place the printing office occupied in the village life of the Western Reserve community before the Civil War, and on the daily experience of the boy who worked there for long hours. During these years Howells transmuted his experiences into soaring literary ambitions that were already beginning to be partially realized. For the boy's leisure was given either to cultivating a "thankless muse" in imitation of the verses of Pope and Goldsmith, or to devouring with greedy eagerness Cervantes' *Don Quixote*, the essays of Macaulay, or the novels of Dickens. Tramping back and forth between the printing office and home, his father talked philosophy and poetry with him as though to a contemporary—a habit which sometimes made it difficult for the elder Howells to mete out even-handed justice when the eight children fell to quarrelling on the kitchen floor.

But for William the pursuit of his "literary ideals" when he returned home in the evening was paramount. So intensely literary was this boy almost from his infancy that it seemed only natural to himself and his family that he should have formed by fifteen a definite ambition to "conquer" in the world of literature. In a little curtained-off alcove William arranged for himself under the staircase of his home, he was studying four or five languages "blindly and blunderingly enough"; he was also attempting many experiments both in poetry and in prose which he seldom finished; and he was "reading, reading, reading, right and left, hither and yon," wherever an author tempted him. After a day of the printing press he, often fruitlessly, labored far into the night over his own writing or over the writing of the poet or novelist into whose world he was peering with an intensity of sympathy which led to a morbid state verging on a breakdown. A "cloud of misery" settled over his mind, which he was able to dispel only after an idle summer in the woods and fields around the village.

As soon as his "nerves" had resumed their tone, William renewed his struggle with languages, this time with the aid of the "sixteen-bladed grammar" which somehow came into his hands. From this collection of literal translations from Latin, Italian,

French, Spanish, and Portuguese, Howells hacked out a knowledge of five foreign languages, which, inaccurate as it was,
enabled him for the rest of his long life to read other literatures
in their original tongues and to converse with writers from many
countries. Though his father had written an English grammar in
his youth, he now offered his son, in whom he had the utmost
confidence, no help of any sort in his bout with languages. He
guided the boy's taste in literature, however, by supplying him
with the best of the English classics, by reading aloud to the
family in the evenings, by warning William against slavish imitation in his own writing, and, finally, by telling his gifted son
that he regarded him as different from other boys.

Howells had in his hand, when he wrote *Years of My Youth*,
a diary, now lost, which he began in the closing months of 1851,
not so much to account for his days or to list the books he was
reading, as to imitate the style of the authors then filling his
mind: Thackeray, Dickens, Scott, Ossian, Heine, and DeQuincy.
Howells, sixty years later, turned these yellowed, foolscap pages
and reflected on the fact that there was scarcely an error in
spelling or punctuation in these consciously imitative descriptions
of the boy's daily life, which were interspersed on every sheet
with exercises in the Spanish he was struggling to learn. The
older man also observed, somewhat sadly, that the writer of the
diary had not known any boys except those in the printing office;
and even those he knew only "in a shrinking sort, not venturing
to take part, except once, in their wild hilarity"—he hardly, in
fact, had known their names. His chief companion had been his
printer-father, who had supplied him with books and had encouraged his versifying.

Indeed the very first item to be listed in the long chronology of
Howells' writing is a poem, "Old Winter, Loose Thy Hold On
Us," which the father in his pride, sent without consulting his
son to the *Ohio State Journal*. William discovered it in print
with mingled dismay and joy; but only joy was confided to his
diary when he found his verses "copied into a New York paper,
and also in the Cincinnati *Commercial*. I mean the piece on
Winter." One evening the father brought home with him an editor
from a nearby town, to whom he showed some of the poetry and
sketches of his son. After that visit, father and son with difficulty
hid their pleasure from each other when they found the piece of
poetry or prose reprinted in the columns of the *Ohio Farmer*.
Under the assumed name of "Will Narlie," one may find such

titles as "The Autumn Land," "The Caged Robin," "Midnight Rain," not only in the *Ohio Farmer,* but also in the *Ohio State Journal,* the *Casket,* the *National Era,* the *Saturday Press,* the Cincinnati *Dial,* and, finally, in 1860, in the *Atlantic Monthly* itself.

Into the family paper, the Ashtabula *Sentinel,* the young type-setter was constantly slipping sketches, stories, poems, and, on one occasion, a serial romance which he was unable to bring to a close without hurrying the heroine to "an untimely death." Not even his father could bring comfort to the author in this "strange disaster." Though Howells filled his spare time with translating from Spanish, as well as with writing stories and tales, essays, and sketches, it was to poetry that he most fervently gave him-self in the winter of 1851-52. At this time the lonely boy met another young printer, John James Piatt, who cherished literary ambition; and with him in 1860 he produced his first book, *Poems of Two Friends.* Most of their collaboration was carried on by letters, before they met in Columbus, Ohio, where they both worked as compositors for the *Ohio State Journal* just before the Howells family moved to Jefferson.

When William Cooper Howells became editor of the Ashtabula *Sentinel,* the county seat of Jefferson was a village of farmers, dairymen, and lumberers who, with their portable steam saw-mills, were busily cutting down the primeval forest which surrounded the little village. Payment for the semi-weekly news-paper was made in farm and dairy produce or in wood to fill the huge stove in the wide, low room which served at the same time as editorial, composing, and pressroom. Not infrequently these subscribers lingered after delivering their payments to dis-cuss politics with their Freesoil editor, who, with the vast majority of his readers, believed that slavery would come to an end if kept out of the new territories.

But brightly as the fire burned in the hungry stove and lively as the discussion grew, neither could soften the wintry cold of that rough, fierce region of northern Ohio, and William's fingers and toes were frequently numb as he bent over his case and listened to the talk that flew about the room. The day the paper came out, the printing office, splotched with ink and littered with newspapers as it usually was, became a civic and social center of the village. The girls of the community (lured by curiosity, rather than interest in politics) flocked in and made the dreary room—wrote Howells in *Years of My Youth* (84-85)—

"like a scene of comic opera, with their pretty dresses and faces, their eager chatter and lively energy in folding the papers and addressing them to the subscribers," while the men, "like the bassos and baritones and tenors of the chorus, stood about and looked on with faintly sarcastic faces."

No doubt the editor at his table was less responsive to these comic-opera scenes than was his son, for William Cooper Howells was a conscientious journalist who addressed himself seriously to the minds and tastes of his readers in this Western Reserve community of the 1850's. Most of these hard-working, plain-speaking men and women who had migrated from New England had brought with them not only abolitionist political views but also a remarkable supply of literary taste and knowledge. The printers themselves were often joined by the village wits who, with their backs to the stove, liked to dispute about such authors as Holmes, Irving, Byron, Poe, and especially Shakespeare. Religion, as well as politics and literature, entered the conversation, for the editor was tolerant of all views if expressed with proper reverence.

Interested as William Cooper was in the literary ventures of his son, his chief concern at this time and for several years thereafter was in producing a paper which would pay for the printing office and the home, both of which were mortgaged. Fortunately for William, a young printer, who is known both in *My Literary Passions* and *Years of My Youth* merely as "J.W." (Jim Williams), made his home with the Howellses from 1853 to 1856. "J.W." entered fully into the spirit of the Howells household, but was recognized as the particular friend of William both in study and in fun. He became the boy's "boon companion" in the study and reading aloud of Cervantes and Shakespeare and in the "self-conducted inquiries" into Latin, Greek, German, and Spanish; with French, William Dean had already become familiar. Without an accurate knowledge of grammar, which, indeed, he never attained, Howells began at once to imitate the literary forms of the authors he was reading and to acquaint himself with the literary histories of their countries.

Everybody in the village of Jefferson except himself, it seemed to Howells in retrospect, either played a musical instrument or sang. "J.W.'s" tenor voice not only shared in the summer serenades under the moon "which was then always full," but also led the apprentice girls and boys in the songs that filled the printing office every afternoon when the compositors were distributing their cases of type. Much as the eighteen-year-old Howells admired the social prowess of his older friend, he could not himself enter freely into "the living world" around him; his very ambition was a barrier between this shy and literary boy and the sleigh rides, the dances at the taverns, the meetings of the newly-formed Lyceum, and the frolics at the Country Fair.

The qualities which separated Howells from many village pleasures, however, admitted him to others. The misanthropic Englishman, William Goodrich, for instance, who played the organ in the little Episcopal Church, and the Yankee schoolteacher Wadsworth lavished books on William and engaged him and each other in heated arguments as to the relative merits of Dickens and Thackeray, Pope and Gray. The young people, too, "with their unlimited social freedom," read and discussed books together and followed the pirated English serials or the latest American works as they appeared in the magazines. Animated discussions about literature and religion—or the latest theories of mesmerism—made winter evenings in some village houses pass as rapidly as games and frolics did in others.

Charming as these village pleasures appeared to Howells—especially when as a novelist he saw in them "the potential stuff of such fiction as has never yet been written"—he became impatient of the village and began to look toward a larger, independent life. For a month during the summer of 1856 he studied law in the office of United States Senator Benjamin Wade, who for many years had fought the pro-slavery forces in Congress. Without attempting to explain his reasons, the young aspirant left the old lawyer's office to return to his father's printing press where he was always welcomed and never questioned.

Indeed, William's labor as a journeyman compositor could hardly be spared until the family should find itself on firmer financial ground. Though a prosperous farmer in the neighborhood had offered to be one of three or four others willing to pay for a Harvard education for this gifted son, who was the pride of the village, the suggestion was, after a family council, quietly dismissed. Howells records in *Years of My Youth* (110) that he did not then question the decision, nor did it seem to him "an unjust hardship" that he could not even be sent to an academy near by; to his older brother, however, it seemed that "an irreparable wrong" had been done him to which Joseph looked back in later years "with poignant regret." Howells, too, came to deplore his "want of schooling" and to do what he could the rest of his life "to repair the defect of instruction" occasioned by family necessity. In later years, when "three supreme invitations," as well as several lesser ones, to become a college professor came his way, he refused them all, for he knew better than any one else "the ignorance [he] had hidden so long, and [he] forbore to risk a middling novelist on the chance of his turning out a poor professor, or none." These decisions came after sleepless nights, he confessed, "of longing and fearing"; and, after each decision, he rejoiced "with the breathless gratitude . . . of one who has withheld himself from a step over the brink of a precipice."

The family newspaper was finally "free and clear" in 1854 and so was the home; but Howells could never remember just when the family ceased to struggle under the burden of poverty. Joseph Howells soon assumed the editorship of the Ashtabula *Sentinel*, which he, in turn, passed on to his son. William returned to this peaceful home, where his parents passed a serene old age, many times during the years he was moving from success to success. But the hardships, as well as the rewards, of those early days left a permanent mark on Howells. Looking back on the years of his youth he concluded: "I think we denied ourselves too much, and that we paid far beyond its moral worth for the house we were buying" (115). The struggle of this closely united family, however, gave the boy a sense of the essential issues of human life which were never absent from his understanding of the meaning of "realism"; these early scenes supplied the novelist with the "potential stuff" of fiction even at the time when he was struggling to carry his share of the family burdens, and solacing himself with the poetry of Pope.

II *The Reporter in Columbus*

Besides the practical problems which absorbed the attention of the elder Howells as publisher of the Ashtabula *Sentinel*, there were those of an editorial nature, which, for William Cooper, meant preventing, as far as he could, the spread of slavery into the territories. Interested as he was in literature, concerned as he was with problems of religion, he grew at this time more and more absorbed in the struggle to stay the pro-slavery aggression which he saw rising on all sides. Politics became his "main worldly interest," though, according to his son, he was not adept at practical politics. Conventions, nominations, certain individual leaders, fought-over measures—all these were discussed and argued by young and old in the printing office while the editor sat at the table at one side and penned his editorials. The burning issues of the day meant little to William as he patiently set his type and heard the discussion swirling about him; "I myself took no interest whatever in them," he wrote in *Years of My Youth* (119); "their realities did not concern me so much as the least unrealities of fiction."

When the father was again sent to the state Senate, this time as one of the House clerks early in 1856, he not infrequently left the newspaper to the "sole charge" of his son, without the least misgiving. At the age of eighteen Howells, though his heart was in the story or sketch or poem which he was musing upon even as he worked, was perfectly competent in his handling of all the practical problems which arise every day in a newspaper office; this dual capacity which marked him then explains in part the place he later came to occupy in the literary world of journalists and publishers, editors and novelists, critics and poets, artists and dramatists. That Howells was already becoming familiar with this cosmopolitan world is reflected in the frequent summaries of the contents of English periodicals, such as *Blackwood's* and *The Edinburgh Review,* which found their way into the *Sentinel.*

Howells' competence in reporting and reviewing, rather than his verses in imitation of Heine, enabled him in 1857 to escape "the village limits" of Jefferson and to set out with his father and his older sister Victoria for Columbus. Though Howells professed to be somewhat unmindful of the political issues of the Ohio Legislature, he nevertheless put together in the form of a daily letter the material about the legislative proceedings supplied by his father. "The letters at once found favor with the editors" of the Cincinnati *Gazette* and the *Ohio State Journal,* and the elder Howells soon withdrew from the work, leaving the whole undertaking to his son.

To Howells and his sister, nothing "grander or gayer" could be dreamed of than a winter in the Goodale House across the street from the State House. On the advice of a friend, he learned to dance and spent all that he could afford to improve his wardrobe. For Howells and his sister during the long winter months in Jefferson had shared "impossible dreams of that great world of wealth, of fashion, of haughtily and dazzlingly, blindingly brilliant society, which we did not inconveniently consider we were altogether unfit for." Together they had gazed wistfully at the romantic illustration on the cover of a piece of sheet music and wondered "whether it would ever be our high fortune to mingle with a company of such superbly caparisoned people as we saw pictured there, playing and singing and listening."

Howells' social experience, however, during that first winter in Columbus was largely confined to the Saturday night hops at the hotel and to "the generalized hospitality" of the large receptions given the legislature (including the correspondents and reporters) by the leading citizens of the town. Great suppers of oysters, ice cream, and, occasionally, champagne were "world" enough for the village compositor until he "began to divine that these occasions were not of the first fashion." However, there was dancing on some of the dignified old mansions, and when the drawing rooms were not sufficiently large for the quadrilles and waltzes, wooded pavilions were constructed in the gardens. On one of these evenings, "amidst the dancing and the feeding and smoking," the young reporter found a corner where he could write out his letter for the Cincinnati *Gazette*, giving it "satirically poetic touches from Heine and bits of worldly glitter from Thackeray."[1]

This letter, and others like it, soon brought an offer to the astonished correspondent to become a subordinate editor of the Cincinnati *Gazette*, at a salary twice as large as the one he was then receiving. Howells made the trip to that city and lived for a few weeks with the kindly, near-sighted editor, who invited him to share his dusty room. But he did not remain; he renounced the chance held out to him "by that university of the streets and police-stations, with its faculty of patrolmen and ward politicians and saloon-keepers." In later years, Howells regretted his timidity with the comment "I think that if I had been wiser than I was then I would have remained in the employ offered me, and learned in the school of reality the many lessons of human nature which it could have taught me."[2]

But Howells, when he made this decision, was a homesick youth, who ate alone in restaurants and "sadly amused" himself by listening to the waiters' orders called down a speaking-tube to the kitchen below or by watching with secret misgivings the women-clerks and shopgirls who frequented these restaurants. What would these "poor, blameless dears" have thought, he wondered later, had they known that the young man in the corner was censoring them for so boldly showing themselves in a public restaurant? Much less could Howells endure the "ravings of the drunken woman," which he heard one night in a police station where the "abhorred duties" took him for "the detestable news of the place." Howells then, as always, longed for "the cleanly respectabilities." Soon he was back in the printing office in Jefferson, with his books and his manuscripts to console him for the long hours of labor and his missed opportunity. But even while he was "eating [his] heart out" during that autumn of 1858, a call came to a place on the reorganized *Ohio State Journal*; he immediately responded with alacrity.[3]

Howells returned once more to the little metropolitan state capital, to the wide, shady streets, and to the pleasant brick houses set amid ample lawns. Now in his early twenties, he enjoyed not only "the thrilling light of evening parties that burst with the music of dancing from every window" of these mansions on summer evenings but also the glow of the winter fires before which he and like-minded young men and women "exchanged impressions of the books new and old that we had been reading." Tennyson and Thackeray, George Eliot and Dickens and Charles Reade—all of these authors were appearing serially in *Harper's Magazine* and in the *Atlantic*, and all were read and discussed month by month. In fact, the verses of Howells himself had begun to be seen in the *Atlantic*, the Cincinnati *Dial*, and the *Saturday Press*. Poetry kept the reporter in "a whirl of aesthetic emotion . . . at that tumultuous time." Before the year was out Howells had become unofficial literary editor of the *Ohio State Journal*. Just at Christmas in 1859, *Poems of Two Friends*, which Howells had written with John James Piatt, came from a press of Columbus, but one of the young poets, at least, was too proud to offer it to any of his friends, in his "haughty aversion from even the shadow of advertising."[4]

Henry D. Cooke, the liberal Republican editor of the *Ohio State Journal*, soon appointed Howells news editor with the special duty of looking through the exchange newspapers which passed across his desk. From them, Howells culled a column or two called "News and Humors of the Mail" to which he appended "applausive or derisive comment" in the light, satirical manner then fashionable. Not infrequently Howells and the other youthful editors clipped from the Southern papers "some violent proclamation against the North" and tagged it with a few words of ridicule, telling themselves that thus they might help to laugh away the madness of the South which seemed to them to be suf-

fering from only a "temporary insanity."⁵ But the insanity proved
not to be temporary; the *Ohio State Journal* became more
markedly Republican as the issues of slavery grew more crucial.

Salmon P. Chase, governor of Ohio, a leading citizen of Columbus, and the personal friend of Cooke, welcomed the editorial
staff of the Republican paper to his Gothic mansion, presided
over by his "brilliant young daughter." To one notable Thanks-
giving dinner only the young editors were invited; perhaps the
talk revolved around the menacing rumors of war, but all that
Howells relates of the occasion is that the turkey was "brought
to the guests by a shining black butler, instead of being passed
from hand to hand" at this, his "first formal dinner," and that
the entire company, including the governor, played charades
afterwards. It is no surprise to learn that "Chase was of course
our man for the 1860 nomination"—nor that the next time
Howells was invited to the governor's house, the busy nominee
had forgotten his young supporter. No doubt Howells deserved
the absent-minded rebuff, for he himself was not deeply interested in the political questions then uppermost in the mind of
Chase, though his pen was engaged in satirizing "the foibles"
of the political enemies of his newspaper in the clever style
which characterized the "new journalism." "I was always trying
to make my writing literature," Howells wrote fifty-odd years
later. "It may perhaps be safely owned that I had mainly a literary
interest in the political aspects and events which I treated."

Howells felt, however, "the ethical quality of the slavery
question"⁶ and certainly had genuine convictions on the subject,
as is attested by "The Pilot's Story," Howells' narrative poem
published in the *Atlantic* in 1860, on the tragic death of a slave-
girl. Though "the shadow of incredible disaster" soon to darken
the whole country "still lurked below the horizon," the slavery
question was uppermost in the minds of the younger men of
the paper as well as the older editors—and especially so when an
escaping slave was seized in the Columbus railroad station and
returned to his owner in accordance with the Fugitive Slave
Law. For, until "the mad skurry" which followed the incident
of Harper's Ferry in 1859, Howells and his fellow editors thought
that war might be avoided while law was still respected and
while humor still flourished on the *Ohio State Journal*: "They
got their fun out of the opportunities which the situation offered,
and they did not believe the worst was coming."⁷

Old inhabitants in Jefferson today remember the tales they heard as children of the time when John Brown himself was concealed by their grandparents in the attics of the town. Howells was a boy at the time and fully in sympathy with the cult which venerated Brown even before his death. "Certain fervent verses" entitled "Old Brown" in *Echoes of Harper's Ferry* were written by Howells late in 1859 and published in the Ashtabula *Sentinel* in January, 1860. Though Howells was "neither ashamed or sorry" that he had thus lauded Brown as a hero and a martyr, he confessed in *Years of My Youth*, that, in the light of the facts later disclosed, he had altered his views. As usual, his approach was literary, a reflection of his feelings rather than of his political acumen. Living from his boyhood in "the din of meetings, of rallies, of conventions," he never attended one. What is perhaps still more surprising is that Howells when an elderly man reported that he never listened to a political speech to the end. Nevertheless, it was Howells' campaign book, *Lives and Speeches of Abraham Lincoln and Hannibal Hamlin,* which proved to be the means by which this enterprising young writer-reporter made his escape from Ohio to the dreamed-of East.

Less than a third of this three-hundred-page volume makes up Howells' very readable essay on Lincoln himself; the rest is a reprint of the speeches of the candidates. Howells admired Lincoln, not only because of his Whig position in relation to the Mexican War and to slavery in the new territories, but also because, like Howells, he was the aspiring son of an impoverished family who had managed, unaided, to gain an education. A glance through the lucid and often humorous pages of this study of a fifty-one-year-old lawyer and defender of the truth by a twenty-three-year-old reporter, convinces one that, though they never personally met, the two men had in common their Western heritage.

Years later, when Howells brought to a close his memorial essay on his friend, *My Mark Twain* (1910), he paid him the very highest tribute with the words that he was "the Lincoln of our literature." Howells connected the name of Mark Twain with that of Lincoln not only because of their frontier origins and their pungent speech but also because both of them dealt in the truth. Of Mark Twain, Howells observed that he was the most honest man he had ever encountered; of Lincoln, Howells wrote, after a study of his congressional speeches: "You feel that he has not argued to gain a point, but to show the truth; that it is not Lincoln he wishes to sustain, but Lincoln's principles" (65). Lincoln's life, like that of Mark Twain, seemed to Howells "singularly pure" and of "an integrity without flaw," though both men were familiar with "the wild Mississippi towns, with their lawless frolics, deep potations, and reckless gambling" (25). The education of these two great figures—and of Howells, too—"took place through the rough and wholesome experience of border life, the promptings of a restless ambition, and a profound love of knowledge for its own sake" (20-21).

Though Howells made full use of the records in the State House across the street from the Starling Medical College, where he now shared a room with a friend, and though he spoke with many associates of Lincoln, he was himself too reserved to seize the several opportunities to meet Lincoln which presented themselves. Once, while standing in the corridor of the White House, Howells tells us in *Years of My Youth* (203), he saw the President approach and felt his "ineffably melancholy eyes" rest upon him for a moment; but the small, slender writer let the chance pass and failed to make himself known to the towering President.

The nearest the diffident reporter could come to the "reality" of Lincoln was in the imagined visit to his home and office in Springfield, based on the actual visit of James Quay Howard, a young law-student friend of Howells, who interviewed Lincoln and brought his copious notes back to his biographer. Howells closed his essay by telling the reader that Lincoln received his guests at his home, quietly and simply, laying aside "half his singularity"; when one knocked unceremoniously at his office, a hearty voice was heard: " 'Come in!' and you find yourself in the presence of a man who rises to the height of six feet three inches, as you enter" (93). This man shook hands cordially and earnestly and addressed his visitor as though he were a fellow farmer.

Had Howells actually knocked at the door of Lincoln's office, he would soon have found himself conversing with him about Burns, Shakespeare, or Poe—all of whom, Howells reported, Lincoln made his constant companions. Howells, in writing the life of Lincoln, was as much interested in the older man's bouts with grammar and with Blackstone—two giants which Howells, too, had found blocking his path—as in his debates with Douglas. Howells' rather quaint paragraph describing "the young student [Lincoln], climbing unaided up the steep ascent," carried a certain personal melancholy; it is a description of Howells' ascent as well as Lincoln's. "He who has begun the journey after the best hours of the morning are lost forever," wrote this youthful biographer, "shall not be without encouragement when he finds the footprints of another in the most toilsome windings of his path." Howells himself was "the rustic boy" on whom Lincoln conferred "a dignity" by the very fact that he was able to rise above the difficulties of frontier conditions "by his own force" and make a place for himself on the national stage.[8] Studying over the notes that his fellow reporter collected for him, Howells felt "the charm of the material," for, as he explained, "the wild poetry of its reality was not unknown to me; I was at home with it, for I had known the belated backwoods of a certain region in Ohio; I had almost lived the pioneer life."[9]

When Lincoln was on his way to his inauguration in Washington, Howells found himself on the afternoon of February 13, 1861, in the thick of a milling crowd in Columbus, looking up at the President-elect on "the great stairway within the State House." Lincoln stood, "passive, submissive, with the harsh lines of his lower face set immovably," and he shook hands wearily with the country folk who pressed about him. Howells himself, strayed "slowly homeward" without having offered his hand.[10]

The visit of Lincoln to Columbus coincided with the resignation of "the kindest master in the world," Henry D. Cooke, who left the *Ohio State Journal* for a position in Cincinnati. Howells' weekly salary of $10.00, paid to him only fitfully, seemed now to be even less certain. When the same venturesome publishers, who had not yet realized anything from *Lives of Lincoln and Hamlin*, suggested that Howells take $175 for his share of the possible earnings of the book and set forth on "a sort of roving commission to Canada, New England and New York" to study the factories he saw on the route, he gladly accepted the proposal. Above all else, he wished "to see the world, especially the world of Boston."

Though Howells was sufficiently known as a poet in 1860 to be included in *Poets and Poetry of the West* (edited by William T. Coggeshall), the work which the publishers had imagined for him was to be a subscription book describing the operations of leading industries in the East. No doubt the young reporter set out in good faith; but, after being refused admission to an iron factory, Howells gave up the whole enterprise. Instead, he saw with delight the glories of Niagara Falls and the St. Lawrence River, as well as the villages and cities bordering them; and these he described in a series of letters to the Cincinnati *Gazette,* entitled "Glimpses of Summer Travel," and in another for the *Ohio State Journal,* called "En Passant."

With several poems already published in the *Atlantic Monthly,* he found Lowell and Holmes and Fields far more approachable than the supervisors of factories. Howells' pilgrimage to Portland, Salem, Boston, Cambridge, Concord, and New York, seen through the haze of thirty or more intervening years, was described in *Literary Friends and Acquaintance* (1900) with the loving detail and the humorous-critical insight characteristic of the author. But the state of mind of America's future realist as he set forth on his first trip East can hardly be appreciated unless we realize that this break with his own youthful environment was a plunge into the larger literary world which had for years filled his imagination. As he tells us in *Literary Friends and Acquaintance,* "in those days I was bursting with the most romantic expectations of life in every way,"[11]—especially in relation to literature, to the poets, essayists and storytellers in the East who were writing it. Though his courage had failed him at the thought of interviewing Lincoln, Howells was determined to meet and converse with the "New England luminaries" he had so long venerated from afar: Lowell, Longfellow, Emerson, Hawthorne, Holmes, and Whittier, all of whom were then in the fullness of their powers.

Before reaching Boston, Howells stopped several days in Portland, Maine, where he sought out Longfellow's birthplace. He paused again in Salem, Massachusetts, ostensibly to visit shoe factories—and here he inspected the House of Seven Gables, Gallows Hill, and the Custom-house. Wandering up and down the streets of this "quaint old town," made famous by Hawthorne, Howells became aware of "a more complex civilization" than he had yet known in Ohio. The fine, square, buff-colored mansions, somewhat withdrawn from the street, represented to his "Western consciousness" for the first time what the East might mean by family and tradition as an "actuality and a force." The part these factors might play in a novel making use of such setting stirred his imagination, but he only dimly grasped at that time their "vital import" to him. The shoe factories could wait until he reached Lynn, he decided, for there the shoemaking was superior and, more important still, Lynn was nearer Boston (the visit to the shoe factories of Lynn was made thirty years later). When Howells actually arrived in Boston on this first great trip East he "released [himself] altogether to the literary and historical associations of the place" (18-21).

III *Pilgrimage to New England*

When Howells descended from the horsecar which carried him early in August, 1860, from Tremont House in Boston to Cambridge, he found himself standing among the beautiful, massed elms of Harvard Square, with no idea at all of how to find the home of the great man, James Russell Lowell. As he strolled across the college Yard and admired "Old Harvard's scholar factories red," he was too abashed to ask his directions of the several people who were casually enjoying a summer afternoon. At last "an ancient man, with an open mouth and an inquiring eye" offered to show him the Washington Elm and set him on his way (22).

Howells, for all his shyness, felt that he could "fitly report" himself to the editor of the *Atlantic,* for he at the time "wore next [his] heart in [his] breast pocket" a note written him by Lowell praising the poems which he had recently printed in the magazine. Nonetheless, he was "inwardly quaking" when he was at last ushered into Lowell's presence; he was conscious of "such feeling as an obscure subaltern might have before his general." Not only was Lowell forty-one, while Howells was only twenty-two, but he was the great antislavery poet of the *Biglow Papers* (read aloud to Howells by his father when the boy was ten years old) and the leading critic and editor of the decade who "held a place in the public sense which no other author among us has held."[12] Quite apart from his literary leadership, Howells had a sense of his "greatness" as a man, which he never entirely lost.

When Howells took his seat in Lowell's study on this quiet summer day, he felt only "the instant charm" of Lowell's whole personality and appearance—his voice, his careful enunciation, his beautiful eyes, his auburn hair flowing loosely over the white forehead. The gentle smile and the curly beard which gave to Lowell's face the "Christ-look" had been made familiar to Howells, as to all Americans, by many portraits. Sitting across from Lowell at his writing table, Howells observed that, in spite of the erect carriage which lent him dignity, Lowell was no taller than he himself, "five feet and odd inches." Lowell, smoking the pipe he loved, put the younger man completely at his ease by talking with him about his journey, about the origin of his name, about Howells' poetry and that of Heine. He questioned Howells about the West and seemed pleased when he praised it, for "he had always fancied that human nature was laid out on rather a larger scale there than in the East"—a comment which Howells in his heart rejected. But " 'it was not for me to bandy words with my sovereign.' "[13]

Though Howells thought at the time that his conversation with Lowell was imprinted on his mind with "an ineffaceable distinctness," he was able to recall little of its substance when he wrote the long essay for the May, 1894, issue of *Harper's*, "My First Visit to New England," which, in 1900, became the opening chapter of *Literary Friends and Acquaintance*. Howells made no notes of his visit with any of the "luminaries" whom he met in Cambridge or Concord; for, though he was busily writing a series of letters describing his trip for "a Cincinnati paper," he "was severely bent upon keeping all personalities out of them."[14] In "My First Visit to New England," Howells described the narrow streets of old Boston, sloping off toward Faneuil Hall and the docks; decorous Beacon Street; the Public Gardens leading to the new Public Library, "newly planned and planted"; "the elmy quiet" of Cambridge streets, lined with yellow colonial houses lurking behind their shrubbery. Longfellow was away at Nahant when Howells looked curiously through the gate at Craigie House; Whittier, he discovered, lived in Amesbury.

Having at least met Lowell, Howells turned his steps toward Ticknor & Fields, on the corner of School and Washington streets in Boston, for he wished "to verify" the publishers as well as the editor of the *Atlantic Monthly*. The encounter was propitious from the start, for the young contributor found Fields, just back from a trip to Europe, seated in the little room at the rear of the Old Corner Book-Store, with the proof sheets of "The Pilot's Story" before him. Ticknor, the senior partner of the firm, asked Howells whether he had been paid for his poem; when he admitted that he had not, Ticknor produced from a "chamois-leather bag" five half-eagles in gold and laid them before Howells on the green cloth top of the desk, with the remark, " 'I always think it is pleasant to have it in gold' " (34).

A few days after this first meeting with Ticknor and Fields, Lowell arranged a dinner for Howells in a small, upper room of the Parker House. His host was already in the dining room when Howells presented himself at the appointed hour of two in the afternoon, and there at his side—to the "inexpressible delight and surprise" of Howells—stood Dr. Holmes. The Autocrat's nimble wit and genial smile put the younger man immediately at his ease. Moreover, Holmes, like Lowell, was "physically of the Napoleonic height" which enabled the younger man to look directly into his face as a peer. Soon after introductions, Fields appeared at the door and the party was complete. When Howells took his seat, Holmes leaned toward Lowell and laughingly said, as he looked toward Howells, " 'Well, James, this is something like the apostolic succession; this is the laying on of hands.' " Howells took "the sweet and caressing irony" of Holmes with appropriate modesty, "but the charm of it went to [his] head long before any drop of wine" (37).

The talk that flowed round the table was such as Howells had never heard before; it ranged from personal anecdote to discussion of language in poetry, and from what New York thought of Boston to an exchange of "thoughts and fancies" between Lowell and Holmes; and "every word was priceless" to Howells. Hawthorne was named among the authors discussed, for Fields had recently come home on the same steamer with the Hawthorne family. When Holmes asked Howells whether he had yet been introduced to Hawthorne and he admitted that he had not even dared hope for such an opportunity, Holmes remarked, " 'Ah, well! I don't know that you will ever feel that you have really met him. He is like a dim room with a little taper of personality burning on the corner of the mantle.' " This comment Howells recalled forty years later.[15]

Not even at the table of Governor Chase in Columbus had Howells experienced such a perfectly served dinner; many courses flew by the traveler from the West, who tasted in the dishes "a sort of literary flavor." By the time the black coffee appeared, followed by the *petits verres* of cognac, on which floated lumps of sugar set afire, the "experience began to seem altogether visionary." The spark of Lowell's cigar glowed magically in the evening light before the four rose from the table, and Howells was left still further bewildered by invitations to breakfast and tea the following day. "The time that never had, nor can ever have, its fellow for me, had to come to an end, as all times must."[16] Lowell overwhelmed him by saying, in parting, that, if he thought of going out to Concord, he would be glad to give him an introduction to Hawthorne.

Breakfast at the home of Fields in Charles Street the next morning might almost be regarded as a prolongation of the dream into which dinner at the Parker House had thrown him. The walls of the breakfast room, the windows of which looked down upon the river, were covered with the photographs and autographs of all the contemporary poets and novelists of England who were only names to the visitor—Tennyson, Dickens, Carlyle, Charles Reade, Thackeray. After Fields, clad in his Scotch tweeds from London, left for the office, Mrs. Fields dazzled the young man by lifting from the bookshelves autographed copies of books, some of them with penciled notes from the authors to the publisher.

The day which began in the clouds ended in the clouds, for Howells took his "tea" with the Autocrat and his wife in "unceremonial domesticity." Afterwards, Howells and his host mounted to a back parlor which also looked across the beautiful river, and they watched "the sunset die over the water and the westering flats and hills." In the twilight Howells talked to the Doctor of his experience as a morbid youth and admitted, before Holmes's "tolerant wisdom," that the effects of his broken health were still felt by him "in fancy and even in conduct." With exquisite tact, subtle sympathy, and quick understanding, Holmes made Howells feel that some such experiences were common to all and possibly beneficial as well. The two spoke of "forebodings and presentiments" and, together, "approached the mystic confines of the world" in terms which remained, in spite of "filmy impalpabilities," strictly scientific. Years later Howells became a near neighbor to Holmes on Beacon Street where the conversations on "the substance of things unseen" were then resumed; in fact, they left their peculiar mark on the writing of both men.[17]

Within a day or two the promised letter of introduction to Hawthorne arrived, and Howells left Boston by stage, first for the town of Lowell and thence to Concord. "The intimacy of the New England country" in all its "summer sweetness" was spread before him as he traveled the country roads. Neat farmhouses, bramble-covered stone fences, and newly mowed grassy meadows —all so different from the farms of the Western Reserve—possessed for him a peculiar quality which never failed to enchant him in later years.

To ease "the unhappy conscience" Howells had about the factories he had been so unwilling to visit, he turned aside from his meditative contemplation of the countryside and actually entered the bewildering world of spools and shuttles of one of the great mills of Lowell. The sight and sound of the factory seemed to him "the death of the joy that ought to come from work"; but he felt no sense of the tragedy of the situation as, "in the cool of the evening," he sat at the door of his hotel and watched the line of girls returning to their barracks after a ten-hour day at the machines. Howells had not yet been stirred from his "pitiful literary antipathy" for the factory worker; at the age of twenty-three he was mainly concerned "to see which was pretty and which was plain."[18]

The "reality" which Howells was seeking at that time was, of course, literary; and this he felt so intensely that he wasted his first evening and morning in Concord before he could summon up sufficient courage to present Lowells' letter of introduction at Hawthorne's cottage, "The Wayside." The door was opened by the tall handsome son of "the romancer," who soon advanced from a room beyond. Hawthorne's somber presence "full of a dark repose" "demoralized" his visitor for a few moments, in spite of his host's hospitable attempts. When the two were seated on a log on the crest of the little hill behind "The Wayside," however, their intermittent conversation wandered from topic to topic as Hawthorne smoked his cigar and Howells had the grace to accept the intervals of silence. Given to abrupt transitions, Hawthorne commented on English and American authors; on the West and its people; on the New England temperament, which he said not only seemed but actually was cold; on the beauty of women (Hawthorne avowed that he had never seen one who was quite beautiful); on the characters and writing of his neighbors, Emerson, Thoreau, and Alcott, whose name was unknown to Howells. When they descended the hill, Hawthorne invited his visitor to stay for tea, for the table was already laid.

Howells accepted "the shadowy kindness" of the novelist and even dared express his preference for the *Blithedale Romance* as he looked over the half-filled shelves of Hawthorne's library after tea. But "there was a great deal of silence" in the kindness, and he was glad at last to shake Hawthorne warmly by the hand after gratefully accepting from him his visiting card as an introduction to Emerson. Hawthorne had scribbled on the back, "I find this young man worthy"; though Howells felt the quaintness and the stiffness of the message, the kindness behind it filled him with joy. Shy as he was, Hawthorne had received the younger man with all the cordiality his nature permitted, and Howells perceived "the entire sincerity of the man" and cherished the memory of this visit as "one of the finest pleasures" of his life. It is to this memory of the author of the *House of Seven Gables,* the *Scarlet Letter,* the *Marble Faun,* and the *Blithedale Romance* that he reverted when, several years later, he and the young Henry James tramped the streets of Cambridge evolving together their notions of the nature of romance and its relation to the writing of fiction in the new mode. After this "important encounter" of 1860 with Hawthorne, Howells returned to his tavern and kept the evening for the reverberations of his thoughts on the "personage" in whose actual presence he had "felt [his] spirits sink."[19]

The "insufficient person" of Thoreau, who was also given to long pauses between "vague, orphic phrases," afflicted Howells to the point of rout. Howells had not at that time read *Walden;* he was interested in Thoreau principally because he shared with him a belief in the cause of John Brown. But when Thoreau came into the room "a quaint, stump figure of a man" and gave Howells a chair "not quite so far off as Ohio," it soon became apparent that, to Thoreau, John Brown was a type, a principle, a cause, and not at all "the warm, palpable, loving, fearful old man of [Howells'] conception." In spite of Thoreau's "noble face," which reminded his visitor of Don Quixote, Howells felt himself "so scattered over the field of thought that [he] could hardly bring [his] forces together for retreat"; for Howells was at that time "a helplessly concrete young person" who was afflicted "like physical discomforts" by "all forms of the abstract."[20]

In spite of the disappointment of his visit with Thoreau, Howells at once presented his card at Emerson's door. Emerson was then only fifty-seven years old, but Howells retained a vision of a "fine old man standing tall on his threshold, with the card in his hand," as he looked with "a vague serenity" at the young man on the doorstep below. Howells felt immediately the "strange charm" of Emerson, who reminded him somewhat of Lincoln though Emerson was shyer, sweeter, and less sad. Howells had read little more of Emerson than he had of Thoreau, but he knew his essays and the poems published in the *Atlantic;* and, with his sensitive awareness of personality, Howells had a distinct feeling that Emerson "was somehow, beyond and above [his] ken, a presence of force and beauty and wisdom, uncompanioned in our literature." Perhaps because of this awed respect for the sage of Concord, Howells was thrown into a state of confusion by Emerson's casual remarks on the writers dear to Howells. Hawthorne's *Marble Faun* Emerson gently pronounced "a mere mush"; Howells' reference to the criticism of Poe was greeted by, "*Oh, you mean the jingle man!*" Emerson who was unfamiliar with the poems contributed by Howells to the *Atlantic*, astonished the younger poet by observing, as he followed Howells to the door, that one might "very well give a pleasant hour to [poetry] now and then." Howells at that time was intending to give "all time and eternity to poetry." Howells left the great presence, returned to his Concord inn, and "passed the afternoon in pure misery," not so much because of Emerson's defective literary sense as because of some supposed rudeness of his own in his confused retreat.[21]

When Howells recounted his adventures to Fields on his return to Boston and touched upon his failure "in point of ceremony" with Emerson, Fields lay back in his chair and laughed and laughed until Howells thought he would fall to the floor. The effect of this humorous view of the matter upon the responsive Howells was surprising enough: "I thought it a favorable moment to propose myself as the assistant editor of the *Atlantic Monthly*," he blandly reports to the reader. He believed that he could very well become the assistant editor "with advantage to myself if not to the magazine." Fields seemed to share this belief, but unfortunately the position was already filled. However, added Howells, it was perhaps Fields's remembrance of "this prompt ambition of mine" which brought Howells to his mind four years later when the position was available. "With dancing eyes," Fields asked the age of the young man from the West who wished to be "settled in something." When he learned that Howells was twenty-three, he commented, "Well, you begin young, out there"; but he did not forget Howells' clear statement of his aims.[22]

Looking back on his youthful self, Howells saw that these aims were at that time beyond his achievements; that he was morbidly sensitive, and, at the same time astoundingly conceited; that he had met with "incredible kindness"; and that he had suffered no more than was good for him on this first trip to New England. Before returning to Ohio, Howells desired "to explore the literary situation in the metropolis" of New York City, and especially the office of the *Saturday Press*. Since Howells was himself a contributor, though an unpaid one, to the *Press,* he was welcomed by the "cynical" editor, Henry Clapp, Jr., with a degree of Bohemian camaraderie which left the young man who neither drank beer nor smoked with the impression that he "had fallen very far" below the level of literary life that he had glimpsed in Boston. His meeting with Whitman at Pfaff's Restaurant was the "chief fact" of his New York experience. The "passionate pilgrim" to the East who had dined with Lowell, breakfasted with Fields, and supped with Holmes, returned to the West to resume his position on the *Ohio State Journal* with the conviction that he "could not keep himself too carefully in cotton" (76) until he should come East once more, this time to say. He felt himself now more sophisticated in literary ways and also more dedicated to literature.

Howells did not return to the Medical College in Columbus, where, the year before, he had shared a room with a poetically inclined medical student. Now he took a room with Samuel Price, a fellow journalist, and enjoyed the sort of life that seemed to him more appropriate to a man with a literary future. Midnight oysters at Ambos in High Street, occasionally accompanied by a claret punch, suggested to Howells and his friends "the literary free lance in New York." More frequently Howells and Price dined in a German restaurant near the office of the *Ohio State Journal,* and here the Bohemian atmosphere was enhanced by the rats which scampered over the wall of the storeroom beyond where they sat. Once Artemus Ward joined the reporters in this restaurant and laughed with them over the rats; on another occasion Whitelaw Reid, then a correspondent on the Cincinnati *Gazette,* shared their "happy world." During the winter of 1860-61, Greeley himself paid them a visit in the office of the *Journal;* and, "sitting on the corner of a table, with his soft hat and his long coat on, and his quaint child-face, spectacled and framed in long white hair," he delivered a lecture on the "misconduct" of the *Ohio State Journal,* to which the young editors listened with "inward disrespect." A visitor more to Howells' liking was the sculptor, J. Q. A. Ward, who had come to the capital of his native state to execute some figures for the dome of the State House. Howells found time to stand by him as he worked and to talk with him "about New York and the aesthetic life of the metropolis."[23] Strangely enough, in spite of mustering troops on the eve of the Civil War, Howells wrote that "of all winters this was the gayest" in Columbus, at least among the young people. Howells had begun to go the rounds of the friendly houses once more; and before the winter was over—"the most memorable of his whole life" (225)—he met Elinor Gertrude Mead, whom he married the following year.

Holmes was not alone in feeling that Howells carried with him the aura of success. Moncure D. Conway, editor of the *Dial*, whom Howells visited in 1860 after returning from New England, saw in the young man the same promise for the future. "Never shall I forget," wrote Conway in his *Autobiography* (1904), "the day when he came to see us in Cincinnati. There was about him a sincerity and simplicity, a repose of manner along with a maturity of strength, surprising in a countenance so young—and I must add, beautiful—that I knew perfectly well my new friend had a great career before him."[24]

As a poet? As a journalist? Certainly, the idea of aspiring to novel-writing had not occurred to Howells at this time.

IV *Four Years in Venice*

In spite of the "tragical events" of the Civil War "crowding in" upon all young men of the time, Howells himself "felt no stress" —nor does he believe that others felt it so much as those of a later generation might think. The simple explanation is that though everyone knew that the worst was coming "relentlessly, rapidly, visibly," no one quite thought that the worst would come. So many threats of disunion which had not materialized lulled people's minds into disbelief in all threats—until the country plunged into the abyss. Even after the shot fired on Fort Sumter in April, 1861, actually precipitated the war, neither Howells nor the other young men laughing and working around the editorial table of the *Ohio State Journal* could believe in the evidences of their senses. Soon, however, the streets of Columbus were filled with singing boys from farms and shops who had hurried to the state capital at the first call to arms.[25]

Howells, for his part, leaned out of his office window and thought he might immortalize the scene below in a novel; looking backward many years later, he realized that the novel might have been written, not about the flushed and swaggering boys in their red shirts, but rather about "the more subjective riddle of one who looked on, and baffled himself with question of the event."[26] Howells remained the brooding observer; he was glad enough, however, to accept an appointment as consul in Venice when the opportunity came in September, 1861. Now he had a small part in war activity, for, as United States consul, he was asked by the State Department to be vigilant in reporting any signs of Confederate privateers in Adriatic waters.

After the publication of his *Life of Lincoln,* Howells had applied for the consulship of Munich. When he was offered a position with no salary in Rome, he went at once to Washington to ask what he might expect in fees. Lincoln's secretaries, John Nicolay and John Hay, were interested in Howells because he was "a young Western man who had done something in litera-ture"; they proposed Howells' name for Venice and succeeded in securing for him a salary of $1,500.[27]

On a visit to Washington just before he sailed in September, Howells met and enjoyed "a young journalist who had given hostages to poetry," Edmund Stedman, who was then Washington correspondent for the New York *World.* Howells' "report" to Stedman of April 16, 1863, on the progress of his literary life in Venice after nearly two years, suggests that they had talked of their future literary plans on that first meeting: "The Novel is not written; the Great Poem is hardly dreamed of; I think Dante 'somewhat grimly smiles' when he regards . . . my halting progress through his Divine Comedy. Nothing written, nothing read."[28] The mock-gloom of this comment quickly changed to his more usual good cheer as he continued his letter to his fellow journalist and poet. "Since we talked together, I have married—most happily, need I say? Witness, content that I have never known before!"

Accompanied by her brother, Larkin J. Mead, Jr., Elinor Gertrude Mead had crossed the ocean only six months before Howells' letter to Stedman, and had married him on December 24, 1862, in the American Embassy in Paris. Though the Howellses experienced their share of tragedy, their "content" with each other never deserted them during the forty-eight years of their life together. As Howells wrote to Stedman, "In every way the union seems perfect." It was certainly perfect "aesthetically," he added, "for my wife is an artist, in all but the profession of art." At the time Howells was writing to Stedman, his wife was illustrating her husband's poem, *St. Christopher,* which appeared in *Harper's* the following Decem-ber. Howells might have added that his brother-in-law was "aesthetically" an asset to him too, for Larkin had come to Italy with the intention of becoming a sculptor and had opened a studio in Florence. Howells, who considered himself insufficiently educated in art, was fascinated, nevertheless, by observing the artist at work; and he recognized at this early period the kinship between artist and writer.

Happy as he was in his balconied apartment in the "Casa Falier" on the Grand Canal, Howells had, in fact, no novel to his credit. Moreover, except for an occasional poem, most of his contributions to American magazines were returned to him with discouraging regularity. Achieving only "a few pitiful successes" in poetry, Howells recalled his successful travel letters and gathered material for those studies of Venetian existence that later became one of his most popular books, *Venetian Life*. These began to appear in the Boston *Advertiser* of March 27, 1863; they continued until May 3, 1865, just before his return to his country. By the time *Venetian Life* came out as a book in 1866, Howells was assistant editor of the *Atlantic* and was established with his family in Cambridge.

During his four years as consul, "the literary intention" was always present to him; during these four years, too, he discovered that this "intention" was to be fulfilled in prose rather than in poetry. Howells was awakened from his "inveterate dream" of earning a living by means of his poetry by receiving one morning a letter from Lowell accepting an article of his for *The North American Review* and at the same time praising Howells' "Letters from Venice" which Lowell had been reading in the Boston *Advertiser*. Howells tells of this change "from a supreme purpose of poetry to a supreme purpose of prose" in an essay entitled "The Turning Point of My Life" (*Harper's Bazar*, March, 1910) which he wrote almost half a century later. When he was in Venice, he writes, his "two selves came face to face and had it out with each other"; yet he was not "instantly sensible of a turning point" in his career. "Things do not happen so in real life," he admitted; Lowell's letter merely reminded him that, while he had been writing his verses in one "dreamland," he had at the same time been writing his sketches in another, and that the sketches were successful, whereas the poetry was not. Lowell's note was "a trumpet call to battle, which echoed and re-echoed in [his] soul and seemed to fill the universe with its reverberation." Though Howells never ceased to write verse, he knew at this moment that his literary future lay with the sketches then appearing in a Boston newspaper, which he, until he read Lowell's appreciation of them, had thought of as the merest potboilers. Since the sketches had been refused both by the *Atlantic Monthly* and by *Harper's Magazine*, it is not surprising that Lowell's praise brought "the thrill of joy and hope and pride" sufficient to move the younger man to renounce "the intention of earning a livelihood by verse" and to dedicate himself "to prose with a constancy which has since been only occasionally corrupted."

Howells' decision proved to be a wise one. At the very same time that he was writing a reply to Lowell and recounting the misery and confusion of his literary career and his hopes for the future, Moncure D. Conway was attempting in vain to persuade a London publishing house to bring out a volume of Howells' poetry. *Venetian Life*, however, was at last accepted by Trübner of London, and it appeared in June, 1866. The plans which Howells outlined on August 21, 1864, in his letter to Lowell, actually came to pass; for Lowell's commendation had solidified his inner resolution so successfully that he now saw his future lying before him. There was to be no more "lotus-eating" in Venice; armed with Lowell's letter, he must seek a publisher for the sketches. He wrote to Lowell: "I shall first offer the book to a London publisher (for a first appearance in England will brighten my prospects in America), and perhaps with your leave I will show your letter. I'm anxious to succeed with this book, for I've got to that point in life where I cannot afford to fail any more." We can well believe that the penning of these words precipitated his half-formulated notion that, in any case, it was time to go home if he were ever to launch himself on a literary career. "Besides," he added, "I'm going to resign my office and go home, (either at Christmas or next March) and as I have no prospect of place or employment in the States, I must try to make this book a pecuniary success."

Venetian Life was, of course, a "pecuniary success"—perhaps the most successful in terms of receipts that Howells ever wrote. During his lifetime, it was reissued more than twenty times, sometimes appearing with illustrations by Edmund Gannett, Childe Hassam, and other artists of the day. But perhaps more important than these business considerations was Howells' intuitive feeling at this crucial point in his career that he wished to establish himself on his native soil, that he feared expatriation. "I go home in this imprudent way," he wrote, in this same letter to Lowell, "because at the end of three years, I find myself almost expatriated, and I have seen enough of uncountryed Americans in Europe to disgust me with voluntary exile, and its effects upon character."[29]

Though Howells realized that he had "by no means fulfilled all the high objects" for which he had gone to Italy, he had at least arranged "a line of study" which he could continue at home. The "notes" he had prepared before he left Italy ("with what unspeakable regret!") sustained him for years to come. Besides a series of lectures on the Italian poets delivered at the Lowell Institute of Harvard in 1870, Howells wrote four novels concerning Americans in Italy: *A Foregone Conclusion* (1875), *The Lady of the Aroostook* (1879), *A Fearful Responsibility* (1881), and *Indian Summer* (1886). He also produced three informal travel books—*Italian Journeys* (1867), *Tuscan Cities* (1886), *Roman Holidays* (1908); a series of essays on Italian poets, *Modern Italian Poets* (1887); and many articles, reviews, and memoirs. All his life he dreamed of returning to Venice and of writing its history, no doubt from the "notes" to which he refers in his letter of 1864 to Lowell, who was able to say the right word at the right time to the young consul in Venice then so in need of direction. The seed would have fallen on barren ground, however, had Howells not already—without fully realizing it—discovered in "the measureless leisure" of his life in Venice his own way of observing and recording the life about him. "My literary life, almost without my willing it, had taken the course of critical observance of books and men in their actuality." It is this touch of "actuality" which gives a peculiar charm to the beggars on the piazzas, the black-clad priests, and the girls looking down from their balconies in *Venetian Life*. Ten years later the same turn for the poetically—or humorously—perceived reality marked his series of Italianate novels and, indeed, launched him on his career as a writer "in the new mode."

The key to the "lesson" taught to Howells by Carlo Goldoni is to be found in Howells' introduction to *The Memoirs of Goldoni* (1877). In this sustained essay on the eighteenth-century dramatist, Howells remarked at once upon his own good fortune in discovering the comedies of Goldoni early in his stay in Venice; for, through the eyes of this kindly observer, whose "true judges were the people in the pit," "the romantic city became early humanized" for him. More interested in "local human nature" than in "the mere manners of the age" (14),

Goldoni gracefully and vividly mirrored the Venice of Howells' day, as well as his own. What, precisely, was the dramatist's technique? Howells asked himself the question for, indeed, he was attempting to discover his own through his latest "literary passion." Goldoni's plays, he noticed, are "simple as to plot, but their movement is very spirited." Why not make use of such "simple affairs," then, as the circumstances surrounding the Atlantic crossing of an attractive New England girl (described to him by an American visitor)? Or "the fearful responsibility" of preventing a visiting sister (Howells' sister-in-law Mary) from falling in love with a handsome Austrian officer? Or of an Italian priest—the one, indeed, then giving Italian lessons to the Howellses—from succumbing to the charms of an American girl to the point of illness? If Goldoni's material "lay in himself and everywhere about him in the Venice he knew so well," so also did Howells', though he did not discover the richness of his own observations until several years after his return to the United States. No doubt Howells' diary kept the scenes, the incidents and, above all, the overheard dialogue clearly in his imagination.

Howells quickly perceived that Goldoni depended for the movement of his plays not so much on incident as on lively but not epigrammatic dialogue. The talk is always "brisk" in his comedies, "with a droll, natural, sarcastic humor in it that smacks of the popular life; it is rarely witty. . . ." (15) A decade before Howells discovered this same lesson in the realistic handling of plot, incident, and dialogue from Turgenev, he had learned it from Goldoni, and at a time when all Venice lay before him with its romantic charm. Howells, fortunately, saw not only the beauty of palaces and churches but also the reality of the present-day scene as he and Mrs. Howells strayed in and out of cafés and museums, or as he helped his wife set up her easel by the side of a canal at sunset. "It is incredible how young I was when I came Consul to Venice in 1861," Howels wrote in 1907, when he re-edited *Venetian Life;* he was not too young, however, to notice in the dazzling beauty of Venice the simple and sometimes sad aspects of "real life."

When Howells, a seasoned novelist of sixty, reread the "exuberant" but still popular Venetian sketches of his youth, he remembered with wonder and embarrassment the youthful journalist and poet, realist and romantic, which he had then been. In 1907, Howells had before him the very diary of his days in

Venice from which he had copied out whole pages, sent them to the Boston *Advertiser*, and won his first real literary success. "I cannot deny," said the author to the reader of *Venetian Life*,

> the dates of the diary which I kept almost from the first day, and with the strong dyes of which I colored my impressions of Venice in this book. I wrote the diary for myself, but I could not help making it rankly literary, such being my nature. . . . [But] in the transfer of whole passages from its pages to [*Venetian Life*], an entire sincerity as to the fact and a fresh hue of actuality went with whatever of rhetorical pose was inseparable from the record (X-XI).

Up to this time in his life, Howells observed, his "experience had been entirely journalistic, with a constant literary intention." In his desperate need for recognition at home, as well as for money to augment the $1,500 he received from the government, Howells merely "wrote out some of those passages from [his] diary and offered them to our first literary periodical, with an audacity at which [he could] but wonder," when, in the ripeness of his experience, he "used the pruning knife on certain exuberances of style in which [his] youth had too eagerly wrecked itself." Actually, Howells' experience as a journalist, his reading of Goldoni, and his tours of Venice with his artist-wife sufficiently controlled the sketches which all of Boston was eagerly reading and which Lowell and many other "private persons" praised in enthusiastic terms. More than that, the very habit of observation and delight in his Italian experience stored up a reserve in the mind of the future storyteller which he called on again and again until he wrote his most beautiful Italian novel, *Indian Summer*.

Since *Indian Summer* was not only Howells' favorite novel but also the last he was to write with a distinctly European background, we shall pause here to consider the personal experience out of which emerged this mellow and meditative story of two middle-aged American lovers in Florence.

In order to refresh his mind, Colville, now a man of forty, "had taken up, with as much earnestness as he could reasonably expect of himself, that notion of studying the architectural expression of Florentine character at the different periods." He had bought a great many books on the subject; he had met many interesting people in the pursuit of his quest; above all he "had revived his youthful familiarity with the city." Colville's delight in Florence, where he had once been an aspiring young

American artist, is readily equated with Howells' own "youthful familiarity" with Florence, which he described in "From Venice to Florence and Back," an early "Letter" to the *Advertiser* (May 25, 1863).

The Howellses enjoyed their first trip to Florence in the spring of 1863, much as Colville enjoyed his first visit to the romantic city where he met but failed to marry the woman he never thereafter forgot. The Howellses' visits to the studios of Larkin Mead and his other sculptor and artist friends, described in Howells' "Letter" to the *Advertiser*, became, twenty years later, the background of *Indian Summer*. The sights and sounds and smells of the lovely medieval city lingered in Howells' mind for many years before he put a portion of himself into the hero of his novel, a weary newspaper man, who returned to Florence, as did Howells, after the lapse of almost a generation. On his second visit Colville encountered Mrs. Bowen, a widow now, who had been the good friend of his first love and, indeed, the one he should have married many years earlier; and he almost failed to marry her once more because of his attempt to re-capture his youth with the romantic young Imogene Graham, who only imagined herself in love with Colville.

In 1883 Howells, too, returned to Florence to prepare for *Century* a series of essays entitled "Tuscan Cities," which were to be illustrated by Joseph Pennell. Richard Watson Gilder, the editor, sent the artist not only to sketch the campaniles, the piazzas, and the scenes in cafés and sunny squares, but also to catch with his pencil the homely details of ordinary daily life which Howells had so successfully recorded in *Venetian Life*. Howells, of course, was also storing up for future use the scenes which might commend themselves to the hero of his as-yet-un-written novel. "Colville," he tells us in *Indian Summer* (119), "haunted the studios a good deal, and through a retrospective affinity with art, and a human sympathy with the sacrifice which it always involves, he was on friendly terms with sculptors and painters . . . there were some among these artists whom he had known twenty years before in Florence, ardent and hopeful beginners." Like Howells and Pennell, Colville preferred "the simple trattoria" with its "companionable smell of stale tobacco" to the hotel table, for there they could sit in the smoky half-light and enjoy the coming and going of the young artists and sculptors.

Howells' leisurely four years as consul in Venice, troubled

as they often were, enlarged his already sensitive powers of observation by bringing him in contact with an old and beautiful civilization. He was helped to understand the significance of this European culture through his reading of Italian literature, especially the comedies of Goldoni. Lowell's kindly letter, accepting his article on "Modern Italian Poets," and—equally important—praising the "Letters from Venice," helped the young consul realize that if he were ever to fulfill his "literary intentions," he must turn toward home. When *Venetian Life* came out in an American edition two months after the British edition, Lowell promptly praised it in *The North American Review* of October, 1866, for its "airy elegance" and "refined humor." That such delicacy and finish could be "a product of the rough-and-ready West" appeared to this Bostonian as interesting a phenomenon of "our shaggy democracy" as it had ever been his fortune to encounter. "The hitherto unfamiliar name of Mr. Howells" was one which Lowell was glad to introduce to a wider circle of readers; however, by the time Lowell's review appeared, Howells was already becoming known as the new assistant editor of the *Atlantic Monthly*.

CHAPTER 2

Editor and Novelist

I *Assistant Editor of the Atlantic, 1866–71*

AFTER Howells, with his wife and their little daughter, landed in Boston on August, 3, 1865, he took his family to Brattleboro, Vermont, to stay with the Meads until he could find a position on a newspaper or magazine. Returning to Boston, he went at once to the office of the *Advertiser;* though there was no opening for him, he was at least urged not to accept a place on any other journal without further consultation.

Buoyed up by this hope, Howells made his way out to Cambridge, where he had "a most joyful little visit" with Lowell. At midnight his older friend lighted a candle and descended into the cellar in quest of "certain bottles," which encouraged the talk to flow on until "the cat-bird called in the syringa thicket" at Lowell's door. In the course of the conversation, Lowell intimated to the aspiring young man that he thought he would do well to return to the West, there to live out his "literary life" in his own air. Howells knew well that, without "an Eastern imprint," he would find it difficult after an absence of four years to establish himself in Ohio. However, in the mellow glow of that evening's conversation, Howells did not take issue with his "hero" and his "master"; he went home at last exalted by the thought that the great Lowell had talked to him as though to a peer.[1]

When Howells again visited the office of the *Advertiser,* he found that there was, after all, no place for him on the paper. The editor even returned to him half a dozen of his unprinted "Letters from Venice" as of no further value to the *Advertiser,* and these Howells dispatched at once to the *Nation* in New York, while he himself took a train for Ohio. After three fruitless weeks hunting for a newspaper position in Columbus, Cleveland, and Cincinnati, Howells returned to New York determined, like Bartley Hubbard of *A Modern Instance,* to "get a basis" on a periodical as soon as possible. Though the New York *Times,* the *Saturday Press,* the *Round Table,* and other periodicals were glad enough to print his poems, sketches, and reviews, he knew that only an established position on one paper would enable him to support a family. To his astonishment, the editor of the *Nation,* E. L. Godkin, unexpectedly offered him just such a place with freedom to do "outside work" for any paper except a rival, the *Round Table.* Though Howells proposed $50.00 a week as a salary, he accepted the offer of $40.00, sent for his family, and settled down in New York—as he supposed "for good and all." So much did he enjoy his association with those who worked for this new and liberal journal that he hated to have each day come to a close. Before long, Howells himself introduced a new department, "Minor Topics," on which he labored "with joy, with ardor," reviewing the latest books and plays, and commenting on events of the day, both here and abroad, just as he had done for the *Ohio State Journal* several years earlier.

Howells was soon renewing his friendships with old literary acquaintants that he had formed before his years in Venice—with the R. H. Stoddards in Lafayette Place; the E. C. Stedmans, who had now moved to New York from Washington; with the Bayard Taylors who had an apartment in East Twelfth Street. On New Year's Eve at a party given by the Taylors, Howells encountered Mr. and Mrs. Fields of Boston, and he smilingly recalled with them all the pleasure of those earlier meetings in the Fields's curtained drawing room overlooking the Charles. The editor of the *Atlantic* had not precisely discouraged Howells when he had, at that time, boldly suggested himself as assistant editor, nor had Fields responded in any practical way when Howells wrote him an outspoken note on his return to Ohio in 1860. "The truth is," Howells then wrote, "there is no place quite so good as Boston—God bless it; and I look forward to living there someday—being possibly the linchpin in the hub." Perhaps Fields remembered Howells' letter of five years ago when he said good-night to him in the dawn of January 1, 1866, and added, mockingly, "Don't despise Boston!" Howells responded gayly, "Few are worthy to live in Boston,"[2] knowing very well that the four or five poems he had sent to Fields from Venice had not been considered worthy of appearing in Boston's *Atlantic.*

The snow was so heavy that New Year's Eve that the Fifth Avenue horse-car which Howells hailed had difficulty making its way through the drifts to his boarding house at 441 West

44th Street. Once arrived, he remained, for he was unable to reach the office of the *Nation* for the next few days. On the fourth day when he at last sat down at his desk, he found a letter from Fields asking him—as though the question had never been raised between them—how he would like to be his assistant on the *Atlantic*. Howells lost no time in submitting the proposal to his editor in the next room, nor in talking the matter over with James R. Osgood, then in New York. After an exchange of letters as to salary and duties, Howells took a train for Boston on February 1 to confer with Fields in his new office at 124 Tremont Street.

James T. Fields, Howells' "kindly chief" until 1871, must have treated this slender young man from the West with respect as he talked over the final agreement with him; for Howells had already established by mail that he was to be paid $50.00 a week rather than the $40.00 which Fields had suggested. Fields now went over with him the duties of the assistant to the editor: he was to read all the manuscripts submitted to the *Atlantic* and correspond with their authors; he would proofread the magazine unaided; and he would write four or five pages of book reviews monthly. In spite of the "unfailing tact and kindness" of Fields, Howells left the office feeling that he had "eaten humble-pie"; it was clear to the young editor with vaulting literary ambitions that Fields valued him not so much for his literary qualifications as for his practical printing-office experience, which, Fields hoped, would count on the side of economy in the publication of the *Atlantic*.[3] However, the agreement was formally confirmed by mail on February 6, 1866.

On March 1, 1866 (Howells' twenty-ninth birthday), the new assistant editor of the *Atlantic* began his work at 124 Tremont Street. It soon became clear that Fields was glad to turn over to his assistant not only the reading of manuscripts but the choice for publication as well. Fields constantly consulted Howells, and was soon willing to exercise "a suzerainty rather than a sovereignty" over the magazine, especially when he left for New Hampshire or Europe in the summer. Five years later when the strain of his busy life was beginning to tell on his robust physique, Fields surrendered the editorship of the *Atlantic* to his assistant.

When Howells wrote that during these years he enjoyed "a relation marred by scarcely a moment of displeasure" on either side, we wonder whether his editorial views actually counted in the *Atlantic* office; whether his tireless reviewing, his long hours of proofreading, his endless correspondence, his friendly interviewing really influenced the essential character of the magazine. Howells himself suggested an answer to this question in "Recollections of an Atlantic Editorship" (*Atlantic Monthly*, November, 1907), where he modestly claimed that the *Atlantic* was already "established in its traditions" when he came to it nine years after it was founded and that all he managed to do for it was to "fix it more firmly" in the traditions defined by its two editors. A perusal of the contents of the *Atlantic* from 1866 to 1881, when Howells resigned the editorship, makes it clear, however, that during these years the New England periodical was transformed into a national publication.

But at the outset of his editorship in 1866, Howells was merely a lonely—and lucky—Westerner who stood in a new relationship to "those gods and half gods and quarter gods of New England" —to Longfellow, Emerson, Hawthorne, Whittier, Holmes, Lowell, Mrs. Stowe, as well as to a never-ending line of lesser contributors, all of them from New England. No doubt Howells himself agreed with his chief that, though the *Atlantic* would welcome "outlying literature," there was in those days "very little good writing beyond the borders of New England." Howells was now in a position to look beyond these borders, since, for the first seven or eight years of his editorship, he composed nearly all the "Literary Notices" of the magazine. "I usually have my say in the critical notices," Howells wrote soon after he became assistant. We are not surprised to discover new names, unfamiliar to Boston, in the list of authors reviewed; Hjalmar Hjorth Boyesen, Björnstjerne Björnson, S. Weir Mitchell, John W. De Forest, Bret Harte, Mark Twain, and Sarah Orne Jewett. The fact is that the *Atlantic* under Howells' unobtrusive influence was growing "more and more American." Though it did not cease to be New England or even Bostonian in tone, it had also become "southern, mid-western, and far western" in sympathy, for the new assistant was perusing the piles of manuscripts with a curiosity and insight beyond the scope of the editor.

Perhaps one reason Howells maintained such a happy relation with Fields was that he moved soon after his arrival in Boston from the boarding house at 22 Bulfinch Street, which was within a few minutes' walk of the *Atlantic* office, to a home on Sacramento Street, Cambridge. The house which C. E. Norton found for him was not far from Harvard Square, where stood the

University Press, printers of the *Atlantic Monthly*. "The carpenter's box," as Howells called it, stood on a dark, unpaved street, hardly more than a country road; but here Howells could read manuscript and correct proofs without interruption and then carry the material to the press.

Equally important to Howells was the fact that Sacramento Street was within walking distance of Elmwood and Shady Hill where almost any evening he might find his two older friends, Lowell and Norton, seated beside their friendly fires or reading under their green-shaded Welsbach lamps. As co-editors of the *North American Review*, these eminent men had placed their official stamp of approval on Howells by publishing his two essays on "Modern Italian Poets"; when Howells moved his family to Cambridge on May 1, 1866, they became his warm friends. Belonging to a distinctly older and already somewhat outmoded manner of thinking, they enjoyed Howells for his fresh modernity; he not only appreciated the mellow wisdom and grace of these literary scholars but looked to them for advice and sympathy as long as they lived.

In February, 1866, before moving to Cambridge, Howells had been invited to participate in the "Dante evenings" held at "Craigie House" where Longfellow read aloud his translation of Dante's *Paradiso*. Norton, who was also translating Dante at this time, had arranged for Howells, who had studied the poet with his tutor in Venice, to be included in this group of "accomplished Danteists."[4] The youngest in the room, Howells listened to the hollow, deep-throated tones of Longfellow's voice and conscientiously noted the translation in the margin of his Italian text; he never drowsed, as some did, by the gentle warmth of the fire. The nine o'clock supper which followed must have been as delightful to Howells as the reading, for over the cold turkey or haunch of venison "Holmes sparkled, and Lowell glowed, and Agassiz beamed."[5] Stories, quips, and wise aphorisms flew around the table, and the youngest guest was more "richly content" than ever that he had become a citizen of "Old Cambridge."

"I do not see how I could well have been more content if I had found myself in the Elysian Fields with an agreeable eternity before me," Howells wrote in 1900. In Cambridge everyone had written a poem, a novel, an essay, or was about to; money counted for nothing, though somehow everyone had been to Europe; intelligence rated higher than family and everyone seemed to have acquired the habits and bearing of good-breeding. These ruminations must have consoled Howells at the close of a "Dante evening" as he trudged down the middle of the road through the snow to his square little house a mile or two away in "a poor suburb of a suburb," where piles of proof awaited him.

Happily the proof was frequently his own, for *Venetian Life* was to appear in an English edition in June, 1866. Before the Dante evenings were over for the year, the book had not only been published but it had been reviewed—and favorably—in the London *Athenaeum* (June 2, 1866). At the last meeting of the year on June 12, Howells had his moment of glory after the many hours he had spent paying silent homage to the great men around the fireplace. The Danteists had seen his *Venetian Life* —or at least they had read the review in the *Athenaeum*. In his next letter to his sister (June 17, 1866), Howells summed it all up:

> My book has been noticed in the London *Athenaeum* more favorably than unfavorably—it was my fear that it would be cut up, there—and all the English critics have treated it very kindly. The other night at Mr. Longfellow's Mr. Lowell declared to the whole company, "It is the best book ever written about Italy." But that is only what he had said before in his letters to me. We've had the last of the Dante readings. On Wednesday night Mr. Longfellow finished the final canto, and we honored the close by sitting at supper till two o'clock in the morning.[6]

The meetings were resumed in the fall, and Howells enjoyed "a whole winter of Wednesday evenings." His association with Lowell extended into the summer and, indeed, into the three summers after that of 1866. "For four years I did not take any summer outing," wrote Howells, "and my associations with Elmwood and with Lowell are more of summer than of winter weather meetings."

Lowell hardly let a week go by without mounting the steps of "the ugly little house" on Sacramento Street—as Howells described it—and inviting the editor, pouring over his manuscripts, to join him in a walk no matter how inclement the weather. Lowell loved every tree and lamp-post of Cambridge; he also loved to talk to his sympathetic, though usually somewhat reserved companion who silently noted the "growing conservatism" of his idol, now "quite past the storm and stress of his antislavery age." Though the ideas expressed by Lowell seemed less arresting to his younger friend than they had on his first visit to Elmwood, the streets of Cambridge, the Charles River Flats, and the "struggling, unhandsome outskirts" of the village left an indelible impression on Howells' sensitive mind. The "squalid Irish neighborhoods" of the refined little village of Cambridge, "fraying off into marshes and salt meadows," caught the eye of the future realist. But Howells' sympathy for the poor at this time was somewhat limited; he had yet to be stirred by the social problems of the post-Civil War era. Indeed, Lowell on one of their walks paused to chide him for his "grudge" against the encroaching Irish who a few years later were to drive the Howellses from Sacramento Street to a new home on Berkeley Street. Lowell "liked to tease and . . . liked to mock, especially his juniors"; perhaps he was partially responsible for the sympathetic tone of Howells' observations on the "bedraggled" occupants of the little frame-houses of Cambridge which one feels in his *Suburban Sketches*.

During the summer of 1866 Howells was preparing *Venetian Life* for an American edition; as he strolled the streets with Lowell, he must frequently have thought of his endless walks through the piazzas and over the bridges of Venice. He was also at this time writing *Italian Journeys* (1867), further descriptions of his own experiences as a traveler in Italy. Howells had learned in Italy the trick of turning his simple observations of street scenes into sketches, and he pondered a similar use of the scenes of Cambridge. "Other people went away from Cambridge to the sea and to the mountains," he wrote, "but Lowell always stayed at Elmwood, in an impassioned love for his home and for his town." For several summers Howells was fortunate enough to share with Lowell his love of Cambridge, and the results of the "pedestrian tours" were soon seen in the "Sketches" which began in the *Atlantic* of January, 1868.[7]

Though Howells claimed that he took no "summer outing" from Cambridge for four summers, he did spend a month in Brattleboro in the summer of 1867. No doubt the manuscripts and the reviews for the *Atlantic,* which he had to consider or write before leaving Cambridge in the middle of August, made him feel that this brief period could hardly be called a holiday, especially since he carried in his bag material for future issues of the magazine. At the same time he had his own plans for *Suburban Sketches* and *Italian Journeys* and even possibly for a novel; he had been thinking for some time of commencing "a romance—the scene laid in Italy, or Venice, rather." Because of his desire to record the many ideas which pressed for expression, Howells began to feel increasingly the burden of his work for the *Atlantic*. He wrote to Norton on August 10, 1867, the week before leaving for Brattleboro: "The magazine went to press, this week, and as usual cost me unspeakable anguish at the last moment. I am not yet so far removed from the event but that I still regard my book-notices as so many elements of Ruin."

Howells then turned to a more cheerful subject: his contact, as both friend and editor, with the clever but puzzling young Henry James, Jr., whose essays on current books were then appearing in the *Nation* and the *North American Review* and whose stories were finding their way into the *Galaxy* and the *Atlantic Monthly*. "I see the Jameses rather frequently," he wrote Norton. "They are all in town"—that is to say, in Cambridge, where the Jameses had come to live in 1866.

Henry James, who had tried the law for a few years at Harvard and then given it up, was now devoting his effort to establishing himself in the world of periodical literature. Howells, six years his elder and an editor, had already recognized the genius of his young contributor; he had published James's story "My Friend Bingham" in the March, 1867, issue of the *Atlantic*. "Harry has just written us another story, which I think admirable," he wrote Norton, who was himself encouraging James to contribute to the *North American Review*. Howells' mistrust of a public which found it difficult to accept this distinctly new writer and his firm belief in James's genius, which he expressed to Norton, mark the beginning of a long literary friendship between Howells and James. "I do not feel sure of the public any longer," wrote Howells, "since the *Nation* could not see the merit of *Poor Richard*. It appeared to me that there was remarkable strength in the last scenes of that story; and I cannot doubt that James has every element of success in fiction. But I suspect he must in a great degree create his audience."

Both Howells and James were, in fact, writing for a public which in 1867 hardly existed. During these years in Cambridge, they were not only discussing new novels from abroad never heard of by their elders but also experimenting with stories and essays which they frequently read aloud to each other. The editor-contributor relationship of the two men quickly developed into a friendship which lasted over fifty years. As Howells wrote many years later, "We seemed to have been presently always together, and always talking methods of fiction, whether we walked the streets by night, or sat together reading our stuff to each other."[8] Before James went to live in Europe permanently in 1875, Howells and James, during their "nocturnal rambles" through the streets of Cambridge and around Fresh Pond, had pretty much "settled the true principles of literary art" along lines quite new to the older writers of New England.

In later years both men wrote of these early encounters, each after his own manner. In *Notes of a Son and Brother* (1914), James "pushed through a thicket of memories," and recalled that in the autumn of 1866 the James parents settled, "virtually for the rest of their days" (437), in Cambridge. He then experienced "a perfect muddle of pleasure," when at Howells' "positive invitation," he "addressed the most presuming as yet of my fictional bids"—namely "Poor Richard"—"to my distinguished friend of a virtual lifetime, as he was to become, William Dean Howells," who had "shortly before returned from a considerable term of exile in Venice and was in the act of taking all but complete charge of the Boston Atlantic." Almost fifty years after James's first encounter with Howells, he was moved to record "the felt felicity . . . the felt ecstacy" of the editor's "glittering response" to the author after he had perused the manuscript of "Poor Richard."

Howells recorded the same events in an essay, "Henry James, Jr.," for *Century* (November, 1882) in terms which make us feel at once the difference in style of these two fellow novelists. James had already published a tale in the *Atlantic* ("The Story of a Year") before Howells was associated with the magazine. When Fields asked his assistant editor whether he would accept the second contribution from the unknown young contributor, Howells at once replied, " 'Yes, and all the stories you can get from the writer.' " Howells then added: "One is much surer of one's judgment at twenty-nine than, say, at forty-five; but if this was a mistake of mine I am not yet old enough to regret it."

In 1869, James uprooted himself from Cambridge to spend a year abroad; communications between Howells and James flew back and forth across the Atlantic, however, for the habit of reading and commenting upon each other's writing was now established. Hardly had James sailed before Howells wrote him a long letter on June 26, enclosing "several reviews" praising James's "Gabrielle de Bergerac." It promises "to make a greater

impression than anything else you've done in the *Atlantic*,"
Howells wrote. Lest James should not have received his copy of
the magazine, Howells tore out the pages containing James's
story and enclosed them in the envelope with "Jubilee Days,"
Howells' own essay which had appeared in the same issue of the
Atlantic. "Your story is universally praised," he wrote. "There
seems at last to be a general waking-up to your merits; but when
you've a fame as great as Hawthorne's, you won't forget who
was the first, warmest and truest of your admirers, will you?"⁹

Though far from the first of Howells' admirers, James had
been as "warm and true" in his appreciation of *Italian Journeys*
when it had appeared in 1868 as Howells was of James's stories.
In the *North American Review* (January, 1868), James said of
Howells' latest book, and of its predecessor, *Venetian Life*, that
"they belong to literature and to the centre and core of it,—the
region where men think and feel, and one may almost say
breathe, in good prose, and where the classics stand on guard."
With remarkable insight into the direction which Howells' genius
was about to take, he observed that the best portions of *Italian
Journeys* are concerned with "the common roadside figures"
whom Howells had encountered on his way through Italy, and
with their "manners and morals."

Before Howells closed his letter of June 26, 1869, he reported to
James that he had nearly finished "something I call *A Pedestrian
Tour*, and which is nothing but an impudent attempt to interest
people in a stroll I take from Sacramento street up through the
Brickyards and the Irish village of Dublin near by, and so down
through North Avenue. If the public will stand this, I shall consider my fortune made." James, at least, knew before he read
"A Pedestrian Tour" in the November, 1869, issue of the *Atlantic*
that it was in just such light but penetrating observations of
"common roadside figures" that Howells' fortune lay. James's
early understanding of Howells' essential quality proved correct.

Suburban Sketches, of which "A Pedestrian Tour" formed a
part, appeared in 1871, the year in which Howells had already
begun to publish *Their Wedding Journey* in the *Atlantic*. In this
same eventful period Howells became editor of the magazine
on which he had labored both as a contributor and an assistant
editor. Before the year was out, Howells had moved his family
from "Cottage Quiet," as he sometimes called 41 Sacramento
Street, to a more attractive home at 3 Berkeley Street. Here the
family remained for the next two years, while the house at 37

Concord Avenue was being built. In September, 1872, Howells wrote James: "The cellar is dug, and the lumber is partly on the ground, and every day Winny and Bua [as the infant John was called] and I visit the place, they to play on the sand and boards, and I to watch the cellar wall a-building, and admire at myself for giving employment to four men, two boys and two horses. The money's all somehow to come out of me, but as yet, the future house and the opportunity of letting the poor earn their bread, seem to be freely bestowed upon me by some good power outside of me."

The power which enabled Howells to build the new house into which the family moved in July was not outside of him but within; in his first five years with the *Atlantic* he not only had become its editor but also had discovered in his sketches both of Italy and of Cambridge the possibility of turning the material of his own experience into something very like a novel in *Their Wedding Journey*. Much as Howells loved and admired the circle of older men who had so graciously welcomed him and made him one of their own, he had discovered by the time his period as assistant to Fields drew to a close that "it was in poetry and in romance that they excelled; in the novel, so far as they attempted it, they failed."[10] Howells realized that this was the gap he might be able to fill.

Editor of the Atlantic, 1871-81

When Fields sailed to Europe in May, 1869, he left the *Atlantic* in the hands of his assistant with no compunction, for Howells had before then taken charge of the magazine during the summer when the Fieldses were in New Hampshire. Moreover, he and Howells had already planned together the issues of the *Atlantic*—as far as it was possible to look ahead—until the return of Fields the following autumn. The stay was to be a long one, both because of the editor's failing health and because he hoped to elicit manuscripts from his many friends abroad.

Both Lowell and Holmes kept the traveling editor well posted as to the affairs of 124 Tremont Street. Howells, too, wrote long informal "reports" of the daily life of the harassed editor he had become. The year before Fields left for Europe, Howells' salary had been raised to $3,500 and he had been relieved of much of the proofreading since the decisions as to the contents of the magazine now rested almost entirely with him. The August,

1869, issue of the *Atlantic* had brought a letter of approval from Fields; and Howells replied: "I'm glad you liked the August number so well: I put in the things you directed and filled out according to my own judgment, from the mass of material, that seems to grow like the liver of Prometheus the more it is preyed upon."[11]

The September, 1869, issue, carrying "The True Story of Lady Byron's Life" by Mrs. Stowe, had only recently appeared when Howells wrote to Fields on August 24, 1869: "Mrs. Stowe's sensation of course benumbs the public to everything else in it. So far her story has been received with howls of rejection from almost every side where a critical dog is kept."

Mrs. Stowe's attempt to vindicate the position of Byron's wife, with whom Mrs. Stowe had talked, by exposing the whole story of Byron's incest, broke like a bombshell on the readers of the *Atlantic*. Though the facts have since been proved substantially true, Mrs. Stowe's presentation was melodramatic and inaccurate. Howells had made every attempt to correct details in the article in type before it finally went to press—with the blessing of both Fields and Holmes. The whole affair was "awkwardly done," Howells admitted, "but I think the story is true and ought to have been told." Since, as he wrote his father a month later, Howells "never saw Mrs. Stowe's article till it was in type,"[12] he was in no way to blame for the devastating effect it had on the subscription list; the list fell off markedly in 1870 and never fully recovered until after Howells' editorship had come to a close in 1881, when there were but 12,000 subscribers.

In January, 1871, Howells nominally became the editor of the *Atlantic Monthly* (at $5,000 a year), though he did not actually assume editorship until the following July. In his 1907 "Recollections" for the hundredth anniversary of the *Atlantic*, Howells wrote: "I recall very distinctly the official parting with my kindly chief in his little room looking into the corner of the Common at 124 Tremont Street," when Fields—who lived for another ten years—told Howells that he feared for his health.

Another observer in the office of the magazine was Miss Susan M. Francis, the "clerical assistant" to Fields, Howells, and the next three editors of the *Atlantic*. In an anonymous essay, "The Atlantic's Pleasant Days in Tremont Street," Miss Francis described for the anniversary issue of the magazine her impression of Fields's "cheerful little room, with an open fire, opposite to which was a sofa for visitors, with prints, mostly portraits,

upon the walls, and Mr. Fields's standing desk in one corner."
Next to Fields's office was that of Thomas Bailey Aldrich, editor
of "Every Saturday" (also published by Ticknor and Fields),
which was larger than Fields's office but was used as a reception room for both publications. Below these two rooms on the
street level was the bookstore of Ticknor and Fields and the
office of the publisher, James R. Osgood. Howells, as assistant
to the editor, Miss Francis noted, "did his work, the greater part
of the actual editorial labor, at his home in Cambridge or at
the University Press" in Harvard Square after she herself had
weeded out the hopeless manuscripts in the Tremont Street office.

Sociable as Howells was, he clearly wished to avoid the bursts
of laughter and the gay luncheons sent in from the Parker
House, a few steps from the *Atlantic* office. No doubt he was
also glad to miss the stream of "literary bores and cranks," as well
as the wise and witty, who made their way every day to Fields's
friendly office—which was, in a way, but an extension of his
home in Charles Street. Miss Francis remembered seeing Emerson, Longfellow, Lowell, Holmes, and Whittier crowded together one winter morning around the fire of Fields's editorial
chamber ("always full of sunshine") when the portly figure of
Bayard Taylor appeared at the door and the company over-
flowed into Aldrich's precincts. "There could not be grayness or
dullness with Mr. Fields, Mr. Aldrich, and Mr. Osgood in
possession," wrote this devoted admirer of her generous, kindly
and hearty employer and his friends. Fields "still retained his
room, though he was in it less," even after Howells became
editor. Then, she observed sadly, "There was no longer a Boston
office" in the old sense; there was merely a place of business on
Winthrop Square.

To the "clerical assistant" to the *Atlantic* editor it appeared that
"clouds and rain began to come when Mr. Fields retired," and
Howells became editor, with James R. Osgood the publisher of
the magazine. The retiring "chief" took with him not only a certain
old-fashioned office good-cheer but also "a desirable element of
conservatism and wise caution"—or so it seemed to the clerk who
watched the changes of the office through the regime of five
Atlantic editors. In 1871, she noticed, "new enterprises proved
costly . . . times were changing." Then, "one winter night,"
November 9, 1872, the building housing the office of the *Atlantic*
"burned to the ground." Miss Francis remembered that, at the
time of the destruction of the office, "many *Atlantic* MSS. were

burned with it, how many I never exactly knew, for the book where they were recorded went too." It was her duty to write to the contributors, few of whom "seemed to have kept copies, even of poems." Two years after this disaster, the *Atlantic Monthly* was sold once more, this time to Messrs. Hurd and Houghton; and, said Miss Francis, "I knew nothing save by hearsay of the making of the magazine" until 1878 when Hurd and Houghton consolidated with J. R. Osgood and Company and some of "the comforts of home, so to speak" returned together with "some of my old work therein."

When Houghton, Mifflin and Company bought the publishing business from Houghton and Osgood in 1880, the *Atlantic* moved to 4 Park Street. But Howells had by that time moved from Cambridge to "Redtop," his country home in Belmont where he lived until 1881, a few months before he left the *Atlantic* altogether. He was seldom seen in the Park Street office overlooking the Common, where "Mr. Howells on his weekly visits had the use of a small, dark room." This was never considered an *Atlantic* office—at least not by Miss Francis, who had known "the pleasant quarters in Tremont Street," so full of good cheer, "even gayety," where "nimbleness of spirit seemed to give quickness and deftness to head and hand."

But of these shifts and changes recorded by Miss Francis we find not a word from Howells in his "Recollections of an Atlantic Editorship." Perhaps a remote reference to the aid he received from her is found in the following remark: "During the greater part of the time [of my editorship] I had clerkly help, most efficient, most intelligent." Howells himself, according to his memory in 1907, "read all the manuscripts which claimed critical attention"; during those long afternoons and evenings in Cambridge, he wrote to the contributors, revised all the proofs, verified all the quotations and foreign words, and corrected "slovenly style and syntax"—often to the surprise of his learned friends. At the same time, Howells was "writing not only criticisms, but sketches, stories, and poems for the body of the magazine; and in the course of time, a novel each year." In spite of this extraordinary output—more than that of any other single contributor to the magazine—Howells felt that he "had always leisure." The secret—"if there was any secret"—lay in his lifelong habit "of doing every day two or three hours' work, and letting no day pass idly."

The two or three hours' editorial work actually stretched into the afternoons as Howells "grew more and more a novelist" and laid aside every morning for his fiction. Reading manuscripts, writing to contributors, correcting proof, putting together the final sheets, and carrying them to the University Press were duties kept for "later afternoons and evenings." Small wonder that Miss Francis seldom saw "Mr. Howells," either in the convivial office at 124 Tremont Street or in the dark little room at 4 Park Street. Howells' own "flitting remembrances" of his editorial labors are "of winter days, and laborious trudges to the printers' through the deep Cambridge snow, when the overwrought horse-car faltered in its track; and of Cambridge summer nights spent far toward their starry noons over obdurate proofs, while the crickets and the grasshoppers rasped together under the open window, and the mad moth beat against the chimney of the lamp."

Though Howells' reputation as a writer was steadily growing during his years on the *Atlantic*, no doubt his renown as man of learning was also mounting, since he gently but firmly corrected the Latin and the French of Harvard's best and since his "fearfully scrupulous" methods included verifying every date and every name in a manuscript.[13] Because his "modest merit" had raised him to "such deserved reputation in the world of letters" and had endeared him to so many scholars, Harvard bestowed an M.A. on Howells in 1867 and prevailed on him to become a University Lecturer on Italian literature in 1869-71. Howells wrote to his wife, visiting in Brattleboro at the time, that, when President Eliot came to urge him to accept the appointment, which he had refused in a letter, "I told him what a superficial fellow I was, and warned him of his risk, but it made no difference." He then added, "So I'm a professor in spite of myself."[14]

Howells' attitude toward the hosts of writers with whom he conferred, whose manuscripts he painstakingly corrected, and whose final successes (or failures) he shared was not unlike that of the extraordinary teacher. Although he recalled in his "Recollections" (605) the names of many forgotten and many still famous writers, he regretted that he was unable to name them all. "Their success could not have been dearer to them than they were to me." As each new talent appeared in the *Atlantic*, Howells "exhulted in it with a transport" which was sometimes— but not always—shared by the readers of the magazine. In editing the manuscripts of unknown contributors, Howells found an "unalloyed delight"—a delight "such as few things in life can give."

The custom of paying for manuscripts upon acceptance had been established at the inception of the magazine; the result was that Howells inherited from Fields a half-barrel—"I will compromise on a bushel"—with which he "grappled" as soon as he became editor. He never succeeded in emptying the barrel or in quieting his conscience in respect to "the patient tribe" of contributors who did not have the satisfaction of seeing their poems or stories in print.

Howells felt a "glow of joy" when he edited his really gifted contributors—Henry James, Jr., Sarah Orne Jewett, Mary N. Murfree, Edward Eggleston, John William De Forest, John Hay, Bret Harte, and, later, Mark Twain, "originally of Missouri, but then provisionally of Hartford, and now ultimately of the Solar System, not to say the Universe." What Howells was looking for in the thousands of manuscripts that passed under his eyes was the writers' sense of "reality" freshly perceived—whether humorously, subtly, starkly, or touchingly hardly mattered. Though Howells insisted that he merely sustained "the essential unity of the editorial tradition" he had inherited from Lowell and Fields, he did admit "coloring the web a little, it seems a very little, from my own tastes and opinions." He wrote the "Literary Notices" as soon as he was appointed assistant editor, and he continued to do so for seven or eight years afterward. In 1871 Howells confided to his old friend, J. M. Comly that the *Atlantic* "still continues of Boston, Bostony—with a shadow of Buckeye."[15]

Just how Howells maintained the "essential unity" of the editorial policy of the *Atlantic,* at the same time "coloring" it somewhat by his own tastes, is suggested by the accounts we have of the relationship of other Westerners to the magazine. Bret Harte, who was the same age as Howells and who was editor of the *Overland Monthly,* had begun to appear in the *Atlantic,* Howells tells us, "in the sixth year of the magazine." But it was not until he had taken the country by storm with "The Heathen Chinee" and "The Luck of Roaring Camp" that he made his triumphant journey from the West Coast to Boston. Here Howells helped Harte enjoy a round of dinner parties, lecture engagements, and receptions before the visiting lion moved on to New York. Howells at that time established a firm editor-contributor relationship which even survived Harte's literary decline. A study of this relationship with a contributor such as Bret Harte suggests both Howells' warmth of friendship with the man and his cool objectivity of critical judgment.

It was late in February—soon after Howells had become editor of the *Atlantic* and had moved to a larger house near Harvard Square—that Mr. and Mrs. Harte and their two sons arrived in Boston. Met by Howells at the station "in the handsomest hack which the livery of Cambridge afforded," and driven to 3 Berkeley Street, they kept the Howells family in an uproar for a week. The Howellses decided that, having lived five years in Cambridge and having accepted more civilities than they had bestowed, they should now give a splendid party to their guest, who seemed to them, at first, "a fairy prince." The party, which took place on February 27, 1871, was indeed splendid; it was provided by a caterer "at *a dollar and a half a head!*", Mrs. Howells wrote her sister-in-law the next week. "The man brought linen, silver, dishes, coffee, chocolate, ice cream, salad, bread, cake," and then, after the guests had left, "washed up the dishes and took them off." She attributed the success of the evening to the fact that the Howellses, comparative newcomers to Cambridge, were able to invite people from various groups who did not usually associate with one another.[16] Some of these notable guests were enumerated after the party in a letter which one of them, John Fiske, wrote to his mother: "Fields, Longfellow, Lowell, John [*sic*] Bailey Aldrich, Henry James, Sedgwick, John Bennett, Shaler, Agassiz, Tom Perry, Ernst Perabo, pianist, and many others were there, so many we knocked elbows. Everyone wore his best bib and tucker, the house is well arranged for entertaining, and the supper was delicious—provided by caterer Smith. Mrs. Howells was very pretty and charming; vivacious and amusing as always. We were among the last to leave shortly before midnight."[17]

The Hartes left the Howells home on March 4, and the next day Howells wrote his father that the household had at last subsided into its usual quiet. Though the visit was pleasant, "one of the pleasantest that we've ever had made us," it was exhausting, for "besides our party, the Hartes were entertained somewhere every night. I dined with him at Longfellow's, Agassiz's and Fields's."[18] As Howells owned years later when, after Harte's death, he described "A Belated Guest" for *Harper's* (December, 1903), "Harte was nearly always late for those luncheons and dinners which he was always going out to, and it needed the anxieties and energies of both families to get him into his clothes, and then into the carriage where a good deal of final buttoning must have been done, in order that he might not arrive so very late. He was the only one concerned who was quie unconcerned; his patience with his delays was inexhaustible; he arrived at the expected houses smiling, serenely jovial, radiating a bland gayety from his whole person, and ready to ignore any discomfort he might have occasioned." Though Howells never ceased to love the sweetness and charm of Harte's flamboyant temperament, he also saw during that first visit Harte's ironic impertinence toward "the old saints," as Fields used to call the "literary eminences" of Cambridge, not to mention the fact that Harte frequently drank too much, failed to pay his debts, and borrowed money from his many friends and admirers—though never from his host.

A curious example of Howells' transmuting power is given us at the end of his description of "the joyous visit" of Bret Harte. Having delivered his "Belated Guest" almost on time to so many luncheons and dinners, Howells longed to taste the triumph of getting him actually on time at the station—which he did "in as much magnificence as had marked his going to meet him there." Howells had boarded the pullman, to enjoy a few more moments of merry conversation when suddenly Harte thought of the cigars he had not bought. Both men rushed to the cigar stand and then boarded the train, which was already moving with that "deceitful slowness" which made Howells realize that he must leap to the platform if he were not to be carried along with it. As Harte blandly waved his cigar from the rear of the car, Howells barely escaped being crushed against the side of an archway. He then sat down in the hansom cab and was for a moment "deathly sick" as he realized the danger he had escaped. Howells, however, was able, almost twenty years later, "to adapt the incident to the exigencies of fiction" in *The Shadow of a Dream* and "to have a character, not otherwise conveniently disposed of, actually crushed to death between a moving train and such an archway."

While Howells was playing the anxious host to the literary star of the Boston season, he was also critically appraising this extraordinary personality; beyond the host, the editor, and the critic, was the novelist who incessantly stored up "experiences" to reappear in a novel or story many years later. In spite of the unending demand on Howells' critical ability, first as assistant to Fields and then as editor of the *Atlantic,* he claimed at that time and throughout his long life—as in *Recollections* (396)— that "I never liked writing criticism, and never pleased myself in it"—for, in fact, he was a novelist before he was a critic. Howells was, nevertheless, a critic of unusual insight, for his criticism grew out of a knowledge of the whole personality of the writer and was not limited to a manuscript spread out on his desk. His final literary judgment of Bret Harte—whose voice and laughter he remembered for over thirty years as "the most winning in the world"—was that he never developed as a writer but "wrote Bret Harte over and over as long as he lived." In "A Belated Guest," Howells' literary judgment and personal evocation of Bret Harte are so mingled that they become a superior kind of criticism—the criticism of a novelist.

In most cases, of course, Howells as editor never saw the author of the sheets before him; nevertheless—as he himself stated in *Recollections* (606)—"it was all very, very intimate, that relation of editor and contributor. I do not mean as to personal acquaintance, for in the vast, the overwhelming majority of cases, it never came to that; but I mean the sort of metempsychosis by which I was put so entirely in their place, became so more than one with them, that any slight or wrong done them hurt me more than if it were done to me." A temperament so sensitive to the inner spirit of "the poor fellows, and still more the poor dears" who aspired to publish their poems and essays in the *Atlantic,* was the source of Howells' critical gifts; it was also the source of Howells' "increasing occupation with fiction," for he was equally responsive to the human demands in the daily life around him, which he perpetually transmuted into literary material. At last he discovered that the manuscripts and the letters "could be pushed into a corner," as he "grew more and more a novelist" and "needed every morning for fiction."[19]

Because of this discovery and because, finally, the strain of being an editor, a critic, and a novelist temporarily undermined his health, Howells resigned from the editorship of the *Atlantic Monthly* in January, 1881. As he wrote to one of his contributors ten days later, "I have grown terribly, miserably tired of editing. I think my nerves have given way under fifteen years' fret and substantial unsuccess."[20] At that time he had to his credit over half a dozen successful novels, several books of poems, a campaign *Life of Rutherford B. Hayes,* and a number of plays,

essays, sketches, and critical introductions—he could well afford
to throw himself upon the market rather than continue the
editing he was conscious of slighting.

III *Early Novels*

Henry James, who had returned to Cambridge at the time
Howells took over the *Atlantic,* wrote to their mutual friend,
Charles Eliot Norton: "Howells edits, and observes and produces
. . . His recent sketches in the *Atlantic,* collected into a volume,
belong, I think, by the wondrous cunning of their manner, to
very good literature."[21] *Suburban Sketches,* to which James
referred, had appeared a month earlier; the sketches themselves,
however, had been amusing and interesting *Atlantic* readers for
the past three years.

When Fields lamented to Howells the lack of humor in the
sober *Atlantic Monthly,* the assistant editor had attempted to
brighten its pages with "little short, sketchy things" such as he
had sent to the Boston *Advertiser* from Venice. "Mrs. Johnson,"
"Doorstep Acquaintance," "A Pedestrian Tour," and other essays
which make up *Suburban Sketches* are Howells' observations of
the American scene as he walked from Sacramento Street to
the horsecar which took him into Boston, or as he paced the
quiet streets of Cambridge with Lowell or James. To Howells
it was more entertaining to jot down these half-narrative accounts
of his daily experiences than to struggle through the pile of
manuscripts which he found waiting for him on his desk. A
month after James's letter to Norton, Howells wrote to James M.
Comly, then editor of the *Ohio State Journal,* about a second
venture into narrative sketches: "I am very busy with a sort of
narrative short-story, half a travel sketch—for the *Atlantic,* to
begin in July. The scene is in America altogether, and I am
trying to make it a faithful study of our American life."[22] So
faithful these sketches seemed to Henry Adams, who reviewed
Their Wedding Journey when it appeared as a book, that he
surmised it might be one of the lasting novels of the generation
because it caught the very tone and atmosphere of the decade.
For the same reason, Theodore Dreiser observed a generation
later that Howells, whom he considered too tame, "did one fine
piece of work, *Their Wedding Journey,* not a sentimental
passage in it, quarrels from beginning to end, just the way it
would be, don't you know, quite beautiful and true."[23]

Howells' sketches of the Marches on their wedding trip to Quebec bore the imprint of actuality because they were the faintly romanticized account of his own family excursion to Quebec the previous summer, into which he wove impressions of his earlier trip from Ohio to Boston in 1860. With a jubilant sense of discovery, he wrote to his father on April 16, 1871: "At last I am fairly launched upon the story of our last summer's travels, which I am giving the form of fiction so far as the characters are concerned. If I succeed in this—and I believe I shall—I see clear before me a path in literature which no one else has tried, and which I believe I can make most distinctly my own."[24]

So great was Howells' success in presenting the wedding journey of Isabel and Basil March that the well-loved pair reappeared in novels, essays, and sketches until their author's death almost fifty years later. When the six *Atlantic* installments were collected into a book (December, 1871), Howells himself had difficulty in securing a copy for his father; for between Tuesday, December 27, when the book was put on the stands, and the next day at noon, all of the 1500 copies were sold. In spite of the fact that it came out too late for the holiday sales, another thousand copies were quickly printed by James R. Osgood & Company and put on sale the following Wednesday. "5000 could have been sold if the book had been printed a few weeks ago," Howells wrote his father in the letter quoted above.

The "new way of writing" which Howells had hit upon was, in the simplest sense, merely a projection of himself as Basil March and of his wife as Isabel into familiar scenes, often involving the Howellses' actual experiences. The Marches were introduced to *Atlantic* readers in the July, 1871, issue of the magazine—the number which marked Howells' full assumption of the editorship; and we can hardly doubt that readers in and around Cambridge and Boston recognized in Basil March, a transplanted Midwesterner, their delightful new editor. Certainly they must have recognized that the half-humorous, half-romantic glance at "reality" was similar to that which they had relished in *Suburban Sketches*, as well as in dozens of reviews and essays by the same deft hand. Howells' fresh touch, as Lowell admitted to Fields, suddenly made the "old fellows" seem dated.

Isabel, in these fictionalized sketches, was described as a Bostonian "of great intensity both by birth and conviction," sufficiently dedicated to local custom to satisfy the feelings of every loyal citizen of "the hub"; Basil, however, was only a Bostonian by adoption. He, then, like his author, viewed the "actual" scene with a somewhat critical aloofness. This objectivity was, at the same time, marked by a quality which left the New England reader pleased by the seemingly simple presentation of his treasured traditions and also aware of the ironic—or sad—smile which gently—or sharply—called in question accepted New England values.

But if Basil March was Howells' spokesman, he was not precisely the author himself. We are constantly aware throughout *Their Wedding Journey* of the keener eye of Howells glancing over the shoulders of the romantic, and sometimes quarrelsome, honeymooners. While the Marches are attempting in vain to remain within their romantic dream into which the trivial and the annoying behavior of their fellow travelers unexpectedly obtrudes, Howells himself finds riches enough in "an ordinary carful of human beings," for he prefers to study his fellow man "in his habitual moods of vacancy and tiresomeness" rather than "in his heroic or occasional phases."

Howells very early in his novel-writing career established, therefore, his essential point of view toward the human race which remained unchanged throughout his more than fifty years of "fictioning." Sometimes this "vast, unaffected dullness" of his characters—including Basil and Isabel—struck him as amusing; sometimes he viewed human mediocrity as pathetic, vain, or even cruel, as his understanding of the social implication of the dullness of ordinary people developed. Though but a shadow of Howells himself, Basil too, grew in apprehension of the reality around him as he passed from story to story, while Isabel remained always the conventional Bostonian. Not infrequently Howells' readers complained that there were no heroes or heroines in his novels—not even the Marches. They were right; for, though Howells studied the people he actually knew, as well as his novel-characters, with loving understanding, he did not see them as heroic.

In the half-dozen novels written between 1871 and 1881, when the young *Atlantic* editor from Ohio had indeed become "the linchpin in the hub," Howells was more concerned with manners and men—and especially with those of Boston—than with larger social problems. In *A Chance Acquaintance, A Foregone Conclusion, The Lady of the Aroostook, The Undiscovered Country, A Fearful Responsibility,* and *Dr. Breen's Practice*—each of which was first printed in the *Atlantic Monthly*—Howells humorously and skillfully pricked the bubbles of our conventional illusions, especially about ourselves. Only by sudden sharp thrusts did Howells give his reader a hint that the amusing stupidities and blindnesses of society were not always to him merely amusing. His ability to perceive the perpetual contrast between the picture of ourselves as we would like to appear and the image of ourselves as we, in truth, actually are is perhaps the source of Howells' ironic detachment from his characters. When asked on one occasion whether he ever lost himself in his writing, Howells replied: "Never. The essence of achievement is to keep outside, to be entirely dispassionate, as a sculptor must be, in molding his clay."[25]

Howells' attitude toward his characters, the story he has to tell, and the theme which emerges can best be seen by a further study of *A Chance Acquaintance*. A year after the publication of his early tentative venture into novel writing, Howells began in the *Atlantic* of January, 1873, a second series of narrative sketches which were gathered into a small volume immediately on their conclusion in June, 1873. We might hesitate to call this neat little book, which we could readily tuck into our coat pocket, a novel; but it has a genuine heroine, Kitty Ellison, and a hero of sorts, Miles Arbuton, between whom a relationship is established which might be taken as Howells' first narrative with a plot.

Kitty had encountered Arbuton "by chance" on the deck of a boat which had transported her, as the guest of her uncle and aunt, to the distant city of Quebec, where they had recently said goodbye to the Marches. The story, of course, is concerned with the ill-fated romance of the chance acquaintances, Kitty and Miles; but on a more significant level it is concerned with the validity of the Boston concept of a "gentleman," which is challenged by a Midwesterner.

Kitty's uncle, Dr. John Ellison, had provided a home and family for his niece as far back as she could remember. Born in West Virginia, "Uncle Jack" had migrated to a corner of northwestern New York since he was too ardent an abolitionist to remain in a slave-holding state. He and his wife had welcomed into their home the orphaned daughter of his youngest brother, a newspaper editor, and a member of the Free Soil Party who had been killed in a border feud in Kansas. Kitty, as she grew up, had become the pet of the older boys and girls of the Ellison family; she was especially her uncle's chosen companion as he traveled the country roads with the little girl on the seat by his side. In the course of these professional trips the doctor educated his niece "in those extreme ideas, tempered by humor, which formed the character of himself and his family" (5).

The Ellison's home in Erie Creek was, in fact, one of the principal over-night stops for runaway slaves during the Civil War, and many an evening was spent around the fire listening to the tales of the cousins who helped them escape to Canada. Kitty remembered one abolitionist visitor who was treated by all with a serious regard approaching veneration—an old man with a high forehead, bushy brows and flaming blue eyes, who took her on his knees and sang, "Blow ye the trumpet, blow!" in a mighty voice which she never forgot. Then John Brown and her uncle talked of some "far-off place that they called Boston, in terms that commended it to her childish apprehension as very little less holy than Jerusalem and as the home of all the good and great people outside of Palestine" (6).

Dr. Ellison had corresponded occasionally with John Quincy Adams; when he had attended the Free Soil Convention in Buffalo in 1848, he had also met some of those very Bostonians he had admired from afar. But he had never fulfilled his ambition of visiting Boston itself; now his niece was to enjoy the opportunity he had missed, for she, with another uncle and his wife, Colonel and Mrs. Ellison, was to visit "the birthplace of American liberty" on her return trip from Quebec. The old doctor at once wrote her a long letter which Kitty thrust into her bag after reading it hastily on the deck of the boat. He reminded her to make the most of her few days in Boston: "There everything that is noble and grand and liberal and enlightened in the national life has originated, and I cannot doubt that you will find the character of its people marked by every attribute of a magnanimous democracy. If I could envy you anything, my dear girl, I should envy you this privilege of seeing a city where man is valued simply and solely for what he is in himself, and where color, wealth, family, occupation, and other vulgar and meretricious distinctions are wholly lost sight of in the consideration of individual excellence" (10). On her brief stay, Kitty was, of course, to visit Faneuil Hall and the Massachusetts Historical Society; even more important, she was "somehow to catch sight of the author of the 'Biglow Papers,'" of "Mr. Whittier," "Colonel Higginson" and many others—all less actual persons to the doctor's "idealizing remoteness" than figures "of a grand historical composition."

Kitty, seated at a writing desk in the Saguenay boat which was about to leave Quebec, dashed off a letter to "the girls" at home and instructed them to tell her Uncle Jack that "he had not rated Boston people a bit too high" (3) if she were to judge from Mr. and Mrs. March from whom she had just parted. They would, she was sure, help her carry out all of her uncle's instructions when she reached Boston.

Meanwhile, a faultlessly dressed gentleman with a flaxen mustache, Mr. Miles Arbuton—whom everyone first decided must be an Englishman—stepped on board and glanced disdainfully about him. To Kitty this unknown young man, whom she soon learned was from Boston, was already "invested with a halo of romance," for she had seen him from afar on the Goat Island Bridge at Niagara. Mr. Arbuton, for his part, had cast a casual look at the Ellisons and at once had decided that he would certainly have nothing to do with them in spite of Kitty's "long-lashed grey eyes." Not, indeed, that the Ellisons had made any overtures, but "he had the habit of thus protecting himself from the chances of life, and a conscience against encouraging people whom he might have to drop for reasons of society." The originality, spontaneity, charm, and intelligence of the free-minded Kitty proved, of course, stronger than all of Mr. Arbuton's Bostonian hesitations. He fell in love with her in spite of himself; indeed, he proposed marriage against his better judgment and was accepted. But a small episode turned the whole course of events. In a moment of fatal hesitation, Arbuton failed to introduce his fiancée to several stylishly dressed ladies from Boston, who had advanced upon Arbuton and stood chatting with him on the hotel piazza while Kitty, simply clad in traveling costume, remained in stony silence outside the charmed circle. When her fallen hero later attempted "to make everything clear," Kitty observed simply: " 'You have been telling me that you were ashamed of me in this dress before those people. But I knew that already. What do you want me to do?' " With that "the whole fabric of Mr. Arbuton's defence toppled to the ground." He was a man of scrupulous honesty—being from Boston—he prided himself upon his ability to look the truth in the face, unpleasant as it might be to him. He saw "with paralyzing clearness" that throughout that "ignoble scene" Kitty "had been the gentle person and he the vulgar one" (267).

We hesitate to say that the editor of the *Atlantic* was transmuting his own bitter-humorous experiences in the slowly unfolding story of Kitty Ellison. However, as an ardent young Westerner, he too had encountered the conventional Bostonian who was peculiarly disturbing to one reared in the midst of Free Soil idealists. Both Howells and his young heroine had vainly struggled to bring together the dream and the reality of Bostonian values. Kitty did not relent and marry Arbuton, nor did Howells ever truly accept a certain complacent Bostonian rigidity, much as he loved all of his life many of the qualities of the New Englander. When in 1884 he wrote *The Rise of Silas Lapham,* he was, indeed, still satirizing the subtly interwoven fabric of Boston snobbery, with which he had become familiar.

In a letter to Henry James, written September 1, 1882, Howells declared that he had finished *A Chance Acquaintance* with "triumphal feelings." But "now I regard it with abhorrence, and work it over, shuddering"—for Howells was reliving, through his outspoken heroine from northwestern New York, his own feelings as an outsider in the Boston he had idealized. Of these personal implications Howells, of course, said nothing to his sophisticated younger friend; he merely remarked, "This too must pass away: anyway I begin printing in January and I dare say I shall be ready to agree, and more, with anybody who praises it."[26] So many readers did follow Kitty's story as it unfolded in the *Atlantic* between January, 1872, and June of the same year that, as Howells wrote James, he was flooded with letters "from people unknown to me—begging for a sequel," which he was unwilling to supply. "The trouble is," he added, "that they are of such various minds as to what the end ought to be."[27] But Howells knew quite clearly that Kitty—as well as he—must reject the Boston snob; only his readers—always a step behind—wondered whether amends might not somehow be made. Howells, however, was already "pushing toward [his] Venetian priest's story," *A Foregone Conclusion,* and never, therefore, supplied Kitty's romance with a happy ending—though he glancingly referred to her in several later March stories.

James, it is clear, did not thoroughly approve of Howells' "new" heroine; however, Kitty's independent attitude toward her laggard lover is reflected in James's story of *Daisy Miller* (1879), who, in her turn, vainly struggled against the snobbish conventionalities of old Europe. Hardly had the first installment of Howells' story appeared before he received from Switzerland James's comment to which he replied at considerable length on March 10, 1873. Howells thanked James "with all [his] heart" for the criticism of his heroine and added that he was "able to check the young person a little before handing her down to the latest posterity in book form"; James's letter, however, had arrived too late to modify the magazine version. It was Kitty's "pertness" which James found objectionable (the same quality in Daisy Miller becomes mere vulgarity, or, as James might have said, "commonness").

Howells' defense of Kitty marks a real difference in outlook of the two friends; it shows, too, how far Howells had moved forward in his ability to objectify his own experience. Kitty's "pertness," he airily explained—never hinting that she was a reflection of his own views—"was but another proof of the contrariness of her sex." He explained:

> I meant her to be everything that was lovely, and went on protesting that she was so, but she preferred being saucy to the young man, especially in that second number. . . . I like her because she seems to me a character; the man, I own, is a simulacrum. Well—or ill-advisedly I conceived the notion of confronting two extreme American types: the conventional and the unconventional. These always disgust each other, but I amused myself with the notion of their falling in love, which would not be impossible, if they were both young and good looking. Now conventionality is, in our condition of things, in itself a caricature; and I did my best for the young man, but his nature was against him, and he is the stick you see.[28]

Though James could not then have known it, this stick of a young man was none other than their mutual friend, Thomas Sergeant Perry, whom James had taken to see Howells in the spring of 1869. Perry, who had asked his friend to introduce him to the assistant editor of the *Atlantic*, was at that time a tutor in French and German at Harvard. According to an article which Perry wrote for the February 25, 1917, issue of the New York *Sun*, the next time they met was in the summer of 1869 when he and a classmate took a summer excursion on a steamer up the Saguenay to Quebec where they encountered Howells. Perry amused himself by giving him "a somewhat depressing account of the trip and spoke without admiration of the brief glance one got at the Capes Trinity and Eternity . . . at which the passengers threw potatoes while the steamboat's whistle shrieked." But the whole excursion appeared to Howells in quite a different light, as Perry humorously explained in 1917 after he and Howells had been for many years intimate friends: "Mr. Howells, being thus prepared for the worst, found everything much better than he had been prepared to expect, as one may recall from the description in 'A Chance Acquaintance.' A sensitive conscience tells me, though Mr. Howells is kind enough to deny it, that it is my unseemly comment on the wonders of nature that he puts into the lips of the supercilious Arbuton. I bear no malice. If one can't be immortalized in one way one must try another" (New York *Sun*, February 25, 1917).[29]

Howells was right to deny that Perry—whom he had invited to write the French and German book notices when he took over the *Atlantic*—was actually that "simulacrum" of a man, Arbuton. Just as Howells later supplied James with "the germ" for the character of Strether in *The Ambassadors*, so had the charming and clever young Perry, disdainfully commenting on his fellow passengers, supplied Howells with the hint he needed for his story. Howells was, in a sense, speaking of himself when he wrote to James: "Of course the girl must be attracted by what is elegant and fine in him, and provoked to any sort of reprisal by his necessary, cool assumption of superiority. She cannot very well help 'sassing' him, though she feels that this puts her at a disadvantage, and makes her seem the aggressor."[30] Howells, too, was attracted by the "elegant and fine" in his Eastern associates, though he was not infrequently very critical of "the cool assumption of superiority" of the New Englander and more especially of the Bostonian.

James wrote on June 22, 1873, after he had received A *Chance Acquaintance* in Berne: "Your work is a success and Kitty a creation. I have envied you greatly, as I read, the delight of feeling her grow so real and complete, so true and charming. I think in bringing her through with such unerring felicity, your imagination has *fait ses preuves*."[31] He expressed his doubts about the ending, however. Howells thanked him, in his letter of December 5, 1873, for his "praise and blame" of the difficult little story. "Your strictures are fairly made," he wrote, "and I know that I ran along the edge of a knife-blade to reach that dénouement. Sometimes it seems to me all clumsily wrong; and again I have the motive as clearly before me, as I had at first, and feel that nothing could drive me from that conclusion."[32]

Nothing drove Howells from walking the knife-edge of romance and reality in this or any of his many subsequent novels. In a letter to Norton, James lamented Howells' lack of "a really grasping imagination";[33] and, in a letter to Grace Norton, he remarked upon the "melancholy spectacle" of seeing his friend's "charming style and refined intentions . . . so poorly and meagerly served by our American atmosphere."[34] To Howells this country seemed to offer a rich supply of material for the "grasping" mind, if one looked beneath the surface of daily experiences, too frequently romanticized, and examined the reality of our conventional attitudes.

Perry, who worked at Howells' side throughout his *Atlantic* editorship, understood perhaps more clearly than James—who in 1875 settled in England for the rest of his life—the intent of the novels Howells wrote during his *Atlantic* years. When the editor was forced by overwork and illness to give up his post in 1881 and to make a prolonged visit to Europe, Perry wrote "William Dean Howells" for *Century* (March, 1882), an essay in which he neatly summed up his appraisal of Howells' literary place. In essence, wrote Perry, Howells' novels reflect an almost scientific questioning of social conventions in the interest of establishing "the dignity of native worth." Perry, though he was himself the supercilious Arbuton, perfectly understood that Howells was sharply questioning his and other Bostonians' "assumption of superiority." With remarkable insight, Perry wrote, just when Howells was about to enter his greatest decade:

> There is a truly national spirit in the way Mr. Howells shows.
> . . . the emptiness of convention and the dignity of native
> worth. . . . After all, what can realism produce but the downfall
> of conventionality? Just as the scientific spirit digs the ground
> from beneath superstition, so does its fellow-worker, realism,
> tend to prick the bubble of abstract types. Realism is the tool
> of the democratic spirit, the modern spirit, by means of which
> the truth is elicited, and Mr. Howells's realism is untiring. It
> is, too, inceasingly good-natured. We feel that Mr. Howells is
> scrutinizing the person he is writing about with undisturbed
> calmness, and that no name and no person can impose upon him
> by its conventional value.

Not even the names and the persons of two well-dressed, sophisticated young Easterners, Henry James, Jr., and Thomas Sergeant Perry, could impose their conventional values on their older friend. These two representatives of the new generation had known each other for a number of years before they met Howells, who, during his period as editor of the *Atlantic* became the third member of "a triangular friendship that time and distance never diminished."[35]

IV *Turgenev and the "New Way of Writing"*

Henry James, who came to know Turgenev during his 1876 stay in Paris, talked to him about Howells and showed him several of his friend's books. Some time later a message came to Howells from "the Master," who said: "I have spent the night reading *A Chance Acquaintance*, and now I should like to visit the country where there are girls like the heroine." We wish we might have Turgenev's comment on the procession of heroines who followed Kitty Ellison: Florida Vervain of *A Foregone Conclusion*; Lydia Blood of *The Lady of the Aroostook*; Lily Mayhew of *A Fearful Responsibility*; and, above all, Marcia Gaylord of *A Modern Instance*. In all these novels Howells was experimenting with "the new way of writing" which was the subject of conversations and of letters between the triangle of friends—Howells, James, and Perry—whose platform was the *Atlantic*.

When Perry joined the staff of the *Atlantic* in 1871, he introduced Howells to the novels of Turgenev, which he was then translating into English. Howells later recognized that the reading of the tales of this great Russian, personally known both to Perry and James, was to him the "most notable literary experience"[36] of his years in Cambridge. Characteristically, Howells at once began to describe his latest literary "passion" in his *Atlantic* reviews of *Smoke, Lisa, Dimitri Roudine, Spring Floods*, and other Turgenev stories; at the same time, perhaps unconsciously, Howells suggested to the reader his own beliefs as a storyteller. What he admired in these novels was precisely what he also was attempting in *Suburban Sketches, Their Wedding Journey*, and *A Chance Acquaintance*: the objective, humane, often humorous presentation of simple experiences, mainly through dialogue.

That the author should trust to his characters, few in number and ordinary in type, to unfold their own inner conflicts, had been revealed to Howells already by Goldoni, by Björnson, by his own literary attempts. Turgenev, however, was ahead of them all; and as soon as Howells began to read him, he recognized that this writer had brought his method as far as art could go. "Here was a master," he wrote, "who was apparently not trying to work out a plot, who was not even trying to work out a character, but was standing aside from the whole affair, and letting the character work the plot out."[37] What a relief, after "the gross darkness of English fiction," after Thackeray, Dickens, Charles Reade, George Eliot, and even Hawthorne. With "joyful astonishment," Howells recognized the "transcendent superiority" of Turgenev, who was of the "great race" of those who are willing to look at human nature "without either false pride or false shame in its nakedness." Turgenev's method, which made character, rather than plot, the center of interest, Howells adopted —as well as Turgenev's reliance on dialogue to bring out theme. A decade later, the impact of Tolstoy made Howells, in his concern for humanity, "impatient even of the artifice that hid itself"; but Howells by then had adapted to his own use the art of Turgenev. Though Tolstoy deepened Howells' thinking, it was Turgenev who influenced his style. "I still think of *Dimitri Roudine* as one of the most interesting books I ever read," Howells observed to Perry with whom in 1912 he again discussed "Recent Russian Fiction."[38]

Perry translated *Dimitri Roudine,* which had first appeared in Russian in 1855, from French and German texts in 1873. Immediately after the publication of Turgenev's novel in *Every Saturday* (January to June, 1873), Perry himself, in reviewing the story in the July issue of *The Nation,* pointed out the psychological realism of this new way of writing which relied on the objective fact and was content to leave moral judgments to the reader. Perry retells the story of Daria Michaelovna, "a faded beauty who has a high opinion of her own abilities," and of her daughter Natalie, "a charming young girl such as Turgenev draws so well," who are spending an idle summer in the country, surrounded by various neighbors and friends. Dimitri Roudine, a middle-aged gentleman from Moscow, becomes quite casually a member of the circle. This clever, experienced, talkative visitor, whose promise habitually exceeds his accomplishment, enlists, first, the pity, then the love of the ardent young Natalie, who romantically believes that she might help Roudine achieve the success which has always eluded him. Daria, however, who regards her daughter as "a mere chit," carries on her own sophisticated flirtation with the same gentleman. Urged on by

Natalie, an elopement is planned; but Roudine is unable at the last moment to sustain his romantic role, both because he fears the anger of Daria and because for too long he has grown accustomed to talking rather than acting. Natalie, being young, recovers from her disillusionment; Roudine fades off into the dim, melancholy future his own character had prepared for him.

Howells, who favorably reviewed this book for the September issue of the *Atlantic,* commented on Turgenev's study of Dimitri Roudine: it is "so complex that there is little to ask of the author in the way of a story." The women, Howells remarks, are very well drawn, especially the young heroine, Natalie, "whose ignorant trust, courage, love and adoration for Roudine, changing to doubt and scorn," are put before the reader dramatically in only a few scenes. Her mother, Daria, "is an entirely different type, a woman of mind, as she supposes, with advanced ideas, but really full of the pride of cast, worldly, and slight of intellect, though not wanting in selfish shrewdness or a strong will."

In the July, 1874, issue of the *Atlantic,* just ten months after reviewing Turgenev's novel, Howells himself began *A Foregone Conclusion,* the story of a mother and daughter, who are confused by an unexpected love affair. The scene is laid in Venice where an American lady is spending a summer vacation with her daughter Florida. Like Daria, Mrs. Vervain is a widow, vivacious, worldly, and attractive to men; again, like Daria, she thinks of her daughter as far too young to fall in love. Like Dimitri Roudine, Don Ippolito, a priest who is recommended to Mrs. Vervain as a tutor in Italian for her daughter, joins the family circle. A man with unrealized potentialities, he is at heart an inventor much more interested in his ingenious experiments than in his priestly duties. Though Natalie hoped in her youthful ardor to bring Dimitri Roudine out of the bondage of his own temperamental weakness, Florida merely hopes that Don Ippolito, by discarding his priestly garb, may achieve success as an inventor in the United States. Florida, amazed to discover that the priest is in love with her, retreats with her mother to Providence, Rhode Island, and leaves in her wake confusion and despair. Both Natalie and Florida recover from their summer madness, since they were moved more by romantic idealism than by love; but both of their lovers remain fatally caught in the dilemmas which lay deep within their characters.

Ferris, the American consul who introduced Don Ippolito to the Vervains, was, in many of his characteristics, Howells himself as a young consul in Venice; Don Ippolito was, as Howells tells us in one of his letters,[39] a brother in the Convent of San Lazzaro, who frequently breakfasted with the Howellses in their apartment on the Grand Canal and talked Italian with them. Howells' tone in *A Foregone Conclusion* is as American as Turgenev's is Russian; but the relationship between the novels, though possibly unconscious, is, nonetheless, real. The kinship of the two girls, for example, can hardly be overlooked in spite of the fact that one is typically Russian and the other totally American. Of Natalie, Turgenev wrote:

> Thin and dark, she had not yet reached her full growth, and she did not hold herself perfectly straight. Her features, although rather marked for a girl of seventeen, were noble and regular. Especially beautiful was the clear, smooth forehead, which rose above her gently arching eyebrows. She spoke very little, but when any one was talking she listened and looked attentively, almost fixedly, at him, as if she was unwilling to let anything escape her. She would often sit motionless, sunk in thought, her arms hanging by her side; at such times her face expressed the profoundness of her abstraction.[40]

Florida, Howells wrote, "was a girl of about seventeen, who looked older":

> She was tall rather than short, and rather full. . . . In the attitudes of shy hauteur into which she constantly fell, there was a touch of defiant awkwardness which had a certain fascination. She was blonde, with a throat and hands of milky whiteness; there was a suggestion of freckles on her regular face, where a quick color came and went, though her cheeks were habitually somewhat pale; her eyes were very blue under their level brows, and the lashes were even lighter in color than the masses of her fair gold hair . . . she had the air of being embarrassed in presence of herself, and of having an anxious watch upon her impulses (19).

In the same year in which Perry and Howells were reviewing *Dimitri Roudine*, James too expressed his views of Turgenev's writing in a long essay for the *North American Review* (April, 1874). Turgenev, he wrote, "belongs to the limited class of very careful writers . . . he is a zealous genius, rather than an abundant one. To describe him in the fewest terms, he is a storyteller who has taken notes. . . . His tales are a magazine of small facts, of anecdotes, of descriptive traits. . . . He notes down an idiosyncrasy of character, a fragment of talk, an attitude, a feature, a gesture, and keeps it, if need be, for twenty years, till just the moment for using it comes, just the spot for placing it." In almost these same terms, James in 1886 described Howells' special gifts—his "work of observation, of patient and definite notation"—in his essay which introduced the new editor of the "Editor's Study" to Harper readers.[41] James, who carried messages back and forth across the ocean between Turgenev and Howells, recognized their kinship and the relation of both to the new way of writing fiction.

Howells' own most extensive description of what he considered to be this new method which so deeply influenced the unfolding technique both of himself and of James is in his essay "Henry James, Jr." in the November, 1882, issue of *Century.* In it Howells not only repudiated the old romantic novels of the English tradition but also announced his allegiance to the more analytical, more objective school of the Continental writers— a type exemplified in his country most particularly by James. Both James and Howells put their trust in the dramatic, the impersonal presentation of their characters in the clear light of day; at the same time, neither scorned the romantic, the poetic, or the humorous glow through which, in various moods, they saw reality. Story did not matter; the meaningful episode was there to be analyzed until character was fully displayed. "The novelist's main business is to possess his reader with a due conception of his characters and the situations in which they find themselves. If he does more or less than this, he equally fails," wrote Howells in his essay on James—and in words closely akin to those used by James several years later in *The Art of Fiction* (1884).

When Howells wrote his essay for *Century,* James's first really important novel, *The Portrait of a Lady,* had just appeared in London in book form after being serialized in the *Atlantic.* Howells' essay, then, stressed James's most recent novel as an illustration of the theory of the new kind of fiction which they had worked out together, with the aid of Perry, largely through reading and reviewing the novels of Turgenev. Just as Turgenev deliberately refrained from telling the whole story of Dimitri Roudine, so James only partially presents the story of Isabel Archer, Howells pointed out. Instead, he contents himself with a part of her history, leaving the rest for the reader to fill in. "We must agree, then, to take what seems a fragment instead of a whole, and to find, when we can, a name for this new kind of fiction. Evidently it is the character, not the fate, of his people which occupies him; when he has fully developed their character he leaves them to what destiny the reader pleases."

In describing the method of James, Howells was restating the lesson he had learned from Turgenev, who, more than Balzac or Zola, more than Hawthorne or George Eliot (all of whom they admired and discussed), was their teacher during the 1870's: "The man who has set the standard for the novel of the future is Turgenev."[42] In order to understand the modern novel, Howells insisted, older, outworn methods, particularly those of the English novelists, from Richardson to Thackeray, had to be discarded, for "the art of fiction has . . . become a finer art in our day than it was with Dickens and Thackeray," who are in "the heavy and awkward tradition of the craft." In his essay on James, Howells was attempting to educate a new generation of readers in his country and abroad for the kind of novels appropriate to a scientific, analytic, anti-romantic fiction which "studies human nature much more in its wonted aspects, and finds its ethical and dramatic examples in the operation of lighter but not really less vital motives." He was inviting his readers to desert "the bad school we were all brought up in," and to explore the "finer art" of the new school.

Though Howells generously asserted that "this school, which is so largely of the future as well as the present, finds its chief exemplar in Mr. James," he himself, even as he was writing his essay, was watching the last installment of his own most ambitious novel up to that time, *A Modern Instance,* appear in the October, 1882, issue of *Century.* The novel came out as a book a month before the appearance of Howells' essay on James.

Not only did *A Modern Instance* show the author's fully developed skill in the new way of writing but it also proved that Howells indeed possessed the "grasping imagination" which James failed to find in his earlier sketches and stories. It proved, too, that Howells intended to seek his material in his own country and not in England where James had found it necessary to transport Isabel Archer, who was born and brought up in Albany, New York. For the question of where a novelist should live, in his own country or abroad, had been uppermost in the conversation and letters of Howells and James since they first came to know each other. While in Cambridge, James had remarked in 1871 to Norton that Howells seemed able to write only of what his "fleshly eyes" had seen. For this reason, James wished he were " 'located' where they would rest upon richer and fairer things than this immediate landscape" of his native land. A few years later he wrote to Howells from Italy on January 9, 1874: "There is something in all the regular New England scenes and subjects, in fiction, which strikes a chill upon my soul." Though Howells had shown in his series of Italianate novels that he, too, was quite aware of the peculiar charm of the international novel, the very thought of becoming an expatriate struck a chill upon *his* soul. As Kitty Ellison and Daisy Miller offered a contrast in the interpretation of American girls on foreign soil by Howells and James in the 1870's, so Marcia Gaylord and Isabel Archer presented themselves as contrasting heroines in the 1880's. By then the issue as to where their fiction should be located was finally settled for both novelists.

James's Isabel was romantically beautiful, full of potentialities, eager, and partially educated after the fashion of the day; her caliber was tested, in James's long novel, by her responses to three possible lovers. Howells endowed his heroine, Marcia Gaylord, with similar traits; she, however, threw herself at the first lover to present himself, Bartley Hubbard; and Howells' tale is the story of the consequences of this impetuous act. Both Isabel and Marcia are girls when we meet them; under the impact of unfortunate marriages both heroines mature—Isabel finally to a dignity and reserve of wisdom which, according to James, marks the "Lady"; Marcia, to a petty, selfish, small-town woman, destroyed by her own "romantic" pursuit of passionate desire. Small wonder that James, after the appearance of the novel, had hopes for Howells as "the great American naturalist." But Howells, in the careful, stroke-by-stroke portrait of Marcia Gaylord, was not, in fact, a "naturalist," as Zola was then defining the word; he was more truly a faithful follower of Turgenev, whose selective art Howells had pondered—and practiced—in half a dozen novels during the decade of his *Atlantic* editorship.

To feel the Turgenev quality of *A Modern Instance,* so full of the infinitely small touches that "compose" a picture of Equity, Maine, in the 1880's, one has only to reread with deliberation the first few pages of the novel, beginning with "The village stood on a wide plain, and around it rose the mountains." Plain and mountain, summer and winter, waving corn and freezing snows— the scene is laid for this slowly moving, deeply felt, epic-novel of passion and relentless law. The village street, with the church steeple at the end; the "cutter" gliding swiftly between snow-

banks, as Bartley Hubbard and Marcia drive up to Judge Gaylord's large, square dwelling; the neighbors peeping between
lace curtains—all against the background of bare hills, winter
twilights, and lighted windows—are in the subdued tone of
Turgenev.

Howells himself was conscious of the change which the reading
of the Russian novelist wrought in him, difficult as it was to
define: "Life showed itself to me in different colors, after I had
once read Turgenev; it became more serious, more awful, and
with mystical responsibilities I had not known before. . . . Who
else but Turgenev and one's own most secret self ever felt all the
rich, sad meaning of the night air drawing in at an open window,
of the fires burning in the darkness in distant fields? I try in
vain to give some notion of the subtle sympathy with nature
which scarcely put itself into words with him."[43]

One of the most remarkable aspects of Howells' growth in
the ten years between *Their Wedding Journey* and *A Modern
Instance* is precisely the increased seriousness of his picture of
human relations, especially as seen in marriage. Before offering
the manuscript of the latter to the publisher, Howells wrote, as
was his custom, a brief résumé of the theme. It is to hinge on
divorce, he said: "We all know what an enormous fact it is in
American life, and that it has never been treated seriously. I
intend to treat it tragically, though of course the story is not to
be wholly tragical; and I feel that I have a theme only less
intense and pathetic than slavery."[44] From the narrative sketch of
the Marches' honeymoon at Niagara, to Kitty Ellison's misjudg-
ment of her Boston lover, through Florida's innocent, but fatal,
abuse of Don Ippolito, to the long-drawn-out moral deterioration
of Marcia Gaylord in her life with Hubbard, we can see that
human relations presented themselves to Howells as "more
serious, more awful" than he had supposed them to be before
his imaginative world was enlarged by wider reading of Russian
literature—especially of Turgenev.

But reading and experiencing were always partners in the
making of a Howells novel. While James moved eastward in his
imagination to find a world large enough to permit Isabel Archer
to test out her romantic illusions, Howells literally moved west-
ward in May, 1881, to gather in the details of an actual divorce
case as it came before the County Court of Crawfordsville,
Indiana. In the creation of Bartley Hubbard, Howells made use
of his knowledge of western journalists—himself among them—

whose easy cynicism sometimes led to lazy, irresponsible journalism. The actual squabbling of a couple he had witnessed in Shirley, Massachusetts, during two summer vacations added to Howells' sense of the possible sordidness of marital relations when confidence has been misplaced. His Boston friends supplied Howells with the prototypes of the well-meaning Clara Kingsbury, the idealistic Ben Halleck, and the over-genteel Athertons. Sensitive as Howells was to the writers who, like Turgenev, became his "passions," Howells' "fleshly eye," and, we might add, ear, were always alert to the sights and sounds around him. Just as Turgenev found the Russian character and the Russian setting sufficient for his uses, so Howells found that the American scene never failed him; and the ways of seeing and feeling came to him from many quarters.

Since both Perry and James knew Turgenev in Paris, it is pleasant to learn that, according to one witness, Howells, too, met and corresponded with the Russian novelist before the latter's death in 1883. Abraham Cahan writes in the story of his life[45] that, as he was saying goodbye to Howells at the end of an evening of talk in 1894, Howells held him back a moment and said, "Wait, I want to show you something." He then went to a desk and took out a letter to him from Turgenev, praising one of his novels, and this he read aloud to his guest. Cahan added, "Howells then told me how he met Turgenev in Paris, and how he corresponded with him. He was very proud of the letter." Though by 1894 Howells' concept of the novel had been altered by further reading and by wider social experiences, he still treasured the enlivening contact he had had with Turgenev at the time when, with his friends, he was discovering the art of novel-writing for a new generation.

CHAPTER *3*

The Creed of a Novelist

I   *Howells and Mark Twain*

HOWELLS' manner of writing was deeply and permanently affected by James, his fellow novelist, and by Perry, his fellow critic; he talked literature endlessly with these two friends, read and published their writings, learned from them of the new European movements, and modified his thinking accordingly. Another side of Howells' nature, however, his Western leanings, remained unaffected by his sophisticated associates of Boston and London. For Mark Twain, Howells felt at once both a personal and a literary kinship: "We were natives of the same vast Mississippi Valley; and Missouri was not so far from Ohio but that we were akin in our first knowledges of woods and fields as we were in our early parlance." Howells, by the time he met Mark Twain, had largely outgrown his own Ohio speech through his "greater bookishness," but he always relished the phrases of Mark Twain "which he employed for their lasting juiciness and the long-remembered savor they had on his mental palate."[1]

Howells talked over Twain's writing with him, edited his stories and other contributions, and reviewed each book as it appeared; Twain, on the other hand, seldom commented upon the books of Howells—indeed, his friend suspected he seldom read them. Of *A Foregone Conclusion*, Twain wrote Howells on August 22, 1872, "I should think that this must be the daintiest, truest, most admirable workmanship that was ever put on a story"; one wonders, however, whether Twain really enjoyed such "dainty" fare. The one critical appraisal of Howells he ever wrote appeared in *Harper's* (July, 1907) toward the end of his life, and in this four-page essay in which Twain extravagantly lauded Howells' "style," he showed no real grasp of the significance of his writing. Understanding flowed from Howells to Twain, rather than from Twain to Howells—perhaps this is the secret of their long and varied friendship.

Howells' subtle critical insight into the unformed writing of this free and vigorous writer from the West not only helped to transform Twain from a journalist to a writer of literary pretentions, but also enlarged Howells' spirit by hearty laughter, by bold ideas, and by exuberant conversations, all of which enriched and deepened Howells' capacities as a novelist as well as his power as a critic. The title, *Criticism and Fiction,* chosen by Howells in 1891 for the small volume in which he stated his creed as a novelist-critic, describes his own character as a writer, for his *fiction* always grew from his *criticism.* Howells' association with Twain between 1869 and 1881 is a prelude to Howells' own greatest period as a novelist, during which he turned from his Turgenev-inspired study of New England society, such as *A Modern Instance,* to Tolstoyian panoramas of New York social conditions, such as those presented in *A Hazard of New Fortunes.* Twain helped put Howells in touch with a larger world, the limits of which were not henceforth to be set by Lowell, Holmes, Norton—or even by James. We shall, in this section, consider only the first ten years of this extraordinary friendship between Howells and Twain.

Just as Howells had welcomed Bret Harte not only to the pages of the *Atlantic* but also to his home, so did he open his heart to Mark Twain the moment he appeared in the Tremont Street office in 1869—a few months after James's departure for a prolonged stay in England. As Fields's "proud and glad" assistant, Howells had written an anonymous review of *Innocents Abroad* (*Atlantic,* December, 1869) in which he had recognized that the book was "such fun as we had not had before." Hardly had the review appeared, before Clemens, clad in his sealskin coat, strode into the *Atlantic* office to shake the hand of his appreciative reviewer.

The fact that Howells praised *Innocents Abroad* before he had ever met its author won Twain's undying gratitude not only because a review in the *Atlantic* meant that he had actually penetrated the literary fortress of the country but also because the unknown critic clearly understood the peculiar quality of "Mr. Clements's [*sic*] very amusing book." Howells had pointed out that "it was out of the bounty and abundance of the author's own nature" that this astonishing saga of a trip abroad had sprung, and that its humor was always good-natured: "even in its impudence" it was charming; it was never indulged "at the cost of the weak or helpless"; and, in spite of its "sauciness and irreverence," it was never insolent. As the reviewer turned the pages of *Innocents Abroad*, he imagined that the author would talk of his experiences in just the same casual fashion as he wrote of them—"and very amusing talk it would be." Mark Twain himself soon justified the supposition during his frequent visits to the office on Tremont Street.

Something of the high spirits of the group surrounding the *Atlantic* in the spring of 1871 can be caught in Howells' description (*Life in Letters*, II, 156-57) of a gay luncheon at Ober's restaurant, given by "that genius of hospitality," Ralph Keeler, another *Atlantic* contributor from the West. How "that lurid lunch which the divine Keeler gave us out of his poverty" was paid for, Howells never knew. The party, indeed, was not a small one: "There was T. B. Aldrich, there was J. T. Fields, much the oldest of our company, who had just freed himself from the trammels of the publishing business, and was feeling his freedom in every word; there was Bret Harte, who had lately come East in his princely progress from California; and there was Clemens," he wrote years later. Nothing remained in Howells' mind of that "happy time" but a sense of "idle and aimless and joyful table-talk" and of good stories soon forgotten. In the midst of the beefsteak and mushrooms, "the shimmer of wit" and the discourse, "so little improving," Bret Harte looked across the table at Mark Twain, whom he had known well in the West, and spluttered, "Why, fellows, this is the dream of Mark's life,"[2] for that lunch was exactly what a "literary lunch in Boston was imagined to be—at least by strangers from the West. "Those were gay years, and bless God, we *knew* they were at the time!",[3] wrote Howells to Aldrich.

The next meeting after the Ober luncheon between Twain and Howells took place in Clemens' new mansion in Hartford, Connecticut. *Innocents Abroad* was by then an enormous success —so much so that "an army of agents" was spreading out over the country and selling Twain's not-yet-written books by subscription. Clemens was rapidly becoming a rich man; and, on the strength of his success, he had married Olivia Langdon and built his splendid house. Howells soon became a familiar figure in Hartford, while Clemens, often accompanied by his wife, frequently stayed with the Howells family in Cambridge and later in Belmont. These visits were exhausting but exhilarating experiences for Howells, who would sit up late while his tall, red-headed friend smoked the last of his many cigars and soothed his nerves at bedtime with his usual hot Scotch. "We both talked and talked and talked, of everything in the heavens and on the earth, and the waters under the earth," Howells said of one visit to Hartford. At the end of two days he returned to Cambridge feeling, he said, as hollow as a locust-shell sticking to the bark of a tree at the close of summer.

On another occasion, Howells and Twain took rooms at the old Brunswick Hotel in New York, and though they wished to sleep, they could not stop talking. Howells remembered Twain as he lounged through their rooms in his long "nightgown" telling the story of his life, "the inexhaustible, the fairy, the Arabian Nights story, which I could never tire of even when it began to be told over again." Twain walked up and down the rooms until dawn, "halting now and then, with a fine toss and slant of his shaggy head, as some bold thought or splendid joke struck him." These "bold thoughts" Howells tells us—quoting Milton's description of the lost souls in Hell— were

> Of Providence, foreknowledge, will and fate,
> Fixed fate, free will, foreknowledge absolute.

They were as characteristic of Twain as his "splendid jokes."[4]

Out of the stuff of these ranging conversations, the endless reminiscing, the "bold thoughts," and the hilarious, sometimes ribald jokes, came Mark Twain's stream of writing, which at this time he himself regarded as entirely journalistic. Howells, a journalist himself who had only recently made his entrance into literature, recognized that Twain's writing might, with editorial direction and wise curbing, become important. As a young reporter in California, Twain had already come under the tutelage of Bret Harte, who, Twain wrote to T. B. Aldrich, "trimmed and trained and schooled me patiently until he changed me from an awkward utterer of coarse grotesqueness to a writer of paragraphs and chapters that have found a certain favor in the eyes of even some of the very decentest people in the land."

During the period when Howells was in charge of the *Atlantic* —"the most scrupulously cultivated of our periodicals"—he was to Twain the editor under whose rule the new contributor most willingly came. Occasionally Twain would try stronger language than the *Atlantic* "had stomach for";[5] once or twice Howells found it impossible to accept what his friend offered him. Twain continued, however, to seek Howells' editorial advice during the rest of his life; he knew that without the curbing of his verbal extravagance he was unpublishable—at least in the magazines of the period.

In "My Memories of Mark Twain,"[6] written soon after the death of his old friend, Howells admitted that his "fainter pencil" could not catch the "graphic touch" of Clemens, who "had the Southwestern, the Lincolnian, the Elizabethan breadth of parlance," which one could hardly "call coarse without calling one's self prudish." Howells often found himself "hiding away in discreet holes and corners" Twain's letters in which he "had loosed his bold fancy" and which Howells could bear neither to throw away nor to look at again. Out of this astonishing disparity of temperament grew one of the great literary friendships.

As an editor Howells undoubtedly curbed and limited his friend's contributions to the *Atlantic*. After receiving several offerings from him while his own novel, *A Foregone Conclusion*, was appearing in the magazine, Howells wrote:

> I'm going to settle *your* opinion of the next installment of *A Foregone Conclusion* by sending back one of your [two] contributions. Not, let me hasten to say, that I don't think they are both very good. But *The Atlantic*, as regards matters of religion, is just in that Good Lord, Good Devil condition when a little fable like yours wouldn't leave it a single Presbyterian, Baptist, Unitarian, Episcopalian, Methodist, or Millerite *paying* subscriber —all the deadheads would stick to it, and abuse it in the denominational newspapers. . . . I've kept the *True Story* which I think extremely good and touching, with the best and realest kind of black talk in it.[7]

No doubt Howells' editorial instinct was correct, for "Some Learned Fables, for Good Old Boys and Girls," which he rejected, was not up to Twain's best. Howells knew precisely what his *Atlantic* readers would accept; Mark Twain, properly guided and encouraged, would be just their fare. Howells wrote to M. M. Hurd, one of the *Atlantic* publishers, soon after the appearance of "A True Story," the accepted manuscript: "Our Bret Harte negotiations *did* fall through, but I've more than made good the loss by securing Mark Twain for a series of sketches next year. I'm glad you liked his little story, for I thought it wonderfully good—one of the most artistic things in its way that I'd ever seen." If all the contributors keep their promises, Howells added, "we shall have a great year in 1875, and I do hope the subscription list will sympathize."[8]

The "sketches" to which Howells referred were immediately published after their appearance in the *Atlantic* as *Sketches, Old and New.* Howells reviewed the volume at once in the columns of his magazine, for he not only backed his friend by publishing his writing but also by commenting on it in order to make it acceptable to a public not yet fully prepared for Twain's peculiar blend of comic and serious.

The "average critical mind," wrote the editor in his review of *Sketches, Old and New,* was confused by "A True Story" when it first came out in the *Atlantic,* for the readers did not know whether to take the tale as humorous or tragic, or merely as "one of Mark Twain's extravagances." Was he to laugh or cry over the story of an old black cook, all of whose children were sold into slavery, and who, at last, after twenty years, found her youngest boy? The critics hardly knew and contented themselves with noncommittal reviews until Howells told them that the story was "a study of character as true as life itself, strong, tender, and most movingly pathetic in its perfect fidelity to the tragic fact."[9] The "rugged truth" of the story, published so soon after the close of the Civil War, might well have endangered the *Atlantic* subscription list; to Howells the tale seemed "artistic" because it revealed the author's gift for "the simple, dramatic report of reality."[10]

When Clemens strayed from Howells' interpretation of an artistic norm—as he frequently did—the editor pruned and cut. "If you wanted a thing changed, very good, he changed it," wrote Howells of his "willful" but "biddable" contributor; "if you suggested that a word or a sentence or a paragraph had better be struck out, very good, he struck it out." Far from harming Clemens by overediting, Howells did what other gifted, tactful editors have sometimes been able to do for overexuberant writers: he turned him into a man of letters.

Clemens himself recognized his practical dependence upon Howells in his dual role of editor and critic, and he wrote in his *Autobiography* that "more than once I took the precaution of sending my book, in manuscript, to Mr. Howells, when he was editor of the *Atlantic Monthly,* so that he could prepare a review of it at leisure. I knew that he would find more merit than demerit in it, because I already knew that was the condition of the book. I allowed no copy of that book to go out to the press until after Mr. Howells's notice of it had appeared. That book was always safe."

Clemens needed from Howells not only his official stamp of approval but also the personal encouragement he was able to give him. Howells remembered, for example, in *My Mark Twain,* how his friend came to him in 1875 with the manuscript of *Tom Sawyer* under his arm and asked him to read it, "as a friend and critic, and not as an editor," after having already written him, "I don't know of any other person whose judgment I could venture to take fully and entirely."[11] Howells at his first glance "thoroughly liked *Tom Sawyer,* and said so with every possible amplification," before he walked with his guest to the horsecar station in Harvard Square "and put him aboard a car with his MS. in his hand, stayed and reassured, as far as I counted, concerning it."[12]

When he had read the manuscript more thoroughly, Howells wrote to express not only his hearty appreciation of the book but also to put to rest Clemens' doubt as to whether the story should be told throughout from a boy's point of view: "I finished reading *Tom Sawyer* a week ago, sitting up till one A.M., to get to the end, simply because it was impossible to leave off. It's altogether the best boy's story I ever read. It will be an immense success. But I think you ought to treat it explicitly *as* a boy's story. Grown-ups will enjoy it just as much if you do; and if you should put it forth as a study of boy character from the grown-up point of view, you'd give the wrong key to it."[13]

Aside from this crucial comment, Howells wrote he had only a few suggestions to make in the first third of the manuscript and these he had placed "in faltering pencil" along the margins. "When you fairly swing off, you'd better be let alone," he added. Twain replied two days later: "It is glorious news that you like Tom Sawyer so well. I mean to see to it that your review of it shall have plenty of time to appear before the other notices. Mrs. Clemens decides with you that the book should issue as a book for boys, pure & simple—& so do I."[14] When Clemens finally set himself "to the dreary & hateful task of making final revision of Tom Sawyer," he found that Howells' pencil marks were "scattered all along." This, he wrote to Howells, made his labor simple, for "instead of *reading* the MS, I simply hunted out the pencil marks & made the emendations which they suggested."[15]

Howells, of course, wanted *Tom Sawyer* for the *Atlantic;* but, since Twain was now outside the price-range of that magazine, he wrote in the letter quoted above, "I shouldn't think of publishing this book serially." He added, "Give me a hint when it's to be out, and I'll start the sheep to jumping in the right places." So much did Clemens depend upon Howells' notices to launch his books that he sent him the proof sheets of *Tom Sawyer* early in 1876. From these Howells wrote his review for the May issue of the *Atlantic,* in which he commended the story's "artistic sincerity" and its "fidelity to circumstances," which made it "incomparably" the best picture of life in the Southwest to be found in fiction.

Howells remarked in *My Mark Twain* that, as Twain's "true and cordial advisor," he never failed his friend; however, he added, that, in backing out of the many "enterprises and projects" which he and Clemens planned together, he was "as false as water"—to his own and Twain's astonishment. Among Twain's proposals for collaboration was his suggestion that Howells help him dramatize *Tom Sawyer.* Howells replied at once in July, 1875, from the office of the *Atlantic Monthly* that no one but Twain himself could do the story justice: "I couldn't enter into the spirit of another man's work sufficiently to do the thing you propose."[16] As for Howells, he was finishing a novel and about to begin a play of his own.

The novel to which Howells referred was *Private Theatricals,* which began to appear in the November, 1875, *Atlantic Monthly.* Whether Mark Twain could sufficiently enter into the spirit of Howells' work to read his latest novel is doubtful. Of this delightful story of a coldly flirtatious woman whom Howells had observed in his New Hampshire boarding house during several summers, Twain wrote merely "Company interfered last night, & so 'Private Theatricals' goes over till this evening, to be read aloud."[17]

Howells himself complained, "I have a feeling that you don't read me as much as you ought, and I sometimes swear off from you on account of it." However, since he was eager for a judgment on his play, he asked Twain to read *The Parlor Car* for him before it was published. Twain, who was as unsuccessful as Howells in his dramatic efforts, was enthusiastic about the play; he suggested only the addition of a touch of Mark Twain humor, a suggestion Howells did not accept.

Though *The Parlor Car,* the first of the thirty-three plays Howells wrote, was never professionally produced, the novelist was at this time eager to test himself as a dramatist. *Out of the Question,* his first full-length drama, never appeared except in the pages of the *Atlantic*; but his next play, *A Counterfeit Presentment*, actually opened at the Grand Opera House in Cincinnati on October 11, 1877, starring the popular actor, Lawrence Barrett. After playing to full houses for several days in that city, Barrett toured the country with Howells' play during the 1877-1878 theatrical season and he brought it to New England in December, where it was greeted for a time by full houses and enthusiastic reviews. In spite of the success of the play, Barrett had already felt its inherent dramatic weakness; and, in his letter of November 4, 1877, to James R. Osgood, he expressed his doubts about a long run. So far, he wrote, the success of *A Counterfeit Presentment* has been entirely "owing to friendly and cultured audiences, but it must now please the popular taste which will not accept fine writing and pretty dialogue in a thin plot." Howells promptly added a new act—about which Barrett demurred—and the play continued its successful run. From Chicago, Barrett wrote to Osgood on December, 1877: "Sold again!—the new act made a good impression and by many who saw it I am told that it is nearly complete as a play which fills me with joy."[18] As the play moved from St. Louis to Providence and then to Springfield, Massachusetts, in December, 1877, Howells must have shared Barrett's joy at the success of their joint venture.

Howells' "presentment" in *My Mark Twain* of an actual *Atlantic* dinner which took place just at this time is more dramatic to the modern reader than his *Counterfeit Presentment* which was soon to falter to a close in Boston in spite of Barrett's acting. On the 17th of December, 1877, Howells, as editor of the *Atlantic*, presided over the famous Whittier dinner party, with Whittier, Longfellow, Emerson, and Holmes seated on either side of him at the head table. Clemens, as "a very valued contributor of the magazine," had been asked to make the speech of the evening; but, unfortunately, it was not called for by the toastmaster until after addresses of varying lengths had been made by Whittier, Emerson, Norton, Longfellow, Houghton, and Howells himself. Clemens then arose and presented, as Howells remembered it, "the notion of three tramps, three dead-beats, visiting a California mining-camp, and imposing themselves upon the innocent miners as, respectively, Ralph Waldo Emerson, Henry Wadsworth Longfellow, and Oliver Wendell Holmes." None of those present entered into the "delight" of Twain's fantasy; encircled by un-smiling countenances he "dragged his joke to the climax and left it there." The silence fell, "weighing many tons to the square inch," and it deepened each moment until finally broken by "the hysterical and blood-curdling laughter of a single guest." The "hapless president"—Howells himself—looked at his plate and now and then stole a glance at Twain, "standing solitary amid his appalled and appalling listeners"; at Longfellow, gazing with "pensive puzzle" at the speaker; at Holmes, busily writing on his menu; and at Emerson, lost in a kind of "Jovian oblivion." How the party ended or how he and Warner and Twain made their way to Twain's hotel, Howells, when he wrote the story in *My Mark Twain,* could not remember. He did recall, however, that he spent the rest of the night with his "wholly innocent" friend and that, "after a haggard breakfast," he put him on a train for Hartford (59-61).

Perhaps something of the baffling puzzlement of this occasion lingered in Howells' mind when he wrote the last sentence of "My Memories of Mark Twain": "Emerson, Longfellow, Lowell, Holmes—I knew them all and all the rest of our sages, poets, seers, critics, humorists; they are like one another and like other literary men; but Clemens was sole, incomparable, the Lincoln of our literature" (101).

Besides a lifelong friend, Clemens found in Howells an editor who relished his humor, understood his extravagant Western ways, modified his profanity, faithfully reviewed him, and placed him ahead of the older writers who for so long had dominated the *Atlantic.* Howells found in Clemens a man with a background very like his own with whom he could really laugh and talk; beneath Twain's humor, Howells perceived the wild streak of satire and the profound sadness.

Just as James, at the close of his ten-year association with the *Atlantic* editor, went off to England for several years, so also did Mark Twain, soon after the Whittier dinner, leave this country for a two-year stay in Europe. Howells' editorship was drawing to an end; and in the spring of 1882 he too left for England and the Continent, where he remained until July, 1883. No doubt he felt, when he mailed his two long critical essays for the September and the November, 1882, issues of *Century*— the first one "Mark Twain" and the second "Henry James, Jr."— that an important chapter in his friendship with these men had come to a close.

Both James and Twain, however, in widely different ways, helped Howells find his way toward his first important novels,

A Modern Instance (1882), and *The Rise of Silas Lapham* (1885). But readjustments of his relation to his publishers, Houghton and Osgood; ill-health brought on by years of close application to his editorial work; a delightful but enervating summer in London, not to mention gay lunches and visits with James and Twain—all of these factors must be considered in studying the development of Howells as a novelist during the interim years between his resignation as editor of the *Atlantic* in 1881, and the assumption in 1886, of his new duties on the staff of *Harper's.*

II *Interim Years*

When Houghton & Osgood, publishers of the *Atlantic,* separated in 1880, Howells found himself in a difficult position; Houghton (now affiliated with Mifflin) continued to publish the magazine, and Osgood continued to publish Howells' novels. Houghton, however, soon claimed the right to bring out in book form any material which had already appeared in the magazine. Perhaps the controversy between the two men contributed to Howells' decision to give up editing at that time; in any case, Howells wrote on February 2, 1881, to Osgood that he had "definitely resigned the *Atlantic* editorship" and that he would be glad to commit to Osgood the publication of his writings thereafter.[19]

Since Osgood was a personal friend of Howells and had published all his major works up to that time, it is hardly surprising that Howells chose to be loyal to his old associate. Osgood agreed to take everything Howells wrote and to put him on a yearly salary. *The Lady of the Aroostook,* which first appeared in the *Atlantic,* was the last of the Howells novels to be brought out by Houghton, Osgood, and Company before its dissolution. *The Undiscovered Country,* which soon followed it in the *Atlantic,* was the only one of Howells' novels published by Houghton, Mifflin, and Company, before Howells resigned from the magazine. During these interim years—from *A Fearful Responsibility* in 1881 until Osgood's failure in 1885—Osgood was both Howells' agent and publisher.

Something of the pressure under which Howells worked after he left the *Atlantic* in 1881 and before he became a member of the staff of *Harper's* in 1886 may be surmised from his letter to Clemens, April 17, 1881. Clearly Howells was absorbed in his own writing and wished to escape from the literary plans made for him by Osgood and Twain. Attempting to temporize, for he was "in the employ" of Osgood, he wrote: "Osgood tells me that you and he are about to strike a bargain, and he wants to know if I'm ready to go to work." *The Library of Humor,* one of Twain's many suggested collaborations with Howells, was to be pushed through immediately, Osgood had told him; however, Howells could not agree to work on it "except in the most leisurely way." Moreover, he added, "I have to get ready a novel for Scribner by November 1st, so as to let them have the opening chapters for January; and I wish to finish it by Dec. 31, and cut for Europe."[20] The novel to which Howells was referring in his letter to Twain was *A Modern Instance,* which, in fact, did begin to appear in *Century* (the new name of *Scribner's*) in December of that year. Before its publication, however, Osgood brought out still another book by Howells, *Dr. Breen's Practice,* the first novel in this country concerned with a woman's conflict between love and career.

Instead of "cutting for Europe" in December, Howells suffered a collapse which made writing difficult and reading almost impossible. Of these last months of 1881 at "Redtop," his Belmont home, Howells wrote: "An important event of these years was a long sickness which kept me helpless some seven or eight weeks, when I was forced to read in order to pass the intolerable time. But in this misery I found that I could not read anything of a dramatic cast, whether in the form of plays or of novels. The mere sight of the printed page, broken up in dialogue, was anguish."[21]

Early in 1882 Howells gave up his Belmont home and returned to Boston to be nearer his publishers and his friends. The Howellses settled into a comfortable old house, 16 Louisburg Square, where they lived until they departed in July for England. Henry James, who had spent the winter of 1882 with his family on Mt. Vernon Street just a few doors from the Howellses, had already returned to London and was able to procure for four guineas a week an apartment for Howells at 18 Pelham Crescent, consisting, he wrote Howells, of "a drawing room, dining room & three good bedrooms, in a quiet, salubrious, genteel, but unfashionable, situation." By August 1, Howells reported to Osgood: "We are here in a very charming lodging, which James had taken for us, and in which we sat down to a dinner that was cooking for us on our way up from Liverpool . . . James has been with me to-day, and has been very kind."[22]

When Howells arrived in London, *A Modern Instance* was still appearing each month in the *Century* magazine where it came to a conclusion the following October. A postcard message from James to Howells of August 1, 1862—"When you come tomorrow, do bring with you, if not inconvenient, the sheets of the Modern Instance"[23]—suggests that these two friends and collaborators settled down at once to their briefly interrupted literary discussions. Not only was James eager to confer with Howells about his latest novel, but he was also anxious to introduce his friend, now quite as well known in England as in America, to "lots of nice people" and to take him to "the best house or club in London." What better cure for a man who had recently been suffering from overwork?

James Russell Lowell, our minister to the Court of St. James, was also ready to open the doors of London society to his distinguished younger friend. Moreover, Bret Harte, Clarence King, John Hay, T. B. Aldrich, Charles Warner were all in London in the summer of 1882, and Osgood himself was soon to appear. Just as Osgood had arranged luncheons and dinners for writers, publishers, artists, journalists in Boston and New York, so did he gather such groups together in London. Howells wrote to Clemens a month after he had settled into his Pelham Crescent apartment: "Couldn't you and Mrs. Clemens step over for a little while? Warner lunched with us on Tuesday, and is to return from Scotland for a big dinner that Osgood gives next Thursday. W., Gen. Hawley, John Hay, Boughton, Aldrich, Tadema and W. D. H. How does that strike you as a time?"[24]

The gatherings—not attended by women—were, of course, the means by which "connections" were made; through Edmund Gosse, for example, Howells was soon to meet Burne-Jones, Whistler, Ruskin, and Alma-Tadema. Contact with these men encouraged Howells to study the paintings at the Grosvenor Gallery and the Royal Academy; as a result, he became more deeply aware of the relationships between painting and writing, which had already been pointed out to him by Norton, Perry, and James and which later were discussed in several "Editor's Study" essays. Many of these contacts were, however, merely social. These friends and others led Howells—as he wrote to Mark Twain on September 1, 1882,—on trips to Oxford ("We . . . almost walked our legs off seeing it"), to Stoke Pogis ("It is the prettiest and most pathetic place I ever saw"), to Cambridge ("I dined in hall"). Howells reported to Charles Eliot Norton, "We have had a most charming sojourn here, and though everybody says everybody is out of town, we have met all kinds of desirable people." More soberly, he wrote his father: "For the rest we have been rushing hither and thither; and now we are beginning to feel the stir of travel again. But I shall be glad when we are settled, and I am fairly at work." For Howells, who was now contemplating his next novel, *A Woman's Reason,* was then planning to exchange the sociability of London for a retreat in Switzerland.

Though Howells soon lamented to Clemens that "we are having a good, dull, wholesome time in this little pension on the shore of Lake Leman, within gunshot of the Castle of Chillon,"[25] the amount of work he accomplished—and planned—must have been enough to compensate for the dullness of Villeneuve. Not only did he complete *A Woman's Reason,* several farces, *Three Villages,* and *Niagara Re-visited,* but he also gathered the material for *A Little Swiss Sojourn* (to appear several years later in *Harper's*), and planned, through Osgood, a series for *Century,* "Tuscan Cities," which the new editor, Richard Watson Gilder, wished to bring out handsomely illustrated by the etcher, Joseph Pennell. All these undertakings required endless correspondence, and Howells' letters are usually genial, always shrewdly (though humorously) businesslike. In spite of the cold rain, soon to turn to snow, and in spite of the "want of companionship," Howells' life was not dull, especially, for example, when the mail brought an invitation to lecture on English literature at the Johns Hopkins; a request to submit plans for "my third novel" (*Silas Lapham*); a letter from Robert Louis Stevenson, objecting, for personal reasons, to Howells' treatment of divorce in *A Modern Instance;* or one from James, reporting "the little breeze" stirred up in London by Howells' essay, "Mr. Henry James, Jr.," which had just appeared in the November, 1882, *Century.* These various communications distracted Howells from *A Woman's Reason,* which, however, was ready for publication the following fall.

The story of Helen Harkness, left by her supposedly wealthy father, to make her own way in the world, takes its place in the line of Howells novels from *A Chance Acquaintance* to *Annie Kilburn* which are concerned with the position of women in American society. Brought up in a Beacon Hill mansion, skilled in the art of painting china and trimming women's hats, Helen is not at all equipped by her education to earn a living. With his usual urbanity and wit, Howells questioned the emphasis placed in his day on "female accomplishments," and he suggested that women stood in need of education for exactly the same reason that their brothers did—in order adequately to support themselves.

By the end of July, 1883, after several months in Italy and Germany, the Howellses were back in Boston after having had "a lovely time in England" on their way home. They returned once more to Louisburg Square, where they rented a house (No. 4) for a year. Soon Howells, entirely restored in health and spirits, was again in the thick of things reading a manuscript for Clemens; arranging a lecture tour for Edmund Gosse; conversing with a visiting lecturer, Matthew Arnold; editing a book of drawings by his little daughter; and writing the libretto of an opera, *A Sea Change*, for which George Henschel composed the music. All these activities and many more filled the winter of 1883. It is not surprising that *The Minister's Charge*, begun at this time, did not appear until 1887.

Twain's proposal—broached even before Howells left for Europe in 1881—that they collaborate on a play about Colonel Sellers of *The Gilded Age*, was repeated as soon as Howells was settled in his new home. Encouraged by the success of John T. Raymond's impersonation ten years earlier of the hero of *The Gilded Age*, Twain imagined that Colonel Sellers could be put through further adventures as a spiritualist, a temperance reformer, and an inventor and that Howells, who had reviewed Raymond's presentation, might help him. Though Clemens could not imitate anyone else's style, Howells said he could "very easily" catch Clemens' manner of writing. The characters remained for the most part Twain's; Howells varied them "only to make them more like his than, if possible, he could." The two men worked all day long at their separate tasks; and then, after dinner, they read aloud with shouts of joy the results of their labors, persuading themselves that the script was triumphantly funny.

Since the name of Raymond was identified with that of Colonel Sellers and since Clemens was at that time engaged in a quarrel with the actor, the play, entitled *The Claimant*, was first offered to several other actors, as well as to many theater managers; but all turned it down as being distinctly "a Raymond play." When, at last, an elocutionist offered to do the play, the enthusiastic dramatists actually engaged a theater in New York for a week of trial performances.[26] But back again in Boston and away from the contagious high spirits of his collaborator, Howells in a "cold fit" realized that things had gone too far; after a sleep-less night, he wrote to Clemens: "Here's a play which every manager has put out-of-doors and which every actor known to us has refused, and now we go and give it to an elocutioner. We are fools."[27] Thus ended the prolonged effort of the two men to work together over a play which was, from the start, essentially unfit for the stage. Howells compressed an account of these colloborations and negotiations which extended over more than four years into one short and entertaining chapter of *My Mark Twain*. In this same period Howells wrote and published his most important novel up to this time, *The Rise of Silas Lapham*, even before he had completed *The Minister's Charge*. Twain's cheerful suggestion, "*Now* let's write a tragedy," made in a letter of December 20, 1883, before the Sellers play was nearly finished, brought forth no response from his collaborator.

Howells was, in fact, dedicating his mornings to planning and writing *Silas Lapham*. Once more established on familiar Louis-burg Square, he brooded again over the whole question of snobs in American society, especially those of Boston as reflected in the homes they built. The "new lands" were then being developed on the far end of Beacon Street; old families were moving out of the mansions on the squares behind the State House. Who was moving in? The newly rich, of course; for they, like the Laphams, had made more money than they knew how to use, while many an old family—the Coreys, for example—was forced to retrench.

Silas and his family from Vermont occupied just such a house as Howells himself was enjoying and on just such an old-fashioned square. Here, on the strength of the wealth he had accumulated in the paint business, Silas bought for his wife and daughters the fine, old mansion on Nankeen Square which was no longer stylish, in the confused hope that Persis and the girls, Penelope and Irene, would find their place in the stratified society of old Boston. Their social troubles mounted when the elder Laphams dimly perceived that their home, comfortable as it was, was not in the "right" neighborhood and that they must, so they thought, build an impressive mansion on Beacon Street if they were to establish their daughters in the station befitting their millions. Howells summoned up for his novel the same Boston characters whom his readers remembered from *A Modern Instance*, some of whom they would meet again in *The Minister's Charge*: Miss Kingsbury, the Athertons, the Reverend Mr. Sewell, and others. To them he added the Corey family, the cultivated, charming, impoverished Boston aristocrats who were to act as foils to the Laphams.

By August, 1884, Howells himself had bought a house on "the new land" at 302 Beacon Street, where he spent a lonely summer supervising the necessary alterations while his family remained at Kennebunkport, Maine. "And here I have been hard at work, and lonesome, of course," he wrote his father on August 10, 1884. "There is not only nobody else in the house, but nobody else I know sleeps in town. Altogether the effect is queer. There are miles of empty houses all round me. And how unequally things are divided in this world. While these beautiful, airy, wholesome houses are uninhabited, thousands upon thousands of poor creatures are stifling in wretched barracks in the city here, whole families in one room. I wonder that men are so patient with society as they are."[28]

These thoughts in almost the same words are expressed by Miss Kingsbury at the famous dinner party in *Silas Lapham*; a similar feeling runs through *The Minister's Charge*, in which Lemuel Barker, sleeping on a bench in the Botanical Garden, inadvertently became implicated in a theft and with difficulty finally proved his innocence. These two novels, on which Howells worked concurrently, reflect in different ways Howells' musing on Boston society. Without alienating his readers, who undoubtedly moved in the very circles he was satirizing, Howells stretched their sympathy to include characters from a wider social range. Mrs. Clemens' comment on *Silas Lapham* is probably typical of the feeling of many readers; she said it "showed more the moral struggles of mortals than any thing Mr. Howells ever wrote. The characters are all so well drawn. You are compelled to like 'Silas' and 'Persis' in spite of their commonness—particularly Silas."[29]

From his new home on Beacon Street, Howells wrote to Henry James on August 22, 1884: "The sun goes down over Cambridge with as much apparent interest as if he were a Harvard graduate," adding, "Drolly enough, I am writing a story in which the chief personage builds a house 'on the water side of Beacon', and I shall be able to use all my experience, down to the quick."[30]

The use Howells made of the material was to show that Lapham's financial rise, which enabled him to build his new home on Beacon Street, was not a real rise since it was based on business practices that his wife, at least, considered unethical. The house went up in flames before it was ever occupied. Silas might still have retrieved his fortunes, even after this staggering loss, had he been willing to deal with a pair of dishonest business-men; instead, Silas "rose" to the moral demands of the situation, perceived at last the shallowness of his social values, and re-turned with his wife to their white farmhouse in Vermont.

Curiously enough, the actual events of the story of the Laphams are paralleled in time with those of *A Modern Instance*. Bartley Hubbard, the journalist in the novel, is the brash young reporter from *The Events* who in the opening chapter of *Silas Lapham* is seeking an interview with the successful head of the paint factory for his series of articles on "The Solid Men of Business." He had recently married Marcia, and only his nonchalant manner, in contrast with Lapham's perfect dignity, suggests that his story will describe a "fall" as striking, in its way, as Silas' "rise." These two novels reflect the atmosphere of the post-Civil War era when sudden industrial expansion brought moral confusion both to businessmen and to journalists.

The anti-romantic attitude toward love in *A Modern Instance* is also reflected in the sub-plot of *The Rise of Silas Lapham*. Penelope and Irene both succumb to "young Corey," and they almost ruin the chance of happiness of all three because of their romantic notions of love. The Reverend Mr. Sewell—well known to readers of *A Modern Instance*—is appealed to by the distraught Laphams, and he manages to restore the young people and their parents to reason by voicing Howells' distrust of romantic un-selfishness in matters of love. Main plot and subplot are easily seen to be basically related, for Lapham's romantic dream of wealth and Irene's romantic dream of love (as well as Penelope's equally romantic ideal of self-sacrifice) are in the course of the novel re-examined in the light of simple honesty and common sense. They are discarded, with a certain Turgenev sadness, in favor of more rational views.

The Rise of Silas Lapham appeared serially in *Century* between November, 1884, and August, 1885; however, it was not Osgood, but Osgood's former friend and rival, Ticknor, who published the book in 1885. By then the firm of James R. Osgood had finally failed, thus breaking for Howells another link with Boston—a relationship already weakened by the death of Fields (1881⁺). Howells wrote to Clemens in October, 1885, "You will have heard from the din of the newspapers that I have contracted to take all of Harper & Brothers' money in return for certain literary services." By this time Howells had signed a contract with Harper and Brothers, giving them the right to bring out all his writing, which must include one short novel a year and at least one farce, as well as the monthly "Editor's Study," which began to appear in *Harper's* in January, 1886. On June 19 of that year, Howells was officially introduced to his widening circle of readers by a special issue of *Harper's Weekly*, carrying on the cover a handsome engraving of the new occupant of the "Editor's Study" and an essay within, by Henry James, Jr., entitled "William Dean Howells." Just as Howells in 1882 had traced the early life of James in his *Century* essay, so James in his equally important article for *Harper's Weekly* went back briefly to Howells' family origins before turning to his literary beginning, which he dated from *Venetian Life*.

Much as one appreciates, wrote James, "the mingled freshness and irony" of his early books, the really remarkable thing to observe is "the separation that has taken place, in Mr. Howells's case, between [his] early and [his] later manner." After his "first cautious attempts in the walk of fiction," Howells had gained rapidly in the power to trust his own way of seeing things, it seemed to James, until he was sufficiently master of his powers to write *A Modern Instance*, *Silas Lapham*, and *The Minister's Charge*.

Returning to his old quarrel with Howells as to the advantages of the American scene for the novelist, James observed: "The American life which he for the most part depicts is certainly neither very rich nor very fair, but it is tremendously positive, and as his manner of presenting it is as little as possible conventional, the reader can have no doubt about it." In this new field, "Mr. Howells has gone from one success to another." In no sense is Howells "a romancer"; "he adores the real, the natural, the colloquial, the moderate, the optimistic, the domestic, and the democratic." *Silas Lapham*, James remarked, struck him as "the author's high-water mark" until he "opened the monthly sheets of *Lemuel Barker* [*The Minister's Charge*] in which the art of imparting a palpitating interest to common things and unheroic lives is pursued . . . to an even higher point." This was the first novel into which Howells introduced the concept of "complicity," which perhaps, in James's estimation, lent to the story of Lemuel's fate a wider meaning.

When James wrote this essay, Howells, almost fifty years old, was a seasoned novelist and critic who was even more acclaimed on both sides of the ocean than James himself. The fact that

Howells had moved his center of action from Boston to New York, from the *Atlantic* to *Harper's,* invited James to glance ahead in his closing sentences. "We cannot pretend not to take a still more lively interest in his future than we have done in his past," James wrote. "It is hard to see how it can help being more and more fruitful, for his face is turned in the right direction, and his work is fed from sources which play us no tricks." Thus James both summarized the work of his friend up to 1886 and looked expectantly ahead to the future. Though Howells was, at this time, still a Bostonian, living in his Beacon Street house and mailing his monthly "Studies" to New York, James was right in surmising that Howells was about to embark on the most important period of his creative life; his face was "turned in the right direction": toward the social novel, the scene of which was New York.

III *Social Novels*

When Henry Mills Alden, editor of *Harper's,* was considering the publication of *The Minister's Charge* in the *Monthly,* he suggested that Howells make more of a hero of Lemuel Barker. In a letter to James R. Osgood on May 12, 1884, Howells discussed the matter with his publisher in the hope that Osgood might clarify for the editor Howells' intention as to his hero as well as his dislike of editors of "faltering faith." Not quite trusting Osgood's interpretation of these delicate matters, Howells added: "Perhaps you will show him this letter." After explaining to Osgood that Alden had written "he would like to reconsider the plan of my story if I would make more of the hero and heroine," Howells protested, "I don't believe in heroes and heroines, and willingly avoid the heroic." He wondered whether Alden expected "something farcical or comical?" Such, however, was not the author's intention:

> I meant to make a simple, earnest, and often very pathetic figure of my country boy, whose adventures and qualities should win him the reader's entire sympathy and respect. . . . Nothing in a story can be better than life, and I intended to make this story as lifelike as possible. But I look at life as a very serious affair, and the tendency of the story would be to grow rather tragical than comical. I do not see how I could re-write the plan so as to present to Mr. Alden's mind the image of a more considerable hero; I can only give him the assurance that he will be anything but a trivial or farcical figure.[31]

Alden—who later became one of Howells' close friends and collaborators—was unprepared for the growing seriousness of Howells' writing during the decade of the 1880's; so also were many of his readers who bitterly complained of the harshness of Howells' insistence upon the "lifelike" in his stories. When Alden turned down *The Minister's Charge* for *Harper's,* Osgood sold it to Richard Watson Gilder of *Century Magazine,* where it appeared from February to December, 1886. No doubt Alden well understood the taste of his readers; Howells himself knew that his story was not liked, and wrote to James on December 25, 1886, when the serial had drawn to a close, that he found the reviewers "extremely discouraging." They hardly stopped short, he said, "of personal defamation" on the "genteel" grounds that, in telling the story of Lemuel Barker, Howells had introduced his reader to "low" company. "I suspect," he concluded, "it's an effect of the frankness about our civilization which you sometimes wondered I could practice with impunity. The impunity's gone, now, I assure you."[32]

But, ironically enough, Joseph W. Harper, Jr., the owner of the firm, read the story in *Century* and considered it so strikingly new and interesting that he approached Osgood with the request that he should ask Howells to write another "Boston story" equal to *The Minister's Charge.* When Harper received in response the manuscript of *Indian Summer,* "he was in no pains to hide his humorous disgust with the Florentine scene."[33] Harper consoled himself as well as he could, and the novel appeared in 1886 as Howells' first serial in *Harper's.*

Indian Summer was followed the next year by *April Hopes,* "a Boston story" very different in tone from the novel J. W. Harper had admired in *Century.* No doubt Howells felt that this charmingly ironic "romance," in which we meet again the old Boston friends of earlier novels, might please both Alden and Harper. He soon learned that the magazine to which he was now attached was willing to accept stories reflecting more closely his own growing sense of the social problems of the decade; the result was *Annie Kilburn* (1888).

Howells' famous defense of the Chicago Anarchists, which he made between the writing of these two novels, gave the editor of the "Study" a clearer concept of his relations to the House of Harper. The Haymarket Riot occurred in May, 1886; and, after a prolonged trial, the case was brought to the Supreme Court, which finally confirmed the verdict of "guilty" in the autumn of 1887. Howells' *April Hopes* began to appear in the February, 1887, issue of *Harper's*, while he was still living comfortably in Boston, talking literature with Perry, enjoying the Tavern Club (of which he was the first President), and corresponding with Twain about their *Library of Humor*. With the last installment of *April Hopes* on November, 1887, Howells' mood had changed. He wrote a letter to the New York *Tribune* to urge his readers to follow his example in appealing to the governor of Illinois to commute the death penalty of the Anarchists to imprisonment. While there was still hope of saving the lives of the accused men, Howells risked his position with *Harper's* and, in fact, his whole standing as a writer by allying himself with an unpopular cause.

Throughout this confused, surcharged experience, Harper & Brothers never dropped a hint that its new editor was endangering the subscription list. As Howells observed in his "Paper," (written in 1912 at the request of J. Henry Harper), his protest was no doubt as distasteful to the House of Harper as it was to the vast majority of the American public. "It raised a storm about my head," he wrote, but "the magnanimous forebearance" of the publisher prevented him from feeling that his position on Harper's was in jeopardy.

The magazine's attitude toward the editor of the "Study" at the time of his letter to the *Tribune* encouraged him to treat more boldly larger issues in his novels. In *Annie Kilburn*, (June-November, 1888), a story of industrial unrest in a small New England village, Howells fully expressed his newly formulated social philosophy. Annie's well-meaning but patronizing efforts to improve the position of the factory girls of the town might seem innocuous enough to a modern reader; to the readers of *Harper's Monthly* in 1888, the doctrines advanced were arresting—even dangerous. A comment of ex-President Rutherford B. Hayes is probably typical of the state of mind of the period. On January 13, 1889, soon after the publication of the novel as a book, Hayes recorded in his *Diary*, "I read, or finished Mr. Howells' last book, 'Annie Kilburn.'" He added: "I do not find a ready word for the doctrine of true equality of rights (expressed in the novel). Its foes call it nihilism, communism, socialism, and the like. Howells would perhaps call it justice. It is the doctrine of the Declaration of Independence, and of the Sermon on the Mount. But what is a proper and *favorable* word or phrase to designate it?"[34]

Howells' plea for "justice, not alms"[35] in this novel, is an extension of the concept of "complicity" which he had already expressed in *The Minister's Charge* and was soon to repeat on a still larger canvas in *A Hazard of New Fortunes.* Hayes was right in his reflection that Howells was merely bringing up to date the age-old doctrines on which his country was founded, dangerous though they appeared to be when applied to actual social conditions of the 1880's. The dramatic failure of "justice," which Howells had vainly attempted to avert in the incident of the Chicago Anarchists, was forcibly presented to him at the very time in his life when he was suffering over the illness of his daughter. He had, furthermore, during this decade, begun to read Tolstoy, who, he tells us, influenced his thinking more deeply than any other writer.

For a sense of how these various elements were fused in Howells' consciousness and of how they affected his writing, we must consider several of his letters written during this period. To Francis F. Brown, editor of the *Dial,* Howells wrote, on November 11, 1887, in response to a note concerning the Chicago Anarchists, "I don't know yet what the governor has done. While I write, that hideous scene may be enacting in your jail yard—the thing forever damnable before God and abominable to civilized man. But while I don't know, I can still hope."[36] From a Buffalo hotel on November 18, 1887, when there was no longer any room for hope, Howells expressed to his sister Annie the profound effect these events had upon him. He and his wife, he said, no longer cared for "the world's life" and would like to live humbly and simply away from the center of things in order to be "socially identified with the principles of progress and sympathy for the struggling masses." The past few months had been "full of heartache and horror" for them, he wrote, "on account of the civic murder committed last Friday at Chicago." The whole thing had been "an atrocious piece of frenzy and cruelty, for which we must stand ashamed forever before history."[37] The Judge's later statement vindicates Howells.

He felt unable at the moment to write about these events, but "some day I hope to do justice to these irreparably wronged men." The next paragraph of his letter makes us realize that, though Howells himself was perhaps not quite aware of the fact, he had already begun to voice his inner feelings in a new novel: "I'm busy," he told his sister, "with another story, which will deal rather with humanity than with love. I think I shall call it *The Upper and the Nether Millstone*, and the hero to be a minister who preaches the life rather than the doctrine of Christ. Have you read Tolstoi's heart-searching books? They're worth all the other novels ever written. . . ." "But it's no use," he wrote hopelessly to his sister, for he could not then clarify his chaotic thoughts.[38] By the following June, however, *Annie Kilburn*, as the book was finally called, had begun to appear in *Harper's*.

Through Howells' letter to his sister from the Buffalo hotel about the "heartache and the horror" of the "civic murder" of the Anarchists, we are aware, too, that he and his wife were experiencing a personal heartache occasioned by the illness of their elder daughter, Winifred. "I ought to try to explain why we are in Buffalo," he wrote. "For the last two months we've been at the Sanatorium in Dansville, where we took Winny when we left Lake George. I think she'll get well there if anywhere, and the doctors have judged it best that we should be away from her."[39]

While in Buffalo he heard Laurence Gronlund lecture. Through him he first became interested in "the creed of Socialism"; he afterwards read Gronlund's *The Co-operative Commonwealth*; Kirkup's *Encyclopedia Britannica* article on socialism; the Fabian essays; tracts by William Morris; and, most important of all, the novels of Tolstoy on which he commented in his letter to his sister.

Howells' inner suffering, however, could not be assuaged, at least for the time, by either lectures or books, for the world in which he had so fully participated in the 1870's had disappeared. In its place he discovered a larger, harsher, more baffling civilization. After the third installment of *Annie Kilburn*, Edward Everett Hale wrote to congratulate him on his story; when Howells answered on August 30, 1888, thanking him for his note, he bared his own dissatisfaction with himself and the world around him. "But if you read it to the end," he wrote, "you'll see that I solve nothing, except what was solved eighteen centuries ago . . . at present it seems to me that our competitive civilization is a state of warfare and a game of chance, in which each man fights and bets against fearful odds."[40] Howells then expressed his regret that, since he was not in Boston at the time, he could not join the newly organized Tolstoy Club being formed by Hale.

Howells had begun to read Tolstoy in 1885, the year he signed his contract with *Harper's*. It was Perry, of course, who first had introduced him to this Russian writer, whose works he reviewed again and again in the columns of the Editor's Study and elsewhere. "*Anna Karenina* is a wonderful book," Howells wrote his Boston friend on October 30, 1885; "I seem to live in it."[41] Annie Kilburn herself, who is more concerned with "humanity than with love," is a perfect example of the lesson Howells learned from Tolstoy's *Que Faire?*, which he reviewed in *Harper's* of July, 1887. Howells wrote that Tolstoy presented his experiences as a census-taker with that terrible, unsparing honesty of his, relating "how he tried to do good among the poor in Moscow, and how he failed to do any good, because he proposed a physical instead of a moral relief, a false instead of a real charity, while he grew more and more into conceit of himself as a fine fellow."

Tolstoy's dilemma was translated by Howells into Annie Kilburn's problem. She returned to her small, Massachusetts town after a long stay in Italy with her wealthy father, who finally died, leaving her an ample fortune. Annie was then eager to establish her life on a firm basis, to make the best possible use of her money and her energies. Like Tolstoy when he took over his estates, Annie wished to live comfortably and, at the same time, rid her conscience of the sight of misery "by feeding and clothing and sheltering the poor."

A closer look at the lives of the poor showed Tolstoy that two-thirds of them were, in fact, working hard and were happy in their work; the other third was miserable because of envy of the indolent idleness of the rich. Like men of wealth, this third really despised labor and, therefore, could not be helped by the rich, for the lives of the poor "were of a piece with theirs, while a great social gulf, forbidding all brotherly contact, was fixed between them." All these facts became clear to Tolstoy as he gathered data for the census in Moscow. But Annie had yet to learn such social axioms. When the women of Hatboro called upon her to ask her help in establishing a "Social Union" for the workers in the nearby factories, she, like the younger Tolstoy, eagerly agreed to aid them. The minister, Mr. Peck, pricked her bubble by voicing Tolstoy's later views—that the only thing one can give is oneself, that money and good works somehow do not suffice. The ideas of "complicity"—that we live not to ourselves alone but in our social relations as well—are pointed out clearly by the minister; they reflect the essential thoughts which moved that "singular Russian," Tolstoy, to give up his wealth and become a worker among the peasants.

We cannot but feel as we read Howells' review of *Que Faire?* and the novel which stemmed from the ideas expressed by

Tolstoy, that Howells was, as he said, indeed, "reading and thinking about questions that carry me beyond myself and my miserable literary idolatries of the past."[42] Tolstoy's "mortifying study of himself," Howells wrote in his review, holds the "kindly well-to-do up to self-scorn" and makes him ashamed of his comforts. Tolstoy acted upon his beliefs when "he sold all he had and gave it to the poor, and turned and followed Him"; the rest of us are content with theorizing. In mock irony, aimed at himself as well as at the others, Howells declaimed: "Come, star-eyed Political Economy! Come, Sociology, heavenly nymph! and soothe the ears tortured by this echo of Nazareth. Save us, sweet Evolution! Help, O Nebular Hypothesis! Art, Civilization, Literature, Culture! is there no escape from our brothers but in becoming more and more truly their brothers?"[43]

The fact that Howells' satiric evocation was not only heard but heeded is revealed in the writing of such people as Richard T. Ely, the political economist, Edward Bellamy, Hamlin Garland, Jane Addams, Henry George, and many others, each of whom voiced his social views in his characteristic fashion. An expression of the social-religious thinking of the time was the Church of the Carpenter, an Episcopal Mission, established in Boston by the Rev. W. D. P. Bliss, which won for a time Howells' interest. In almost every issue *The Dawn,* the publication of the Mission, announced *Annie Kilburn* as among the important socialistic novels recommended to its members; its author, however, never in any formal sense, allied himself with this group.

Howells' dissatisfaction with the "civilization" of his time is reflected in a letter to Henry James of October 10, 1888; his mood found expression in his writing rather than in allegiance to groups or movements. Howells admitted to his friend in London: "I'm not in a very good humor with 'America' myself. It seems to be the most grotesquely illogical thing under the sun; and I suppose I love it less because it won't let me love it more." He then added: "I should hardly like to trust pen and ink with all the audacity of my social ideas; but after fifty years of optimistic content with 'civilization' and its ability to come out all right in the end, I now abhor it, and feel that it is coming out all wrong in the end, unless it bases itself anew on a real equality. Meantime, I wear a fur-lined overcoat, and live in all the luxury my money can buy."[44] Howells wrote, he said, from "a wide-verandahed villa in forty acres of seclusion." As a matter of fact, the Howellses had spent "this non-ended summer" in Little

Nahant, Massachusetts, not to enjoy "all the luxury that money [could] buy" but in the vain hope that "poor Winny might get a little better possibly."

In an endeavor to save Winifred's life, the family finally moved to New York in November, 1888, and settled in an old-fashioned house on Stuyvesant Square (330 East 17th Street), across the Park from St. George's Episcopal Church and the Friends' Meeting House. Here they were living when Winifred died in a sanitarium the following March, and here Howells found what solace he could in writing his next novel in which his old friends the Marches also quit Boston and hazarded their fortunes in New York. At his desk in "an uppermost room" in the house, Howells wrote at top speed the serial which opened in *Harper's Weekly* on March 2, 1889. The first chapters of the serial—those dealing with the Marches' distracted search for an apartment in the noise and confusion of New York—are the ones he wrote at the very time of his family tragedy. When he began writing the book, he said, "I reeled about in it, for I had to write it while the heaviest sorrow I had known was a staggering load on heart and brain; but when I had struggled up and found my footing, I believe I went forward with no uncertain tread."

Howells had been meditating *A Hazard of New Fortunes* during the painful months of the summer and autumn of 1888. It was undertaken with the full encouragement of J. W. Harper, whose letter to Alden from Saratoga was forwarded to Howells by the editor in September, 1888. In this communication Harper suggested that Howells be urged to prepare "a *feuilleton* for the *Weekly*, which would be a powerful presentation of the life of our great metropolis, social, educational, economical, political." In these weekly numbers, not only "the rich & the poor, the idler & the worker, the silly men & frivolous women" but also the elevated railroads, the monopolies, the civic nuisances, the schools and churches, were to be presented in such a way as to "command the interest of all classes." No more fascinating invitation could have been placed before Howells than this suggestion of Harper's during his summer of restless distress, both personal and social. The fact that *Harper's Weekly* had already begun to cover the streetcar strikes of Brooklyn in handsomely illustrated articles supplied Howells with the central scenes he needed for the longest and perhaps the most important novel of his career.

But it was not these stirring articles which first launched Howells into his novel. In the "Preface" to *A Hazard* (1907) he recalls that he amused himself the most in writing the early, house-hunting chapters of the story and that he thus regained his ability to contemplate "the vast mass of life" which was to fill to overflowing the most ambitious of his novels. Whether or not the characters of Basil and Isabel March are sufficiently individualized to sustain this "largest canvas" Howells had yet allowed himself is an important critical question. Beginning as a *feuilliton* of the many-sided life of "our great metropolis," the novel never achieves the structural strength we ask of the greatest novels; on the other hand, the very fact that the wide variety of scenes is held together only by the rather shadowy figures of the Marches lends the panorama an objective quality which might have been lost had the Marches been more implicated in the action. Though Basil and Isabel remain throughout the novel hardly more than peripheral observers to the struggles of others, they nevertheless change and develop in their contact with the city; and they reflect, at a distance, the growth of Howells at that period of his life when he too was "trying to catch on to the bigger life" of New York.[45]

As editor of *Every Other Week,* March, like Howells, became painfully aware of the contrast of the rich and the poor—one made all too apparent by a series of streetcar strikes which resulted in riots and bloodshed. Less fortunate than Howells in his publisher, March edited a journal owned by an ignorant and brutal oil-magnate, Dryfoos, who did not hesitate to drop from the staff of *Every Other Week* a fine old socialist, Lindau, though March vainly tried to defend him. Events come to a climax with the fatal shooting of Conrad, Dryfoos' son, who, as a dedicated Christian Socialist, took part in one of the strikes. With Lindau as his spokesman, Howells tests the ideas of Tolstoy that one's beliefs should be matched by one's actions. Conrad literally "lays down his life" for the poor, illustrating in so doing the full meaning of the Christian concept of the Crucifixion. Conrad's death exemplifies the demand, made on professing Christians and Socialists as well, of the sacrifice of "self."

But what of ordinary people, like the Marches, with children to bring up? Not only did they worry about schools, salaries, family illnesses, but they also enjoyed dining in little French restaurants, sitting on the benches in Stuyvesant Park, and associating with their friends in the ordinary ways of the world. Though March defended Lindau in his conflict with Dryfoos and though he witnessed and comprehended the Christlike sacrifice of Conrad

Dryfoos, the only real resolution of the wide range of problems presented lies in the summarizing conversations of Basil and Isabel March; in which they sadly agree that this is a "chance-world" anyway, in which one struggles, suffers, and is also amused—entirely according to chance. Behind it all, *perhaps*, lies a kind of hope, in as much as occasionally a man is willing to die for the sake of others. Concerned as March was with liberal causes, he had no intention of adopting the role of Christian martyr—nor, indeed, had his author. Howells recognized, however, that *A Hazard of New Fortunes* began after the first few chapters "to find its way to issues nobler and larger than those of the love-affairs common to fiction"[46]—but to them he frequently returned in the many novels he was yet to write.

In the late spring of 1889, the unfinished manuscript of *A Hazard* was packed away when the Howellses gave up their apartment on the Square. It was taken out again "in a country house in the Belmont border of Cambridge," where Howells rapidly "pressed it to conclusion before the summer ended." The long novel was issued in weekly installments until the end of the year; it came "so easily from the pen" that Howells had misgivings, he said, as to its value. Nor did he hear any responses from his readers. "As a serial," Howells wrote, the story "crept a sluggish course" before a public which gave no sign of either liking or disliking it. However, in October, 1889, Howells signed to his own advantage a new agreement with *Harper's*; so we may assume that the success of the serial was apparent to those in the office at Franklin Square. When the novel appeared in a volume at the end of the year, it "stood on its feet and went its way to greater favor than any book of his had yet enjoyed."[47]

IV *The "Editor's Study"*

When Joseph Wesley Harper in 1885 invited Howells to join the staff of *Harper's Monthly*, he wished him to continue to be heard as a critic as well as a novelist, for now Howells was as well known for his criticism as for his fiction. He therefore engaged Howells to supply his magazine not only with a serial a year but also with a critical appraisal of current books from home and abroad. Harper suggested that these monthly pronouncements should issue from a new department for which the editor himself should find a title. Howells chose to call it the "Editor's Study."

The story of Howells' early association with the House of Harper is told in a "Paper," written in 1912 at the request of J. Henry Harper. After the publication of several early poems in *Harper's*, Howells' contributions had been rejected so consistently that he had ceased submitting them. Now, however, with Henry Mills Alden as editor and Harper as publisher, the attitude changed. After an exchange of letters and telegrams in the autumn of 1885, Howells came down from Boston to lunch with the head of the House "in a fine great room" at Franklin Square, where, "under the roaring eves of the elevated railroad," the details of the agreement between author and publisher were worked out. "For a certain salary" ($10,000), Howells was "to write at least one short novel every year, with at least one farce, and as much more as I could or liked in the various kinds I was supposed to be expert in." Having agreed to this much of the bargain, J. W. Harper then "made a set at" Howells to do what he had already refused to do in letters to Alden—conduct a regular monthly department. Howells knew that book reviewing would be detrimental to novel writing; he urged his reasons against his "amiable chief" but at last gave way—for $3,000 additional salary. "I still think I was right," Howells wrote in 1912, "and that turning aside to critical essaying at that period of my career, when all my mind tended to fictioning, had the effect I feared. A novelist should be nothing but a novelist. . . ."[48]

Howells never had had the experience, however, of "being nothing but a novelist" even before he signed away the privilege in his contract with Harper. In the five-year interval between his resignation from the *Atlantic* and his association with *Harper's* he had, it is true, published six notable novels; during the same years he had also written many critical essays, most of which appeared in *Harper's* new rival, *Century*. When J. W. Harper made a bid for Howells against Richard Watson Gilder, he wished to engage the whole man; for he recognized that Howells' philosophy of realism, illustrated by his novels, was as important as his fiction. The moment was propitious, for James R. Osgood had recently failed in the publishing business and had himself become connected with Harper.

Though Howells often chafed under the double burden placed on him by Harper, it actually enriched his writing both as a critic and a novelist. His wide reading of Continental literature and his critical appraisal of European writers for American readers not only made him an arbiter of taste in his day but also added a new dimension to his own fiction; and *A Hazard of New Fortunes*, which he considered his best novel, reflected something of the "breadth and depth" of the European writers. Faithful to his contract with Harper, Howells produced his annual novel and farce, in spite of the monthly demands of the "Editor's Study"; and he maintained in these various fields a remarkably high literary standard. When Howells' agreement with Harper lapsed in 1891, the House continued to serialize many of his novels and then to publish them in book form. Since Howells was no longer contracted to publish only in *Harper's*, many of his stories and essays appeared in other publications; these, too, frequently came out later in books bearing the imprint of Harper and Brothers. The fact that Harper not only was a publishing house but also the owner of several monthlies and weeklies which reached somewhat different publics made an association with it of great value to Howells in his double role of novelist and critic.

It was understood by Howells and Harper in their initial talk in Franklin Square that the new editor was to make the "Editor's Study" what he liked. At the same time, Harper clearly stated that there were certain things (capital punishment, among them) that a man "might not say in the Harper periodicals," and that he "rang a little bell" in his office when a member of the staff infringed. Howells, apparently, never suffered from the disapproval of his publisher: "The House left me free to say what I pleased on whatever topic I chose to talk about. Their tolerance put me on my conscience, and I tried to catch the tinkle of the little bell when it was not actually sounded."

It was, then, as a seasoned critic that Howells was invited by J. W. Harper to open the door of the "Editor's Study" in January, 1886. After "a silence of some years," he wrote in his first "Study" essay, he had gathered "a very pretty store of prejudices to indulge and grudges to satisfy," as well as "some opinions, honest as opinions go." These prejudices, grudges, and opinions, Howells proposed, while sitting "at fine ease," to talk over with his reader, who was "invited to look at the same books and consider the same facts with him." The "Study," in short, was to be "a sort of free parliament, but for the presiding officer only; or, a symposium of one."

With this agreeable introduction, the editor regarded the piles of books already gathered on his desk and laid down in his genial way the basic principles which, in fact, guided him throughout his six rather tumultuous years in the "Study." "For our own part," he wrote, "these novels strike us in their range and tendency as admirable'"—not that all of them are good or that any of them is wholly good, but because "we find in nearly every one of them a disposition to regard our life without the literary glasses so long thought desirable, and to see character, not as it is in other fiction, but as it abounds outside of all fiction" (322). To Howells this unromantic view of actuality distinguishes the American novel from a similar group of English novels and "relates American fiction to the only living movement in imaginative literature," that of Continental fiction. Because of their "superior freshness and authenticity," these American novels have "the same good right to be as the like number of recent Russian novels, French novels, Spanish novels, Italian novels, Norwegian novels." This was Howells' firm position as a critic; from it he never deviated.

His repudiation of the old-fashioned romantic novels of England reminds us of Howells' essay, "Mr. Henry James, Jr.," which stirred up an inter-ocean argument in 1882. His appreciation of the freshness and authenticity of American fiction recalls his delight in Twain's Huck Finn. His comparison of American novels with those of the Continent makes us remember that from the early days of his editorship of the *Atlantic* he had urged upon his readers Björnson's tales and those of Turgenev. Howells' standard of judgment remained the same when he moved to *Harper's Monthly*; further reading and writing had only strengthened his convictions.

The new editor of the "Study" made use of these beliefs when he picked up "one of the best of these new fictions of ours" from the pile on his desk, Miss Murfree's *Prophet of the Great Smoky Mountain*, to illustrate his theories of literature. He commended the author for the simple and natural presentation of "those Tennessee mountaineers of hers," which is "marred only here and there by the traditions of the bad school we were all brought up in"—the verbiage and "hysterical emotionality" of Charles Dickens and Victor Hugo. Occasionally, Miss Murfree is romantic, "which is worse than uninteresting," in her presentation of the "lank-bodied, religious, unmoral, primitive-passioned people" of Tennessee; but her attempt to catch "the actual speech and manners" of the mountaineers—when not spoiled by "a certain romance of motive"—is admirable. In the columns of his first "Study," Howells played this same light of reason over a dozen books by American and European writers.

Howells found space, too, for a brief essay on language—especially the American language—as it is actually spoken and written. In spite of disparaging comments from critics abroad, the American writer must be sensitive to "the parlance he hears" and not be enslaved to "the parlance he reads," for "no language is ever old on the lips of those who speak it, no matter how decrepit it drops from the pen" (324). Go into the shops and fields to learn this "near-at-hand truth" which realism taught before she was named, Howells urged aspiring storytellers. If our writers should attempt to use what the critics imagine to be "English," they would only succeed in being priggish; as for the editor of the "Study," he would "like to hear them speak true American, with all the varying Tennesseean, Philadelphian, Bostonian, and New York accents" (325). Grammarians and purists suppose that language is static, but languages, like all other "gifts of God," are freely used by "common people" and are therefore always changing. How the "common man" expresses his feelings, as well as what he does, is important to those who become a part of the new literary movement of realism, which is basically a democratic movement. Truth again—this time in his use of language—is the standard set by Howells for the aspiring novelist. "Being born Americans, we would have them use 'Americanisms'" in spite of the critics; the tone of the novelist's language must be true to that of the people in the same sense that the tone of the morals and manners of his characters must subtly reflect those prevailing in the American society he knows, dull and commonplace though they may appear to those who still long for the old, outworn, romantic fiction of another era.

During the next six years, Joseph W. Harper never had occasion to sound the little warning bell—not even, as we have noted, when Howells in 1887 defended the Chicago Anarchists. Before he took over the "Editor's Study" Howells' position on "the new realism," which was the literary reflection of the scientist's belief in objective truth, was well understood by all readers of *A Modern Instance, Silas Lapham,* and *A Minister's Charge.* It was, in fact, his insistence that heroes and heroines are less interesting than the ordinary man or woman that first attracted J. W. Harper to the Howells novels appearing in *Century.* He encouraged Howells to study even more searchingly the rich and the poor, the beauty and the ugliness, and the order and the disorder of the metropolis in which he had come to live. In his letters to Howells about these matters, it is to be noticed that no reference is made to problems involving sex. The reader must be reminded that the restrictions which Howells laid upon himself in his treatment of the relationship of men and women were precisely the ones shared by such outstanding writers as Mark Twain and Henry James, as well as by Harper, Gilder, and all other publishers of the day, who well knew the tastes and opinions of their readers. Since writers, publishers, and reading public alike were breathing the air of Queen Victoria, it is hardly surprising that Harper was never tempted to ring his bell because of the "love business" in Howells' own novels.

All of Howells' editors and advisors were in agreement on this matter of restraint; his Ohio "chief," when Howells left for Venice, advised him never to write anything objectionable to women; Lowell repeated this same admonition; Holland and Gilder of the *Century* and Alden and Harper reflected a similar attitude. With one accord these men took as their standard the taste of the vast throng of women who were the main supporters of the magazine and book business of the era. Frequently, when Howells, as an editor, curbed Mark Twain and other contributors, he did so from a practical point of view. Suppose an American writer should produce an *Anna Karenina* or a *Madame Bovary*, he wrote, "What editor of what magazine would print such a story?" The question raised by Howells was a valid one.

It is noteworthy that, from the "Editor's Study" and later from *Harper's Weekly*, Howells was permitted to defend the art, if not the ethics, of Tolstoy's *Kreutzer Sonata*, censored in this country; to review favorably Flaubert's *Madame Bovary*, still under the cloud of the Paris trial; to point out the strength and truth of Zola's naturalism, which was raising a heated controversy in Europe; to insist that *Jude the Obscure* should be published as Hardy wrote it, when Harper himself asked him to modify several chapters; to urge that Ibsen's *Ghosts*, banned in London, should be applauded in New York; and to review favorably the stories and poetry of that harried young writer, Stephen Crane.

It is again surprising to the modern reader to learn that Howells did not allow the books he defended to lie on his own living-room table and that he personally refrained from writing in any of his novels a love scene which might bring a blush to the cheeks of "the tenderest bud" at a dinner party. Partly influenced all of his life by the simple morality of his Sweden-borgian family, partly swayed by the well-established taboos and restrictions of his period, Howells was a sensitive individual who enjoyed by temperament what he called "the cleanly respectabil-ities." This preference does not in the least imply that he suf-fered from any serious "sex complex." How strange the very phrase would have sounded to that pre-Freudian generation!

Many critics have observed that Howells tended to avoid the "palpitating divan" in his novels; they have also noted that he stressed "the smiling aspects of life," which he believed "the more American." We must remember, however, that implicit in his very belief in realism was his conviction that American conditions were unlike those of Russia, France, Italy, or Spain. In the United States, he pointed out, we do not execute or banish to Duluth our political enemies; nor, as a general rule, do we accept the double standard in morals which is common abroad. Those who persuade themselves that we do, and seek to make accounts of life in the United States more exciting, more wicked, than the actual circumstances warrant, are, according to Howells, either romantic in their views, or, what is worse, purveyors of sensa-tionalism. Howells' insistence that the novelist look steadily at *things as they are* gained for him in his day the reputation of ruthless objectivity; in the 1920's because he did not as a realist step beyond the "customs and manners" of his time, Howells was considered timid and prudish. He was neither the surgeon with a long sharp knife—as he was pictured in a cartoon of the period —nor the maiden aunt of American literature, as H. L. Mencken dubbed him. He was, in fact, the novelist-critic who made use of the inductive method of the scientist in his own clear glance at the shams and subterfuges of the life about him and who recog-nized a similar quest for truth in the great novels of the more outspoken writers from abroad. These he interpreted to a new generation of American writers—to Hamlin Garland, Stephen Crane, Theodore Dreiser, and Frank Norris; but he also warned that to exaggerate is to romanticize; to be false to the humbler scene is to be unrealistic.

Howells' "polemics" against the sentimental and the romantic in fiction brought angry retorts from critics on both sides of the Atlantic; it is doubtful whether the reverberations of battle caused by his pronouncements would have been felt by the writ-ers of the next generation had he not brought out *Criticism and Fiction* (1891) when he decided that the time had come for him to quit the "Editor's Study." Before he left, J. Henry Harper persuaded him to selected from the hundreds of columns of the "Study" the portions of his essays which seemed to him the best expression of his literary beliefs. The result was the volume which, when it appeared, made Howells "an issue in the literary movement of the day." His monthly "Studies," Garland observed, had the effect of "dividing the public into two opposing camps."

In the last essay of the "Study," March, 1892, Howells warned his readers that he had already bottled his "monthly ministrations of gall and worm-wood" and offered them to the public. The small bottle contained nothing more distasteful than Howells' concentrated attack on "the old romantic ideals" of Scott, Balzac, Victor Hugo, Dickens, Thackeray, and even Hawthorne. The "fungus-growth" of romanticism is the true poison; truth, no matter how unpleasant, is at last salutary and with this alone the novel, as opposed to the romance, is concerned.

"The tests are very plain and simple," declared Howells, "and they are perfectly infallible. If a novel flatters the passions, and exalts them above the principles, it is poisonous; it may not kill, but it will certainly injure." Much more poisonous are "the whole spawn of so-called unmoral romances." These are deadly; they do kill, for they depict a "world where the sins of sense are unvisited by the penalities following, swift or slow, but inexorably sure, in the real world." Howells, in short, believed in the punishment of wrong-doing in exactly the sense that the Greek dramatists believed in the Eumenides and the Furies. Indeed, he first thought of calling A Modern Instance—which is the story of the inexorable penalty visited on romantic passion—The New Medea, for he recognized the kinship between Marcia Gaylord and Euripides' heroine.

The "gaudy hero and heroine," Howells insisted, are responsible for much suffering in the world since they throw themselves on the altars of Love and Duty and overlook the humdrum virtues of "prudence, obedience and reason." Such characters are merely barbarians, full of obsolete ideas, moved by "the motives and ethics" of savages. Novels that "tickle our prejudices and lull our judgment, or that coddle our sensibilities or pamper our gross appetite for the marvelous"—all such writing tends to "clog the soul with unwholesome vapors of all kinds." They "weaken the moral fiber, and make their readers indifferent to 'plodding perseverance and plain industry,' and to 'matter-of-fact poverty and common-place distress.'" Is "love," mistaken or

real, the central concern of life? Or is there genuine novel
material to be found in the hidden struggles of daily existence—
with paying off a mortgage, holding a job, supporting a hopeless
invalid, or dealing with a romantically confused son or daughter?
Howells thought there was and used his powers, both as a
novelist and as a critic, to maintain the beliefs that "the light
of civilization has already broken even upon the novel" and that
the responsible novelist avails himself of this illumination.[49]

To Howells, "civilization" meant "enlightenment," in the eighteenth-century use of the term; it meant the free use of "reason"
in quest of "truth," a pursuit to which the writer as well as the
scientist is dedicated. This standard of judgment carried Howells
beyond the realm of fiction alone to a consideration of "any
work of the imagination." It led him, too, far beyond the moral
conventions of the 1890's to meditations on the final relation of
morality and art in the light of truth. "I confess that I do not
care to judge any work of the imagination without first of all
applying this test to it," he wrote. Above all, we must ask,

> Is it true?—true to the motives, the impulses, the principles that
> shape the life of actual men and women? This truth, which
> necessarily includes the highest morality and the highest artistry—
> this truth given, the book cannot be wicked and cannot be weak.
> . . . In the whole range of fiction we know of no true picture of
> life—that is, of human nature—which is not also a masterpiece of
> literature, full of divine and natural beauty (49).

Limited though Howells was in certain areas, the extraordinary
fact is that he opened the door to the literature of the twentieth
century when he insisted month after month in his "Editor's
Study" that *reality* has more to offer both reader and writer than
romance. "Let fiction cease to lie about life," he wrote; "let it
portray men and women as they are, actuated by the motives
and passions in the measure we all know." The important phrase
in this dictum is "in the measure we all know" (51). To Howells,
the naturalism of Balzac, Dickens, and Zola lay outside this
measure; it was therefore essentially romantic.

After six years of belaboring the writers of romance, the
editor packed up his "literary divinities" from France, Italy,
Norway, Russia, and Spain and quit the scene of battle. "With
so good a cause of his, the cause of Common Honesty in literature," he admitted in the March, 1892, issue of *Harper's*, he had
really achieved very little. "The followers of fraud and humbug,"

once aroused, "had returned blow for blow, and much mud from afar." The best the editor could do was to bottle his potent mixture of wormwood, put a title on it, *Criticism and Fiction*, and send it forth into the world to cure as best it might the ills of romanticism. Before leaving the "Study," Howells wrapped up the pictures and busts of the "canonized realists," dusted off those of the romanticists, and reinstated them in their niches. He came at last to "that great first of all realists, the supreme artist, the incomparable master of fiction," Tolstoy. The place that had known the master would know him no more; Thackeray was duly reinstated on his pedestal and all was restored to the order which marked the quiet "Study" before Howells entered "this haunt of the muses."

Thus Howells gathered up his "exiled gods," his "moral bric-a-brack," and made a bundle of them as best he could, not so much "with the intention of setting them up in another place" as of saving them from "derision and dishonor." "What is this hanging here?" he exclaimed aloud, "A map of Altruria? It is an outlandish region inhabited by people of heart, a sort of economic Pays du Tendre. It ought not to be tolerated."

At the very time when Howells wrote this farewell to the "Study," he had completed his arrangements with John Brisbane Walker to become co-editor of the recently reorganized *Cosmopolitan*. So to an office on the corner of Broadway and 21st Street Howells transported his literary busts and his map of Altruria for an uneasy six months. One wonders whether he ever unpacked his bundle of bric-a-brac; we know, however, that he studied his map so intently that life in Altruria became to Howells, for several years, more absorbing than that of New York. Between November, 1892, and October, 1893, the series of essays entitled "A Traveller From Altruria," appeared in the *Cosmopolitan* and were followed the next year by a second series, "Letters of an Altrurian Traveller."[50]

Howells' tireless and resourceful experiments, both in criticism and in fiction, had brought him to a position of prominence in both fields at a time when the country stood in need of writers who could look more searchingly at the rapidly changing social scene. Conscious of the limitations of the realistic novel, and also aware of the subtle shift in public taste in the 1890's, Howells turned for a while, to romance, poetry, and drama; he remained, however, essentially the novelist-critic, straying into what he called "the flowery fields" of other literary forms.

CHAPTER 4

Romance, Poetry, and Drama

I *Altruria, a Romance*

I WISH to goodness that you could take a week off and run
up to this White Mountain Village," Howells wrote on August
9, 1885, to Clemens from New Hampshire. He added: "I think
the landscape would be a revelation to you, and if we were not
always insulting our maker you would be amazed at the affront
offered him by the ugliness of the little Yankee town dropt into
the beauty of his everlasting hills."[1]

The "affront" offered "our maker" by the ugliness, both physical
and moral, of Hatborough, Massachusetts, was presented to the
reader a few years later in *Annie Kilburn*; it was described again,
even more vehemently, in *A Hazard of New Fortunes*, with New
York as the scene. Between November, 1892, and October, 1893,
a series of essays appeared in *The Cosmopolitan*, in which our
entire industrialized civilization was surveyed by a traveler from
a more advanced—because more Christian—culture. When these
essays came out as *A Traveler From Altruria* in 1894, the title-
page declared the whole to be a "Romance"; it is, in fact, an
unromantic expression of Howells' sense of the ugliness of our
civilization in contrast to its possible grandeur. The vehemence
of Howells' social thought destroyed, for a time, his confidence
in the novel form as a vehicle for his ideas.

Howells wrote the Altrurian essays, for the most part, in a
comfortable New Hampshire hotel situated in the White Mountains, where he spent several summers with his family. Hard-
working New England school teachers waited on the tables in
this country hotel, while poor farmers in the neighborhood
supplied the guests with food and services. Howells had brooded
over the contrast of rich and poor a number of years before he
finally hit upon the character into whose mouth he could put
his ideas—Mr. Aristides Homos, a traveler from an imaginary
island, Altruria, lying in the blue Aegean Sea. At the same time,

Howells created Mr. Twelvemough, the dapper little novelist whose uncomfortable duty it was to welcome the Altrurian as his guest in the very hotel in the White Mountains which his author knew so well. This writer of light fiction is also a mouthpiece for his author, voicing by word and gesture Howells' more hesitant and conventional attitudes. *A Traveler From Altruria* is, then, a dialogue between Howells the social-religious radical and Howells the popular novelist, on the subject of conditions in the United States at the moment when it was beginning to suffer from the depression of the 1890's. Howells calls his loosely connected essays "Romance," and over the whole he throws a gossamer veil of fantasy in order to soften the impact of his increasingly liberal thought.

Where did Howells' Christian Socialist thoughts come from? One might well point to his Swedenborgian and Quaker background; to his youthful rambles in the woods and fields of Ohio and his association with country folk; to the idealistic bent fostered by his poetry-reading father; to his interest in the Shakers of New England; to his connections with the Abolitionist group of Boston as assistant editor and editor of the *Atlantic*, when Howells grew to love Lowell, Longfellow, Holmes, and the outspoken Unitarian minister, Edward Everett Hale; and to his reading of William Morris, Edward Bellamy, Henry George, and others. However, the greatest social influence on Howells during his six years in the "Editor's Study" of *Harper's* was undoubtedly Tolstoy, as he himself declared a decade later in *My Literary Passions*.

Soon after writing to Clemens in August, 1885, Howells began to read the works of Tolstoy, discovering something of the nature of the problem suggested by a Yankee village. Since Howells in this same autumn signed his contract with Harper and in January opened the door of the "Study," it is not surprising that he reviewed Tolstoy's novels, stories, and essays in these columns as they appeared in translation during the latter half of the 1880's. The reviews make it apparent that the effect upon Howells of Tolstoy's mighty novels was not literary, as we have seen Turgenev's to have been, but ethical, social, and, above all, religious. Because of Tolstoy, both *Annie Kilburn* and *A Hazard of New Fortunes* gained in seriousness of purpose. At the same time, *A Hazard*, Howells' longest and most searching novel, was also his most formless.

Perhaps Howells, in calling his Altrurian essays a "Romance," admitted that his Tolstoyan ideas had destroyed the form of the more limited realistic novel which Turgenev had taught him to write. It is certain that when Howells left the "Editor's Study" he had grown, for the time being, impatient of "literary" ideas, which according to his new master were less important than "ethical" considerations—and that he carried with him the bust of Tolstoy, as well as the map of Altruria. As Howells packed away the likeness of Tolstoy, he studied again the Russian's "look of the baffled peasant, the troubled diety, whose plain sad face is perplexed with the vain endeavor to live some Christ-like solution of the riddle of the painful earth." Howells' own endeavor to find a solution to the riddle of American civilization is expressed first in two contributions to the "Editor's Study" (December issues of 1890 and 1891) and then in *A Traveler From Altruria,* over which broods the face of Tolstoy.

In the same issue of *Harper's* of March, 1892, in which Howells bowed out of the "Study," his new novel, *The World of Chance,* began to appear; and in it the concepts of Altruria are also explored. This deftly turned narrative, which recounts the first experiences of a clever young writer from Midland, Ohio, in the publishing world of New York, is a link between the "chance world" of *A Hazard* and the ideal society of *A Traveler;* it reflects, therefore, a stage in Howells' thought. Percy Bysshe Shelley Ray, a young poet-journalist-novelist, is temporarily lost in the same "chance world" in which his older colleague, Basil March, found himself several years earlier. He—like Basil and Howells—is forced to consider the grim facts of a great city; he is aided in his thinking by a gaunt old Socialist, David Hughes, who bears a striking resemblance to Lindau, the friend and mentor of Basil, who, in turn, resembled Howells' old German teacher in Ohio. Though Hughes, a former member of the Brook Farm community, had read and admired Tolstoy, he had also discovered his weakness. "I appreciate to the utmost the spiritual grandeur of the man's nature," he said to Ray, "but practically I don't follow him." The reason he gave for not accepting Tolstoy as a leader was that which Howells expressed at this time: Tolstoy's "unpracticality." Altruria or the "good society," is to be gained only by the vote. Howells wrote in *The World of Chance*:

> We shall never redeem the world by eschewing it. Society is not to be saved by self-outlawry. The body politic is to be healed politically. The way to have the golden age is to elect it by the

Australian ballot. The people must vote themselves into possession of their own business, and intrust their economic affairs to
the same faculty that makes war and peace, that frames laws,
and that does justice. What I object to in Tolstoy is his utter
unpracticality. I cannot forgive any man, however good or great,
who does not measure the means to the end (91).

Hughes attempted to give form to his social ideas in a book entitled *The World Revisited,* but his essays never found a publisher. Howells embodied Hughes's concepts in two very publish-
able books, which, by their titles, show their relationship to
Hughes's manuscript. *The World of Chance* (the real world) and
A Traveler From Altruria (the idealized world) were, in a sense,
two aspects of the American world of 1894 "revisited" by Howells,
who was painfully aware of the actual social scene, and dreamed
of its improvement.

David Hughes shared the socialistic views of his predecessor,
Lindau, of *A Hazard of New Fortunes.* His belief in the vote,
and his insistence on the relation between "the means to the
end" in social reform are a reflection of Howells' own discussions
with a group of practical reformers, the Christian Socialists, with
whom he associated when, after the death of his daughter, he
moved his family back to Boston in December, 1889. Hamlin
Garland, who was a member of this group, many years later
recalled a conversation he held with Howells at this time which
reflects the reading of the Christian Socialists and the mood of
Howells early in the 1890's. According to Garland (*The Boston
Evening Transcript* of May 22, 1920), "Those were the days of
Bellamy's 'Looking Backward,' William Morris's 'News from No-
where' and Henry George's 'Progress and Poverty,' and it was
impossible to keep from discussing these books when we were
together. [Howells] was always much more inclined to Socialism
than I . . . , but we never argued—we merely stated our beliefs."
Garland then added:

> He confessed that he had been deeply moved by Bellamy's
> eloquent pages, and he told me that Clemens had been awakened
> by the book. Then he passed to a sadly accusing description of
> the long row of mansions on the Back Bay, shuttered and empty,
> while the poor sweltered in their overcrowded South End tene-
> ments unable even to get a glimpse of the beach so close to their
> doors. This was a subject on which he felt deeply and to which
> he returned again and again in the years which followed. He

could not reconcile himself to the waste of the idler and the hunger of the poor.

He was at work at that time, if I mistake not, on "The Traveler from Altruria"; at any rate he was in the mood of such writing, and passionately alive to the novels of Tolstoy and other authors who voiced the "noble discontent" of the times.

Howells had already expressed his "discontent" with the problem of the rich and the poor in *The Minister's Charge, A Hazard,* and other novels; he now sought to make his thought more clear in *A Traveler.* Having read and reviewed Bellamy's *Looking Backward* for *Harper's Monthly* (June, 1888), Howells saw the possibility of bringing to a focus his teeming thought in another utopian romance to which he could add an air of reality by placing the discussion on the long piazza of a New Hampshire hotel. Bellamy and Howells were soon exchanging letters; and, in the winter of 1888, Howells came to know the author himself; Howells was, in fact, one of the charter members of Bellamy's Nationalist Club in Boston. Here he met again old friends, such as Edward Everett Hale and Thomas Wentworth Higginson, and new ones, such as Gronlund and Vida Scudder. All of these men and women hoped to find practical means of making Christian Socialist ideas prevail. Reform was in the air; Edward Everett Hale organized a Tolstoy Club in Boston at this time, and Hamlin Garland attempted to established a National Theater for the dramatic presentation of social problems. Howells, though not an active member in either of these undertakings, went to meetings of the clubs when he could, and attended several of the plays. He was drawn into the atmosphere of reform and discussion during his two winters in Boston, and he shared with his friends a desire to give expression to Tolstoyan ideas, which were to him basically Christian.

When W. D. P. Bliss opened the Church of the Carpenter in April, 1890, as a Mission of the Episcopal Church, three hundred persons, Howells among them, attended the first meeting of the Mission in Brunswick Hall. The following week, the Brotherhood of the Carpenter began to hold its Sunday evening suppers and discussions, and many of the outstanding men and women of Boston met to talk over the problems common to Nationalists, Christian Socialists, Single Taxers and to the reformers of American drama. Bliss himself, through the pages of *The Dawn,* gave to the group such coherence as it had until he was absorbed in

1892 into the activities of the People's Party; the movement then
faded away as quickly as it had begun. In the columns of *The
Dawn,* however, Bliss recommended to his readers, for their
further education as Christian Socialists, not only Tolstoy's
Que Faire?, Bellamy's *Looking Backward,* and Richard T. Ely's
The Social Aspects of Christianity, but also Howells' *Annie
Kilburn. A Hazard of New Fortunes,* which Howells was finishing in Boston during these months, was deeply influenced by
these Boston associates; in turn, it influenced them as it appeared
in *Harper's Weekly.*[2]

A *Traveler From Altruria,* written when the Christian Socialists
were disbanding, bears the imprint of Bliss's urgent plea for a
return to the beliefs of primitive Christianity. These beliefs
Bliss wished to see embodied in every phase of living, and he
therefore looked forward to the establishment of actual communes
modeled after those of the early Christians. Hoping to realize his
dreams practically, Bliss advertised in the November, 1891, issue
of *The Dawn,* for a piece of land near Boston on which to
establish a group of Christian Socialists. The plan never materialized, but Howells, a year later, described his vision of such a
community in the serial which opened in the November, 1892,
issue of *The Cosmopolitan.*

In *A Traveler From Altruria,* Aristides Homos parries comments and questions with a circle of complacent American gentlemen—a banker, a lawyer, a professor, a minister, and a merchant
—as they are seated on a long hotel piazza facing the beautiful
White Mountains. By shrouding his views in the Altrurian's
pleasant flow of humor, irony, and kindly satire, Howells tones
down David Hughes's unpublishable tome, *The World Revisited,*
which, as Ray had said, "condemns the whole structure of
society." Just as readers a few years earlier had taken *Looking
Backward* "at a gulp," as Howells put it, not knowing that it
was "the rankest sort of socialism," so did the readers of *The
Cosmopolitan* accept Howells' fantasy embodying the basic ideas
of Christian Socialism without fully grasping its implications.
Bellamy supplied Howells with the suggestion of expressing his
ideas in the form of a utopian romance; and Tolstoy gave
Howells "heart to hope that the world may yet be made over
in the image of Him who died for it";[3] but it was the gatherings
of Christian Socialists in Boston which helped him to see the
need of the rational use of the vote in a society based on Christian
brotherhood.

The amazement of Aristides Homos at our rudeness, stupidity, and cruelty grows from his knowledge of the teaching of Saint Paul, who preached long ago on the island of Altruria, and of our Declaration of Independence, a document known and studied by the school boys of Altruria. To the Altrurian it had seemed apparent, before he had reached American shores, that Christian teaching was the basis of the Declaration and that from the belief in the equality of men grew the concept of democracy. He soon learned, as he talked to the circle of summer visitors, that somehow he was mistaken.

The Age of Accumulation (through which the Altrurians had passed even before the visit of Saint Paul) had made the Americans blind to the plight of such people as the destitute farmers living in desperate poverty not far from the hotel, to the hideous scars left by unrestricted lumbering of the neighboring forests, to the cruelty of the assumption on the part of the wealthy that poverty must always exist. Howells' "Romance" ends, not with a love affair, but with a long speech by Aristides Homos to hotel guests and country folk as well, on the obvious shortcomings of a competitive, capitalistic society. These, the Traveler assures his audience, could be obviated at once, without bloodshed and without strikes, by the simple method of using intelligently, for the good of all, the vote which they already possess. If altruism, which is as much a part of human nature as selfishness, were allowed to prevail, said the Traveler, the United States (which Howells named "Egoria"), like Altruria, might evolve toward a society marked by genuine equality.

During the summer of 1892, news reached Howells through his daily paper, of the strike over the question of the employment of non-union labor at the Carnegie Iron and Steel Company in Homestead, Pennsylvania. Acrimonious threats on both sides ended on July 1 in an all-day battle in which nine Pinkerton men, imported in barges by the company, and eleven workmen were killed. Accounts of this tragic occurrence, which filled the first pages of all the papers, provided Howells with just the evidence he needed to convince him that lawless use of power by either side was wrong and that social change must come about through the vote—by the slower processes of evolution rather than by violent revolution. Howells wrote to his father on July 10, 1892, as the news of the disturbances in Pennsylvania became even more disturbing: "I suppose you have been as excited as I have been, by the Homestead affair"; and he then observed "it is hard, in our sympathy with the working class, to remember that the men are playing a lawless part." Strikes, he said, are no remedy; they are only reminders that "trouble must go on as long as competition goes on, . . . every drop of blood shed for a good cause helps to make a bad cause." Remembering, perhaps, the death of Conrad Dryfoos in the Brooklyn streetcar strikes, Howells added: "How much better if the Homesteaders could have suffered the Pinkertons to shoot them down unarmed. Then they would have had the power of martyrs in the world."[4]

On July 24, Howells read that Henry C. Frick, president of the Carnegie Iron and Steel Company, had been attacked in his office by a humble compositor on a New York paper who had traveled to Pittsburgh for that purpose. Howells, writing immediately to his father, lamented this "wicked and foolish mistake," which only makes "a blood mist through which the situation shows wrong." Though labor's demand might be just, the method the workers employed was to Howells both shortsighted and wrong. "It has the majority of votes and can *vote* the laws it wants, and it won't, but prefers to break the laws we share."[5]

Howells' impatience with the laborers who threw away their strength at the beginning of every quarrel was at once incorporated into the essays he was writing. The banker, as he puffs on his cigar on the hotel piazza, quietly assumes the ascendency in the little group surrounding the Altrurian, and asks: "What does the worker gain by violence?" He answered his own question by adding, "*That* was settled once for all in Chicago." If the workers want an eight-hour law, "they could *make* it the law in six months by such overwhelming numbers that no one would dare to evade or defy it. They can make any law they want, but they prefer to break such laws as we have . . . If they chose, it would take only a few years to transform our government into the likeness of anything they wanted" (225-26).

Howells' belief in the democratic process, as expressed by the fair-minded but somewhat cynical banker, is the most cogent defense of the American civilization offered the inquiring visitor from Altruria. The banker calls himself "almost an Altrurian." Like Howells, he did not consider the Socialists the instigators of strikes, for they proposed "to vote their ideas into laws." Whatever may be said against the Socialist, the banker observed, he is, nevertheless, the man who "has generally thought himself into a socialist." Then he added hastily, as Howells himself might have, "I am not talking of anarchists, mind you, but of socialists, whose philosophy is more law, not less" (227).

The exact tone of Howells' social views was widely commented upon after the appearance of *A Traveler From Altruria* as a book in 1894. Though the reviewer of *Annie Kilburn* in the New York *Daily Tribune* (December 23, 1888) had remarked that "Tolstoy dashed with Anarchy might be said to be the most conspicuous flavors in the book," the reviewer of the New York *Herald* (September 23, 1894) listed Howells among the Socialists. His series of essays, which followed the publication of *A Traveler*, concerned such questions as "Are We a Plutocracy?," "Equality as the Basis of Good Society," and "Who are Our Bretheren?" These amply justified the description of Howells in *The Labour Annual* of 1896 as "a Socialist of the Bellamy School." *The American Fabian* commented and summarized Howells' contribution to socialistic thought during the 1890's in two articles, "Mr. Howells' Millennium" (July, 1896) and "Mr. Howells' Socialism" (February, 1898).

Though the banker voiced Howells' belief in the vote as a practical method of democratic advance, it was the Altrurian himself who, in the final chapter of *A Traveler*, expressed Howells' deepest sense of the "evolution" through which American society must pass, even as the Altrurians had several centuries earlier. In his address to the throng of hotel guests and neighbors, Aristides Homos opened with the remark that his own countrymen—who had once been as greedy, warlike, and cruel as Americans—were able to evolve from the frightful conditions which marked their Age of Accumulation only because they had heard "His message to the world" from "the apostle cast away upon our heathen coasts." Saint Paul won them with the story of the "earliest Christians, who loved one another and who had all things in common."

Howells was a Christian Socialist who, like Tolstoy, like Richard T. Ely, Bellamy, Gronlund, Garland, Jane Addams, and many other social thinkers of the day, felt that a rebirth of the concepts of Christian brotherhood must precede any real reform. Association with members of the Church of the Carpenter at the time when Howells' thoughts had become less literary and more social helped to clarify his ideas. "What is Christian Socialism?" is the title of an article by W. D. P. Bliss in the June, 1892, issue of *The Dawn*, in which he stresses the belief in evolution toward the ideals of primitive Christianity. Howells' answer to the same question was *A Traveler From Altruria.*

So pervasive was the dream of Altruria in Howells' thinking that he returned in 1907 to the same meditations—but with somewhat less confidence and belief—and wrote his third Altrurian romance, *Through the Eye of the Needle.* Nor was the dream wholly forgotten when he evoked once more the New Hampshire scene for the background of his last novel, *The Vacation of the Kelwyns* (1920); in it he again considered the ugliness of Yankee civilization set among "the everlasting hills" of New England—our national "affront to 'our maker.'" Although Howells' indignation at the wrongs and stupidities of society made him break away from the novel form in the 1890's, the abstract perfection of "Altruria" soon bored him, and he returned once more to writing realistic novels. But *The Vacation of the Kelwyns* is in a sense a philosophic romance, though it purports to be only a simple New England tale.

II *The Poetry of a Novelist*

When the Howellses came back to New York in October, 1892, they did not return to their old haunts on Stuyvesant Square but took an apartment overlooking Central Park at 40 West 59th Street. The new decade was well advanced, and Howells' outlook had subtly shifted since his resignation from *The Cosmopolitan* the summer before. Glancing out of his window at the "bit of Altruria" below, or contemplating from the wooded paths of the Park, the ugly, unharmonious buildings surrounding the beautiful stretch of green, Howells continued to meditate on the problems of an industrial society where the wealthy dashed by in handsome carriages, unmindful of the poor seated on the benches of the Park. He could, however, now forget for the moment the confusion of the great city in his pleasure in unpacking his library and arranging his books on the shelves of his airy apartment. Though he continued to produce his annual novel throughout this decade, his thoughts returned at this time to the story of his own youth.

To his Boston friend, Charles E. Norton, he wrote on October 16, 1892, "We are sinking into such quiet as we can find in this hurly-burly, and I am getting my old books about me again, out of the boxes where they have been shut up for five years."[6] Holding once more these precious volumes in his hands—"Most of them are pangs, wounds from the past, with its manifold associations"—Howells was set dreaming, not of a remote world of Altruria, but of an equally remote world of his youth in Ohio, Venice, and Cambridge. Out of this dreaming came a series of autobiographical studies: *A Boy's Town, My Year in a Log Cabin, My Literary Passions, Stories of Ohio,* and *Literary Friends and Acquaintance.*

The prevailing mood of this period is also reflected in his "Bibliographical Note" to the 1911 Library Edition of *My Literary Passions,* where nearly twenty years later Howells looked back with a half-amused smile at himself in the early 1890's. He remembered that he wrote *My Literary Passions* "some time in the year 1893 and 1894, in a New York flat, where he could look from his lofty windows, over two miles and a half in Central Park, and haloo his fancy whenever he chose in that faery realm of books which he re-entered in reminiscences perhaps too fond at times." Between his resignation from *The Cosmopolitan* and his assumption of a position on *Harper's Weekly* in 1895, Howells "halooed his fancy" by re-entering his own past by means of his old, familiar library.

The contemplation of his earlier, more poetic self no doubt tempted him to gather up the poems which had been appearing in *Harper's Monthly* since 1891 and to venture once more into the realms he thought he had forsaken. Accordingly, before he turned his back once more on the Muse of Poetry, and accepted again a regular position with Harper and Brothers,

> "He touch'd the tender stops of various Quills."

Milton's *Lycidas,* which he perhaps discovered in his box of books, supplied the title, *Stops of Various Quills.*

The reluctance with which Howells had renounced, many years earlier, the "inveterate dream" of "living a poet by [his] poetry" is recounted in an essay, "The Turning Point of My Life," which he was invited to write for the March, 1910, issue of *Harper's Bazar.* Howells tells us that long ago, while still a young poetizing consul in Venice, he had come to "the intersections of ways" in his writing career. He was "in danger of taking the wrong road," that of poetry, when a letter came from Lowell accepting an essay of his for publication in the *North American Review,* at a time when his rejected poems were returned to him with discouraging regularity. The communication from his old friend and counselor made him realize that he was clearly more successful as a writer of prose than of poetry. He did not, however, entirely give up the writing of poetry; he merely "turned from the Muse in her penury," when he discovered that "prose was a steady support." He perceived, too, "that prose which sold so much better might also be poetry . . . while poetry might play one false and be a masquerade of dull commonplace."

Right as Howells was in his choice of the Muse of Prose, the very fact that he addressed the Muse of Poetry and "invoked her divine forgiveness" every year of his life thereafter indicates that the spirit of poetry was always strong within him and deeply affected the quality of his prose. It is the poetic overtones of Howells' novels—which he himself frequently smiled over—that lead us to wonder whether his novels were indeed truly "realistic"; for Howells, who began as a poet, was always poetic at heart. "Brazen it out as we will in behalf of prose," he wrote in his reminiscence for *Harper's Bazar*, "there is a mystic power in verse which utters in a measured line the passion and the aspiration which a whole unmetered volume cannot express."

Did Lowell's letter mark a real turning from poetry to prose? asked Howells in his essay, for he, too, realized that he had always attempted to give his prose something of the quality of poetry. "I do not believe there has really been any such change in me as I began pretending. From my earliest remembrance, from the time before I could read, when I made up stories to match the pictures in the first book I ever looked at, 'one continuous purpose' of literature has run through my life." Poetry and prose were subtly blended in Howells' mind; he was, he admitted, "translated to a region of pure bliss" in his exploration of both realms. "The vista has widened before me as I have advanced, and charmed me more and more," whether it happened to be that of poetry or prose, he observed. "I have found it full of divine surprises, of invitations to stray apart, and break wildflowery by-ways to the right and left."

Stops of Various Quills appeared in 1895, embellished by the pen-sketches of his Swedenborgian friend, Howard Pyle, who was both storyteller and artist. The somber, allegorical headpieces and end-designs catch the mystical, symbolic spirit of many of Howells' poems on death, pain, loneliness, care; they also make clear to the modern reader the limitations of Howells' poetry. When he followed the beckoning finger of his Poetic Muse, he, like Pyle in his popular illustrations, was apt to stray—after the fashion of his day—into vague abstractions. How differently his verses struck on the sensibilities of the 1890's is suggested by a letter Howells received from William James commenting on a group of eleven of these poems which had first appeared in the December, 1894, issue of *Harper's Monthly*. "Dear Old Howells," wrote James on January 5, 1895, "I have just been reading your verses in the December Harper, and don't know when I have had a greater pleasure—if pleasure is the word for so solid a sense of gratitude. They are well forged—no fumbling and no spatter, and I do hope that with others of their predecessors they shall be 'collected' soon."[7]

Many of the poems in *Stops of Various Quills*—and, indeed, many in his earlier collections, *Poems of Two Friends* (1860) and *Poems* (1873)—commend themselves to the modern reader of Howells chiefly because they are written by a poet with a story-telling impulse—or by a novelist with poetry in his veins. Howells believed that narratives in verse might become as popular with "the common man" as storytelling in prose. "The turn of the narrative poem may come again," he wrote in an essay on poetry in 1901; "for some reasons I hope it may; it might do such office for our common life as the short story has done in prose."

"The Pilot's Story," the first offering in *Poems of Two Friends* and the poem which had won him acclaim beyond the borders of Ohio, is a dramatic narrative in ballad form based on the suicide of an actual slave girl. The love lyrics in *Poems* carry narrative suggestions, after the manner of Heine, of half-told romances, arising like a faint perfume from, perhaps, a pair of yellowing gloves or "a mysterious box" of ancient love letters. In "Sweet Clover," for example, written while he was still in Venice, Howells thrilled "all through with delicious pain" at the "ghost of fragrance" from such a box of letters:

> And under these December skies,
>   As bland as May's in other climes,
>   I move, and muse my idle rhymes
> And subtly sentimentalise.

In *Stops of Various Quills,* Howells "subtly sentimentalizes" the experiences of a man in his middle fifties. Sadder, more disillusioned, Howells was still the narrator, pausing for a moment to put down in verse tales which were often later expressed in prose.

The thin wall, in Howells' mind, between a narrative poem and a poetic narrative is exemplified in *Stops of Various Quills* by a poem entitled "Material of a Story." The opening lines remind one at once of Howells' two studies of criminal characters in *The Quality of Mercy* (1892) and in "A Circle in the Water" (1895). The "friend" might well have been Edward Everett Hale, clergyman, poet, and story writer.

> I met a friend of mine the other day
> Upon the platform of a West End car;
> We shook hands, and my friend began to say
> Quickly, as if he were not going far,
> 'Last summer something rather in your way
> Came to my knowledge. I was asked to see
> A young man who had come to talk with me
> Because I was a clergyman; and he
> Told me at once that he had served his time
> In the state-prison for a heinous crime,
> And was just out. He had no friends, or none
> To speak of; and he seemed far gone
> With a bad cough. He said he had not done
> The thing. They all say that. You cannot tell.
> He might not have been guilty of it. Well,
> What he now wanted was some place to stay,
> And work that he could do. . . .'

Though Howells followed Lowell's advice and "sweated the Heine" out of his verse, he continued to be haunted by the ghosts of other poets more eminent than he. Lowell himself, Longfellow, Holmes—all of them storytellers in verse—left their traces on *Stops of Various Quills*. In "Heredity," for example, one is aware of the near presence of Oliver Wendell Holmes, the doctor-poet-wit and Howells' friend for over thirty years. Who but Holmes could have inspired Howells to observe a fellow guest at a dinner party in quite these terms?

> That swollen paunch you are doomed to bear
> Your gluttonous grandsire used to wear;
> That tongue, at once so light and dull,
> Wagged in your grandam's empty skull;
> That leering of the sensual eye
> Your father, when he came to die,
> Left yours alone; and that cheap flirt,
> Your mother, gave you from the dirt
> The simper which she used upon
> So many men ere he was won.

Your vanity and greed and lust
Are each your portion from the dust
Of those that died, and from the tomb
Made you what you must needs become.
I do not hold you aught to blame
For sin at second hand, and shame:
. Evil could but from evil spring;
And yet, away, you charnel thing!

Holmes, too, had meditated the roots of character as he
gazed on his family portraits; the professor of anatomy of
Harvard College had pondered the effects of heredity upon
the intelligence of students seated before him. "If you are a
teacher," he remarked in the opening chapter of *Elsie Venner*—
which appeared in the *Atlantic* during Howells' assistantship—
you know from experience what to expect from "two different
aspects of youthful manhood," the country boy, robust but in-
elegant, clumsy in gesture, uncouth in feature, "the eye unsym-
pathetic, even if bright," and the youth of the Brahmin caste,
slender, graceful, bright and never "clownish." The country boy
might even surpass his classmates occasionally: "That is Nature's
republicanism; thank God for it," wrote Holmes, "but do not let
it make you illogical." The "large uncombed youth who goes to
college and startles the hereditary class-leaders by striding past
them all" is a rare phenomenon, for ancestors with libraries and
family portraits do make a difference. Many years later—but
soon after the publication of *Stops of Various Quills*—Howells
tested out the doctor's theory by choosing a country "rube," Jeff
Durgin, for the hero of *The Landlord of Lion's Head* (1897);
sending him to Harvard; and tracing his brilliant, erratic, arrogant course among his Brahmin mates. Both Holmes and Howells
were fascinated by the contemplation of the roots of character;
both of them expressed their essentially narrative thoughts
either in prose or in poetry.

Howells' early conversations with Holmes in 1860 in his
study overlooking the Charles left their imprint also on such a
novel as *The Shadow of a Dream*. In 1884 Howells moved into
his new home on Beacon Street, just two doors away from Dr.
Holmes, and here the conversations were continued until he left
Boston in 1889. After the writing of several of Howells' social
novels, Howells' thoughts turned during the next few years to
the problem of making use of the somewhat romanticized scienti-

fic concepts which were suggested to him by Dr. Holmes, the
neurologist, who was himself a spinner of romances.

Hamlin Garland, in his description of his first visit to Howells'
summer home, in Auburndale, in 1887,[8] records his surprise at
Howells' questioning him, a younger and then unknown writer,
about half-formed plans for writing *The Shadow of a Dream*.
Garland remarked that such a story, based on the psychological
question of the effect of dreams on our waking action, seemed
rather a departure from his usual style. Howells replied that he
realized he was proposing a "romantic" tale and observed that
perhaps he would abandon the whole idea. However, Garland
visited Howells the following summer at Mount Auburn, and
again they discussed the proposed story. He found Howells
living in "a large, old-fashioned structure" which "stood in the
midst of a broad, unkempt, but very lovely garden, filled with
rank tangles of neglected vines and vivid blooms, a scene quite
like that which formed the setting of 'the Shadow of a Dream.'"
The story appeared in 1890, and showed unmistakably the imprint of Dr. Holmes's rational interpretation of the neurotic
dreams which haunt the mind of a jealous husband. The neglected garden, as well as the recurring dream of the illicit love
of his wife and his own best friend, evoked the spirit of evil
which finally led to tragedy. That Holmes, too, felt the literary
possibilities of such scenes is suggested by a charming little
episode having to do with romantic old gardens and the sad
tales which haunt them, which is told by Howells in his essay,
"Oliver Wendell Holmes," *Harper's Monthly*, December, 1896.

In this essay on Holmes, written soon after the death of his
elderly friend, Howells recalled the last conversation he had held
with Holmes after they had encountered each other at a luncheon
in a summer home near the ocean. Howells spoke, among other
things, of some humble ruins he had driven past on the road to
Gloucester. The tumbled foundation-stones of poor bits of houses
gave the wayside a very aged look. "Ah," interrupted Holmes,
"the cellar and the well?" He then quoted his own verse about
the deserted farmhouse:

> Its starving orchard where the thistle blows,
> And mossy trunks still mark the broken rows;
> Its chimney-loving poplar, oftenest seen
> Next an old roof, or where a roof has been . . .
> All the poor shows the curious idler sees,
> As life's thin shadows waste by slow degrees,

> *Till naught remains, the saddening tale to tell,*
> *Save last life's wrecks—the cellar and the well.*

Ten years later, in a little-known poem, "Black Cross Farm," written by Howells for the *Spectator* (January, 1904)[9] the author evokes a mood similar to that of *The Shadow of a Dream* and one clearly reminiscent of the poem quoted by Holmes at their last meeting. A reading of "Black Cross Farm" reminds one again of the thin wall, in Howells' mind, between poetry and prose, for the poem is as narrative in feeling as *The Shadow of a Dream* is poetic. The poem begins with a simple description: one morning in summer the writer, accompanied by a friend, made his way to an empty farmhouse—"theme for tale or song?" —known in the neighborhood as "Black Cross Farm." Through "shadowy woods" the two rode behind their old horse until the "faint wheel tracks" came to an end in

> A lane, now hid by weeds and briars between
> Meadows scarce worth the mowing, to a space
> Shaped as by Nature for the dwelling-place
> Of kindly human life: a small plateau
> Open to the heaven that seemed bending low
> In liking for it. There beneath a roof
> Still against winter and summer weather-proof,
> With walls and doors and window perfect yet,
> Between its garden and its graveyard set,
> Stood the old homestead . . .

Against the "vast gray barn" a black cross was nailed, "the bigness of a man." Howells glanced toward his country host—did it have a meaning,

> Other than chance? He slowly shook his head,
> And with his gaze on the symbol said:
> 'We have quite ceased from guessing or surmising,
> For all our several and joint devising
> Has left us finally where I must leave you.
> But now I think it is your part to do
> Yourself some guessing . . .

But "what, after all, would be the gain/Of making the elusive meaning plain?" Thus they

> . . . left the mystery to the summer day
> That made as if it understood, and could
> Have read the riddle to us if it would;

while they wandered through "birch pastures" and "stony meadows" trying

> . . . to find the lane
> That to our coming feet had been so plain.
> And lost ourselves among the sweetfern's growth,
> And thickets of young pine-trees, nothing loath,
> Amidst the wilding loveliness to stray,
> And spend, if need were, looking for the way,
> Whole hours; but blundered into the right course
> Suddenly, and came out upon our horse,
> Where we had left him—to our great surprise,
> Stamping and switching at the pestering flies,
> But not apparently anxious to depart,
> When nearly overturning at the start,
> We followed down that evanescent trace
> Which, followed up, had brought us to the place.

Howells' feeling for the ruined farm recalls Holmes's verses;
they also suggest the poetry of Robert Frost, whose narrative
poems, in the same tradition, are often closely related to prose.
In this instance, Howells chose "song," but in another mood he
might have settled for a "tale"; in either case, the tone would
have been poetic narrative. As Thomas Hardy wrote Howells
after reading one of his stories: "You, too, have always upheld
the truth that poetry is the heart of literature."

In responding to the imaginative appeal of neglected gardens
and deserted farms, Howells was reflecting not only his latent
poetic impulses, but also a shift in public taste toward the
romantic. On October 28, 1894, an interview appeared in the
New York *Times,* signed by Stephen Crane, which began:
"William Dean Howells leaned his cheek upon the two out-
stretched fingers of his right hand and gazed thoughtfully at
the window—the panes black from the night without, although
studded once or twice with little electric stars far up on the west
side of the Park." Had Howells not "observed a change in the
literary pulse of the country?" the young reporter asked. Yes,
Howells replied, he was aware of a certain new atmosphere.
Romanticism was again in the ascendency; realism might have to
wait.

Howells himself, in following the Muse of Poetry, turned away
from the realism of streetcar strikes and breadlines. *A Hazard
of New Fortunes,* filled with realistic pictures of labor strife,
had presaged what was then the new mood which marked

Howells' writing on his return to New York. But now the "literary pulse of the country" had changed again, and many of the half-told narratives in *Stops of Various Quills* were distinctly romantic in tone in spite of their pseudo-scientific suggestion. Following the lead of his doctor-neighbor, Howells explored in his poetry and his stories possibilities of finding "reality" in psychological rather than in social terms. Howells as well as Holmes discovered the romance latent in the new psychology. For the intensification of Howells' psychological interest, in the 1890's, we may consider the stress on hidden motives (*A Pair of Patient Lovers*); the influence of one person's state of mind on the action of another (*Shadow of a Dream*); the effect of miscegenation down to the fourth generation (*An Imperative Duty*); the ability of a New England farmer to shake the faith of a Congregational minister ("A Difficult Case,") all these psychological stories, and others, indicate that Howells was sensitive to the "literary pulse" of the new decade. That his interest in incorporating some of the concepts of Holmes into his stories as well as into his poetry is interestingly illustrated by "A Circle in the Water" (1895). This tale of a slowly widening circle spread by an evil deed is, in narrative form, similar to that suggested by the poem from *Stops of Various Quills*, quoted above. Tedham, who has served his term in prison, is the same man who, in the poem, "had served his time. In the state-prison for a heinous crime,/And was just out. . . ." From his neighbor, the professor of nervous diseases, Howells had learned something of the possibility of introducing a new psychological note into both his fiction and his poetry. In this sense, Howells' experiments in poetry contributed to his experiments in novel-writing, the field in which he was more at home.

Early in 1896 the Howellses gave up their comfortable apartment overlooking Central Park, and bought a house in Far Rockaway, Long Island, which they sold at the end of the summer. The quest for a suitable home near New York had begun in the summer of 1895, for now their son John, who had completed his architectural studies at the Beaux Arts in Paris, had established himself in New York, near which his parents hoped to find a summer home. Torn, as usual, between New England and New York, the family moved for many years from hotel to apartment to rented house, with the half-humorous melancholy of Basil and Isabel March. Like the Marches, Howells and his wife found a certain exasperated pleasure in their frequent moves in New York, as well as in their summer jaunts to resorts in New England and New Jersey. This restless quest at least supplied Howells with "copy" for the endless flow of essays which accompanied his novel-writing for the rest of his life. A letter from Long Beach, New Jersey, to C. E. Norton, August 11, 1895,[10] reflects Howells' pleasure-pain experience in searching for a home; it reflects, too, a certain boredom with "ordinary" people, whom the realist thirty years earlier would have found inspiring, for now Howells had become interested in more complex personalities:

> I have come down to Long Beach again to look up that 'home' which I begin to doubt we shall not find short of heaven. Our notion is that we ought to be in some village near New York where John can easily reach us during the summer, and where we can live the year round when I write less and earn less. But whenever I go back to New England I find that so much lovelier that my gorge rises at this region, and I am renewing the home-seeking with repugnance and a secret hope of finding nothing. Of course, this wave-whipped desert is not to be thought of; I am only here till the weather changes, and I can really begin looking. Yet it is not cool, even here, tho' the Atlantic raves along the sand for seven miles, and the south wind blows all day. Meantime, it is rather interesting. The hotel is about fifty-feet wide and a thousand feet long, and is perhaps half full of human beings. They are all very quiet, well dressed and amiable, and if I knew any of them I dare say I should like them. But I know only the clerk, who has given me a vast saloon of a room because he said he "knew all about" me, and wished me to be comfortable. He is a shrewd, humorous, intelligent fellow, and we might easily be "known all about" by worse people. He put a red rose in my buttonhole last night, and talked long and wisely about hotels, and the people who frequent them, and the changes that have made them non-society.

After their uncomfortable summer at Far Rockaway, the Howellses came back to New York, and settled into the Westminister Hotel in Irving Place, not far from Stuyvesant Square. In returning to lower New York, to the old world of magazines and newspapers, Howells brought to a close the several years' withdrawal from editorial commitments. During this period he had surveyed his own literary past; he had again "touch't the tender stops of various quills." Like Milton's sorrowing shepherd,

> At last he rose, and twitch'd his mantle blue;
> To-morrow to fresh Woods and Pastures new.

The "fresh woods and pastures new" were the editorial offices of Franklin Square, the drawing rooms "down in University Place," the studios of Saint-Gaudens and other artists—above all, the Broadway theaters. City pavements, especially those of New York, were the wooded paths most enjoyed by this tireless commentator in prose and poetry, much as he longed for the "flowery meadows" on either side.

III *Theater Critic of the Nineties*

Howells' interest in drama goes back to his early days in Ohio when he enjoyed the country fair, the reappearance of the circus tent in the spring, and, occasionally, Shakespearean plays presented by traveling repertory companies. During their years in Venice, Goldoni and Italian Opera supplied the young consul and his wife with endless amusement and interest. As assistant editor of the *Atlantic,* Howells attended several "vulgar and indecent" burlesque shows given in the environs of Boston by an English company and described his disgust with this foreign invasion in "The New Taste in Theatricals" in the *Atlantic*; he remarked that "The new taste . . . is not our taste [and] draws no life from our shores." Just as Howells always argued for the American scene in fiction, so he also enjoyed, whenever the opportunity offered, all forms of native drama.

For thirty-five years, from *The Parlor Car* (1876) to *Parting Friends* (1911), Howells sought to encourage "our taste" in American drama with a series of little plays of his own—most of them humorous and none profound. Enjoyed as parlor-skits designed to be given in family living rooms and church parish-houses, they were never really successful on the legitimate stage. So popular with amateur actors, however, were these half-ironic farces and dramatic interludes that a yearly play, which usually appeared at Christmas time, was a part of Howells' contract with Harper's. These playlets were reprinted in the United States and in England, soon after their magazine appearances, in delightful little gift-volumes. Howells' English friend, Edmund Gosse, wrote to him on October 12, 1882, "I see ladies giggling over little books in the train, and then I know they must be reading 'The Parlor Car.' "[11] Indeed, something of the brightness and wit of Oscar Wilde and George Bernard Shaw still lingers in these gay reminders of the taste of another day; a similar skill in dialogue delighted the readers of Howells' novels, from his earliest efforts in *Their Wedding Journey*.

Although Howells wrote thirty-three plays, farces, skits—and even a comic opera—and though he remarked to Mark Twain, when they were involved in one of their unsuccessful efforts at dramatic collaboration, "I would ten times rather write plays than anything else," Howells never really doubted that he was, in fact, a novelist experimenting with a related literary form. Concerning the play, *Out of the Question* (1877), for example, Howells wrote that this "long story in dramatic form" was "too short to have any strong effect, I suppose, but it seems to me to prove that there is a middle form between narrative and drama, which may be developed into something very pleasant to the reader and convenient to the fictionist."[12] This "middle-form" between drama and fiction Howells discovered in pointed dialogue, which, as a novelist of the "new school," he did not think he needed to "explain."[13] Curiously enough, Howells' dramatic dialogues were more successful within his novels than they were on the stage.

Though, as we have noted, *A Counterfeit Presentment* with the support of the able actor, Lawrence Barrett, was said to herald "a new era in a distinctly American drama," the play was soon found to be too subtle in character analysis and too tenuous in plot-interest to be continued as a part of Barrett's repertory. Just as Howells, a confirmed "fictionist," glanced with a certain nostalgia into the "flowery fields" of poetry, so he also not infrequently wandered into the equally flowery fields of the dramatist. The very stage directions of *A Counterfeit Present-ment*, however, betray the fact that his proper medium was narrative. Like Shaw, Howells relished his long and leisurely introductions; but he knew as he wrote that his description of "a lovely day in September" was "meant for part of the literature in things to be read rather than seen."

The trepidations, hesitations, confusions of a novelist endeavoring to be a dramatist were expressed by Howells in *The Story of a Play* (1898) in which the struggling playwright, Brice Maxwell, becomes hopelessly caught between the suggestions of his wife, the egotism of a well-known actor, the business plans of several stage-managers, and the tantrums of a temperamental actress. Eager to write a "strong" drama depicting the crimes of Hazard, the hero, in order to prove that "the wages of sin is more sinning," Maxwell dreamed of "a new effect" in American drama. What he actually achieved was a confused play, stressing the "love business"; $300 in box-office receipts for his six-months' effort; and a series of quarrels with his eagerly cooperative wife. Howells himself, like Brice Maxwell, was too delicately attuned by temperament to cope with the pragmatic demands of Broadway—nor were the financial returns sufficient to tempt him from his long-established habit of quiet mornings dedicated to composition in his study. His steady work as a journalist—which, at its best, rose to distinguished novels, and, at its worst, sank to the rather thin, but always interesting, comments of a columnist —proved not only more remunerative to Howells but also more consistently satisfactory to his particular temperament than his attempts to become a dramatist.

Howells in his essays for *Harper's Weekly* discussed with his accustomed urbanity any subject which came to his mind after a perusal of his library or a stroll in the city streets: tipping among coach drivers, for instance; the games of tenement-house children; the poetry of Matthew Arnold; the East-Side bread-line in winter; the American custom of spitting in public places; or the equally familiar American habit of daily Bible-reading. But by far the most interesting of his eighty-eight contributions to "Life and Letters," are those having to do, directly or indirectly, with drama.

The opening critical essay for *Harper's Weekly* of March 30, 1895, written before he had agreed to a regular weekly department, was "The Play and the Problem," which reflects the keen critical views of an habitué of the theater. Howells, "during the past theatrical season," had had the good fortune, he tells his readers, to "see three or four of the new sort of plays which the English are now making"—Bernard Shaw's *Arms and the Man*, Henry Arthur Jones's *The Case of Rebellious Susan*, and Oscar Wilde's *An Ideal Husband*. These plays seemed to Howells "vastly better" than "the old sort of novels . . . [the English] are now writing." Beneath "the brilliant little comedy" of Shaw, for example, one discovers "a pitiless satire on what we are agreed to call civilization"; beneath Jones's "merry play" lies a "serious problem" which is not, after all, too serious; Wilde's *tour de force* is "not only an excellent piece of art, but an excellent piece of sense as well." The "problem" which Howells proposed in his essay in relation to these plays was whether, in compressing into dramatic form the crises of "ordinary life," the playwright does not necessarily depart somewhat from the truth of "ordinary experience." When Howells observed that, "without more room than the drama can give itself," it crucial event cannot be shown in "its real relation of life, in its proportion, its value," he was, of course, merely declaring himself once more to be a novelist rather than a dramatist.

Just as Howells constantly pressed the claims of American novels in opposition to those being written in England, so did he jealously uphold the hope of a truly native drama. The last paragraph of his penetrating three-column review of the plays of Shaw, Jones, and Wilde astonishes the modern reader—and perhaps some readers of his own day—by setting up, in opposition to this brilliant trio, a defense of such forgotten American dramatists as Denman Thompson, James A. Herne, and Edward Harrigan. "I am going to prove myself of a very common, or at least very simple taste to people who love titles and gowns, by saying that I think *The Old Homestead* and *Shore Acres,* with all their defects, are built upon broader and sounder lines, and that Mr. Harrigan's Mulligan series of comic sketches is the effect of a more genuine dramatic artistic instinct" than that of the contemporary English dramatists. His suggestions to future American dramatists are similar to those made to aspiring American novelists in *Criticism and Fiction.* To improve the American stage, he observed, "it remains for some American to imagine an honest treatment of our average middle-class life, with the rich variety of possibilities in motive and incident native to our society, and the same success will be his, as the authors of those plays of our rustic life and low life have enjoyed."

Howells' own plays were clearly an attempt to achieve "an honest treatment of our average middle-class life"—and, indeed, they succeeded in their limited aim; however, the "rustic life" and "low life" plays and sketches of Harrigan, Thompson, and Herne maintained a popular appeal on the stage which Howells recognized as more important to any native drama his country might evolve than his own plays. Actor, playwright, and manager of half a dozen New York theaters, Edward Harrigan had delighted Howells with his broadly humorous sketches of the Irish politician, Dan Mulligan, which Harrigan had written and produced between 1873 and 1884. Indeed, Howells devoted more than two columns of his July, 1886, "Study" to commending the art of Harrigan which, he said, was akin to that of Goldoni.

For the February 2, 1899, issue of *Harper's Weekly*, Harrigan had explained his own interest, as playwright and actor, in the joys and sorrows of common people and his use of Irish, German, Italian, Negro types. Howells, whose theatrical interests ranged far beyond the confines of the polite plays of upper Broadway, recalled with delight that "the first successful attempt to represent the life of our streets was in dramatic form." He cited Edward Harrigan in his full-page article "New York Low Life in Fiction" for *The World* of Sunday, July 26, 1896.

In a later essay in "Life and Letters," Howells welcomed the "gentle charm" and "broad human ground" of *Shore Acres*. In his review of Herne's play, *Rev. Griffith Davenport*, he stated again his hopes for the "new drama" in terms akin to those he used about the "new fiction." Herne's play, said Howells, is "the suggestion, possibly the prophecy, of a drama which shall be to the old drama what Tolstoy's fiction is to the old fiction. To this hope one can readily forgive it something of Tolstoy's apparent formlessness and inconclusiveness."[14]

So strongly, indeed, did Howells feel the relationship between "the universal impulse" of European naturalism reflected in the translations of the novels of Tolstoy and the plays of Ibsen that he frequently linked their names as the two "most potent influences for good or evil in our lives." What is the novel, after all, Howells asked, but a kind of "portable theater"; what is a play but a projection on the stage of the "real" scenes from the lives of ordinary people? Both novel and play are basically related, for their moral intention is the same. The publication, in 1889 of translations of three of Ibsen's plays (*Ghosts, The Pillars of Society,* and *An Enemy of the People*) gave Howells an opportunity, even before his readers had seen these dramas on the stage, to associate Ibsen's name with the realistic movement in fiction for which he was arguing in the "Editor's Study."

Howells rejoiced in the hope that the "fat optimism" of American theater-goers was about to be shaken by Ibsen—as it certainly was. During the first half of the 1890's New York audiences had the chance of seeing most of Ibsen's more important plays, *Ghosts, Hedda Gabler, A Doll's House, Little Eyolf,* and, finally, *An Enemy of the People*. Howells' long discussion in *Harper's Weekly* of April 27, 1895, of Sir Beerbohm Tree's presentation of the character of Dr. Stockmann in *An Enemy* begins with a résumé of the past five years of Ibsen productions on the New York stage, "that haunt of the decrepitudes and imbecilities of the past." The "vast hope" and the "deep consolation" which Howells felt as he reviewed *An Enemy* lay in the fact that Ibsen, like Tolstoy, saw that beauty is found only in truth and that both depended for their effectiveness on simplicity and objectivity. In Tree's portrayal of Dr. Stockmann, "the dramatist obtruded himself no more than the actor; they were both there to express a most important conviction in ethics and in aesthetics, and they were jointly absent, as far as any personal effect was concerned. For one of those moments so rare in the theatre the spectator had a sense of absolute drama."

To connect this "theatrical event," Sir Beerbohm Tree's interpretation of *An Enemy of the People* (which was for Howells "the very greatest" he had ever known) with the humble Mulligan skits of Harrigan, with Thompson's *Old Homestead,* and with Herne's *Shore Acres* is perhaps a far stretch for any critic of American drama. Yet the qualities Howells admired in Ibsen were precisely those he was hopefully encouraging in plays by Americans. The "marvelous skill" with which the character of Dr. Stockmann was put before the spectator was "by the simplest means, in the barest terms, and in language so plain and common that nothing of it remained with me afterwards but the last words of Stockmann's crucial experience distilling itself in the phrase, 'He is the strongest man who stands most alone!' " The effect of this simplicity is that actors and playwrights alike are forced to relearn their art, to forget their conventional clichés and gestures, and to live the parts they hope to evoke. Even the modern British playwrights, Pinero, Shaw, and Jones, are, said Howells, attempting to simplify their speech and deepen the problems they present.

Unlike lesser dramatists, Ibsen avoids all dramatic tricks; the problem upon which a play of Ibsen hinges is "as wide as the whole of life, and it seeks a solution in the conscience of the spectator . . . [he] makes you feel the import of what has happened civically, socially, humanly, universally." Ibsen, "above all a moralist," addressed himself to the future rather than to the present, and, like Tolstoy, taught men to forego a quest for personal happiness in the nobler pursuit of social betterment.[15] "Both of these just men perceive that, in the scheme of a just God, there is no room for such happiness; and that, wherever it tries to force itself in, it pushes aside or crushes under it the happiness of some other human creature."[16]

The message is as relevant to an audience in America, Howells pointed out, as to European audiences: *An Enemy of the People* is the Ibsen play which "appeals more intimately than any other to the intelligence of an American audience" because the little Norwegian town where the action takes place is "the image in little of our own vast political hypocrisy." In it are also found the ruthless boss, the cynical journalist, the selfish citizen. Though Tammany was never heard of in Norway, Tammany is there, Howells reminded his readers. Of course, since New Yorkers demand action, hysterics, heroics, and plenty of "love interest," Howells hardly expected "any great acceptance for Ibsen himself on our stage." For "Ibsenism," however, there is "already great acceptance," which will become even greater; "he is the master who has more to say to our generation in the theater than any other, and all must learn his language who would be understood hereafter."

Though Howells in his own plays did not even attempt to reach such heights or depths, he clearly perceived that this was the aim of the naturalistic drama of Ibsen and other Continental dramatists. He saw, too, in the humble sketches produced in East Side playhouses, the promise of a sort of "low life" naturalism akin to Stephen Crane's *Maggie* and to Abraham Cahan's *Yekl*; for the objectives of the writers of plays and of novels was essentially the same: both pointed the way to a more genuinely humane life for ordinary men and women. In "New York Low Life in Fiction," Howells lauded Harrigan for "his sublime moment of absolute fidelity"—in spite of his lapses into romanticism—to the sights and sounds of East Side hoodlums. "It is to the honor of the stage," he wrote, "that it was first to recognize the value of our New York low life as material; and I shall always say that Mr. Harrigan, when he was not overpowered by a tradition or a theory, was exquisitely artistic in his treatment of it. He was then true, and, as Tolstoy has lately told us, 'to be true is to be moral.'" Fiction, said Howells, turning to Stephen Crane's *Maggie*, has been much slower than drama in perceiving that "there is no other standard for the arts but life"—no matter how rough, rude, or terrifying. Howells, in this essay, linked drama and fiction, for which he upheld very similar standards.

And how he sponsored such "rude" and "rough" drama may be

seen from his reactions to American dramas. *The Old Home-stead,* by Denman Thompson, which first appeared in New York in 1886 and remained popular for twenty years, was a homely rural drama of Yankee life that gave Howells hope for native "rustic" drama. *Shore Acres,* by James A. Herne, opened in Boston in 1893, and was, when Howells referred to it, enjoying the five-years' success which enabled Herne to recover his fortune after the failure in 1891 of his earlier play, *Margaret Fleming.*

Howells himself had seen Herne's *Margaret Fleming,* a stark drama of marital infidelity, when, with the encouragement of Hamlin Garland and other liberals, it was presented in Chickering Hall, Boston, on May 4, 1891. Though the play received a cold welcome from shocked Bostonians, and ran for less than two weeks, it was, in another sense, a success. As an early sample of Continental naturalism transported to these shores, the tragedy had much to do with pioneer dramatic movements of the 1890's. Howells remarked of *Margaret Fleming* in "The Play and the Problem" that the awful seriousness of this "great play" was "so dreadful to the conscience" of the audience that finally "the ushers remained almost alone to agonize over it." He nevertheless recognized it as an example of realistic drama attempting to cope with problems of American life.

So strongly did Howells believe in the theater as a means of educating the public that he devoted one of his last papers for *Literature* (April 14, 1899) to a proposal for "A Subscription Theater." Such a theater should not be controlled by a group of wealthy men, he said, for then no essential criticism of "our industrial conditions" would be permitted:

It is not imaginable that their management would approve of such a play as Ibsen's 'Enemy of the People' or 'Die Weber' of Hauptmann, or even 'Die Ehre' of Sudermann. If Mr. Herne wrote a playing dealing as frankly with life in a mining town or a factory town as his 'Griffith Davenport' deals with life on a Virginia plantation, it could never pass the censorship of such a body of subscribers. Mr. Bernard Shaw's satire of 'Arms and the Man', if they felt its irony and realized its implications, could not be given twice in their subscription theater, which would in no wise be a free theatre. No dramatist who knew American conditions and American character could write freely for a theater sustained by the subscription of a limited number of rich men, unless he were of their thinking.

Howells, as a critic of the New York theater of the 1890's, foresaw not only a native, naturalistic drama familiar to us today but also a free theater—such as City Center—where American plays, as well as European dramas, might be presented. He saw, too, that audiences and actors must be re-educated to accept the simple, unconventional, living presentation of drama which Stanislavsky was then introducing in Russia and which has in its turn become a convention in our modern theaters. But clearly as Howells perceived the importance of the "new drama," his own plays were in the tradition of Goldsmith, Sheridan, and Oscar Wilde. Howells' real experiment, when he could escape from journalism, was in the "new fiction," which, for him, grew out of Ibsen's plays as well as from Tolstoy's novels.

Howells himself never mistook his vocation, as the ironic presentation of himself in *The Story of a Play* attests. When Henry James thanked him with kind words for a copy and added a few comments, Howells replied:

> It was good of you to speak those friendly words about my *Story of a Play*, which I found very just. You know my experience of the theater was comic, rather than tragical, and I treated of it lightly because it was light. Of course the husband-and-wife business was the chief thing; and I was glad you recognized that. It is strange how the stage can keep on fooling us; what the burnt child does *not* dread is the fire, or at least the blue fire of the theatre. I have lately been fool enough to dramatize *Silas Lapham* for an actor who wanted it, and now does *not* want it. What a race! Their obligations are chains of flowers.[17]

Toward the end of the decade James A. Herne asked Howells to attempt, with the help of his cousin, Paul Kester, a dramatization of *Silas Lapham*. Nothing came of the effort, either then or later, for Howells' touch as a dramatist was too light; his more serious thought belonged where it first appeared, embedded in a slower-paced novel. Writing to Mark Twain of Herne's rejection of his play, Howells remarked, "While I was working at that thing I piled up the riches until I felt as safe from poverty as if I had laid up treasure in heaven,"[18] which suggests that his interest in writing plays was not entirely literary.

Like Mark Twain, Howells discovered that the western lecture tour, under the management of Major J. B. Pond, was a surer way of laying up treasure on earth than writing dramas. Though he was not unsuccessful as a lecturer, he found this direct contact with the public quite as demoralizing for his temperament as his struggle with actors and stage managers. His mixed feelings are clearly reflected in a letter to his sister written immediately after an evening at Smith College in May, 1897. "I had a very joyous time giving my lecture at Northampton to 500 girls," he wrote, but it left him terribly tired, and he resolved never to lecture again. "The fact is I find that I hate compliments, and thanks, and tributes. If I could take them ungraciously, all right, but I hang out a grateful grin, which I find stereotyped on my face when I go to bed, and which tires me almost to death." Howells was not enough of an actor ever to enjoy the lecture platform.

Whether because of the strain of the lecture tour, because of the unrelieved effort of the last few years to feel "safe from poverty," because of the precarious health of his wife, because of a restless desire to find fresh "copy" by means of travel, or because of a combination of all these factors, Howells took his family to Europe the following summer—only to return again unexpectedly in the fall.

Something of the torn state of mind which kept the Howellses moving back and forth across the ocean (as well as hither and yon on the East coast of the United States) can be felt in the letter Howells wrote to C. E. Norton some weeks after his return to New York and his old haunts on 59th Street. "We all got home the 6th of November, and as you see we are now at our old place on 59th Street. It is almost being out of New York, for I can escape at once into the Park."[19] However, Howells added that he and his wife had really intended to spend the entire winter in Europe and hardly knew why they had returned; perhaps they were "over-traveled," for they had visited Carlsbad, Nuremberg, Ansbach, Würzburg, Weimar, Mayence, Cologne, Düsseldorf, Brussels, and finally, Paris! "Mrs. Howells was worn out, and I was so 'rattled' by registering our baggage, that one day we gave up wintering in Rome, and took our passage for New York. We were rather ashamed of arriving, and we are not yet fully repatriated, in our taste and feelings. It is so ugly it *hurts*, whichever way I turn. But I have my desk, and I am well enough to work. What more can I ask?"

The "work" in which Howells was soon absorbed was, he wrote to Mark Twain, "a kind of story for Harpers, which I am rather enjoying." He was "taking up the couple who figured in *Their Wedding Journey*, and putting them through *Their Silver Wed-*

ding Journey, with the changed point of view, and the evening light on everything." But by the following June he wrote again to his old friend to say that he had agreed with Major Pond to embark on a second western tour, in the course of which he was to deliver "twenty-five or thirty" lectures between October 7 and December 20, 1899. Though the second trip, like the first, was a great success, Howells came home exhausted from the loss of "natural sleep."

On his return, "after the misery of a night in a sleeping-car," Howells picked up the New York *Tribune* to read with amazement that the House of Harper and Brothers was in the hands of the receivers. "It was as if I read that the United States had failed."[21] When early in 1900, Howells wrote to Mark Twain a long letter in which all these events were amusingly jumbled, "that misery of lecturing" seemed to haunt his mind even more than the "Harper collapse." The most painful aspect of the failure of the publisher seemed to Howells, as he was writing to Clemens, that the special holiday edition of *Their Silver Wedding Journey,* which he had persuaded Harpers to issue, had not in the confusion appeared in time for the Christmas sales![22]

Howells had returned once more to his established habit of novel-writing. Refreshing as he found his excursions into romance, poetry, and drama, his deepest impulse was toward the realistic recording, in simple narrative, of the life he observed about him. Howells' "realism," however, was always illumined by a poetic, often romantic, quality; and it was, at its best, made more pointed because of his love of drama. His power as a novelist was greatly enriched by his experiments in other forms.

CHAPTER 5

Novelist in the 'Easy Chair'

I *The "Easy Chair"*

ON CHRISTMAS EVE, 1899, Howells sat down at his typewriter, to which he was slowly becoming accustomed, to write his weekly letter to his family in Ohio. He addressed it to his sister Aurelia whose "tender words" about "our lost Winnie" in a recent letter had set Howells to musing upon "the gay memories of earlier Christmases" before the death of his daughter. At the same time, Howells looked ahead to the new century about to open with a mistrust he had not felt ten years earlier. "I cannot forecast the future by any effort of faith or imagination," he confessed to his sister, "but I am getting to be an old man."[1]

Howells had returned from his second lecture tour exhausted and dispirited. "I look back on my lecturing with terror," he wrote at the time, "what a hideous trade!"[2] When he made his way down to Franklin Square, he found only chaos and confusion in the once serene office. "Where the kind Harper brotherhood and cousinhood had abounded at low desks or high," he at first could find not "one familiar face."[3] Moreover, his wife's health had become a constant concern to him. To his friend, Mark Twain, who had left for his "Following-the-Equator" lecture tour several years earlier, he wrote at this time: "Mrs. Howells is having rather a miserable winter, and suffers from a lowness of spirits, which does not cheer me up very much."[4]

Besides these personal causes for weariness of spirit, Howells suffered then as always from his deep awareness of social wrong, this time on a world-wide scale. The Boer War and the Spanish-American War combined to affirm Howells' aversion to imperialism and war and to remind him of the confusion of the press on these issues. Howells ended his letter to Mark Twain with the comment that the only thing that kept himself and his wife cheered up at all was "the succession of brilliant British victories, which always leave the Boers on top." He added: "I should not think your English acquaintance would find the last chapter of *Following the Equator* very joyous reading, but it is nuts to us. You may be sure that whatever the newspapers say, the heart of the Americans is with the Boers. But we are engaged in a war of conquest ourselves, and so we can't speak out, and own ourselves the friends of republics everywhere. This is politics."[5]

When Howells turned to his Christmas-Eve letter to Aurelia in 1899, however, the new century was dawning; neither in his personal world nor in the larger scene was the outlook without hope. "You know," he wrote, "father said: 'Age is the time to trust,' and I am not unwilling to trust. As usual, I am full of schemes of all sorts, and am by no means looking forward to quitting work."[6] Already new plans were being made for the most distinguished member of the reorganized Harper publishing company. Several weeks later Howells wrote again to his sister that he was very happy in a new arrangement he had made with the editor according to which he would take all Howells wrote at a fixed price and make him "literary adviser of the House."[7]

The story of the rescue of Harper and Brothers in 1899 by J. P. Morgan, its reorganization under Harvey, and Howells' place on the staff is told by J. Henry Harper in *The House of Harper* (1912). Howells himself described these difficult days in a lengthy communication to J. H. Harper, which Harper included in his book as "Mr. Howells's Paper." Written twelve years after the events recorded, Howells' "Paper" recalls the confusion of the transition days when he at last summoned up the courage to climb "the winding stairs to the editorial rooms." There he found J. Henry Harper, who gave him "comforting reassurances" as to the continuation of the *Monthly,* soon to be confirmed by Henry Mills Alden, the editor, who remained in his position after the reorganization. Howells went off, however, to Annisquam, Massachusetts, that summer of 1900, "with a very uncertain mind." As the months passed he grew "more and more anxious for the future" which, he confessed, "stared at [him] rather vacantly." All he had on hand was *Heroines of Fiction,* and in his heart Howells feared that "the House itself had come to an end."

From his "largish" summer home at Annisquam, Howells wrote his friend, Thomas Bailey Aldrich, then editor of the

Atlantic, that he looked forward to the long summer of work "which must be done for a living."[8] To be sure, "Father and Mother" had just appeared in the May *Harper's* and "A Difficult Case" was about to come out in the July and August issues of the *Atlantic.* Nevertheless, Howells felt that he, as well as the House of Harper, must do what he could to put himself on a firmer financial basis. By July he was able to write to his sister, "I am almost half through my 'Heroine' series," (which had already begun to appear in the May issue of *Harper's Bazar*; and, before the summer was over, he had on hand the opening chapter of *The Kentons.* Having at that time "no invitations from editors," Howells returned to New York early in the fall to "look after [his] chances personally," and there, for the first time, met Colonel George Harvey, the new head of the House. "He received me," wrote Howells in retrospect, "as if he had been the president of the old House; I could not say better."[9]

Harvey immediately invited Howells to come down to his home at Long Branch, N. J., to spend the night. After breakfast the following morning, the agreement between the two was discussed on the veranda, and an offer made which reunited Howells' fortune to those of Franklin Square. In Howells' rather vague words, "I was to give them so many thousand words for so much a year, and I was to be a literary adviser, however much or little that meant." Looking back on those days, Howells felt that, "as an adviser I grew more and more reticent as I perceived that the general equipment of the house enabled it to deal more modernly with its literary enterprises than if I had counseled them." Howells had an office in Franklin Square, "like the other editors," and for a while he acted both as reader and contributor to the Harper publication. "But that phase of the affair scarcely outlasted the winter,"[10] he wrote, and this in spite of the fact that in the autumn of 1900 he had moved with his family to 115 East 16th Street in order to be near his office.

J. H. Harper, in *I Remember* (1934), describes Howells in his new quarters with a warmth which Howells' own words lack. "At first," writes Harper, "he seldom appeared at Franklin Square" (53). Then Francis A. Duneka, whom Colonel Harvey brought with him from the *World,* persuaded Howells "to take a more active part in the affairs of the House," and saw to it that an office on the second floor was fitted up for him according to his taste. For a time, at least, the new editor actually occupied his "Easy Chair" and came down to the office with his customary regularity, lending something of the old informality and grace to the "modernized" organization.

Admired by such younger writers as Stephen Crane, Theodore Dreiser, and Frank Norris, Howells was ready to welcome to his precincts still another generation of literary aspirants. Harper reports in his account of this period that ". . . many a now successful author remembers with gratitude the wise sympathy which he was always ready to extend to beginners on the thorny road of authorship." Harper pointed out that, "He liked young people and they in turn liked him and were ready to be guided by his counsel. Although at that time Mr. Howells stood in the very front rank of American letters, there was never a trace of condescension in his unaffected courtesy; it simply was not in him to put on 'side'" (53).

Undoubtedly, the reorganized staff of the House of Harper welcomed the editor who had never really strayed very far from them. Howells was now at the height of his popularity. Not only had be been heard every month for a decade in the Harper publications—*The Weekly* and *Literature*—as well as in many other magazines, but he was "good copy" any Sunday morning for the New York *Herald,* the *Sun,* or the *World.* Young Theodore Dreiser's interview for *Success* of April, 1898, bore the title, "How He Climbed Fame's Ladder"; the subtitle was "William Dean Howells Tells the Story of His Long Struggle for Success and his Ultimate Triumph." Dreiser's article is only one of many which indicate that the readers of newspapers and magazines of the day were eager to learn what Howells thought about poetry, war, the modern novel, and Henry James; they also wished to know where he lived, what objects ornamented his desk, when he took his daily walk, and how he felt about "the coteries and cliques" of New York society.

Howells himself, however, did not assume that he had attained "ultimate success." Two letters to Thomas Bailey Aldrich, written just before and after he had assumed the duties of the "Easy Chair," show that he was troubled at this time by the same misgivings which he had harbored when he undertook the "Study." The first of these letters he wrote on November 4, 1900, soon after he had put the finishing touches on his opening essay for the "Easy Chair." "You will find a word about you in the first number of the Uneasy Chair, which I hope will please you," Howells wrote; he then added unreflectively: "It might have been wiser for me to have kept out of that place, but at 63 one likes a fixed income, even when the unfixed is not bad. Essaying has been the enemy of the novelist that was in me. One cannot do both without hurt to both. If I could have held out fifteen years ago in my refusal of the Study, when Alden tempted me, I might have gone on and beat *Silas Lapham.* Now I can only dream of some leisure day doing better."[11]

Six months later, in a mood of exasperation still more marked, Howells again wrote to Aldrich. "I have done no fiction since last spring—except a short story—the Easy Chair and the N[orth] A[merican] *Review* papers having been quite enough for me. I hate criticism; I suppose my feeling must be much like your own. I never did a piece of it that satisfied me; and to write fiction, on the other hand, is a delight. Yet in my old age, I seem doomed (on a fat salary) to do criticism and essays. I am ending where I began, in a sort of journalism."[12]

Howells was wrong on at least one count. He was in no sense "ending," for he had before him twenty productive years and of these he made full use in all fields of writing—novels, critical essays, travel books, plays, and poetry—to which his hand had become accustomed. The purchase in 1902 of the home at Kittery Point, which at last satisfied Howells and his family, perhaps contributed to his remarkable vitality. Moreover, he made frequent trips to England, Spain, Germany, and Italy in quest of health for himself and his family, as well as copy for magazines. Sometimes he stayed a few months, sometimes as long as a year; but he faithfully mailed his contributions to the *North American Review, Harper's Weekly,* and *Harper's Monthly Magazine,* all of them published by the House of Harper, now owned by Colonel Harvey.

Though Howells claimed to "hate criticism," his distinguished series of essays for the *North American Review*—edited as well as owned by Colonel Harvey from 1898 to 1916—must have brought him more satisfaction than his essays for the "Easy Chair" of *Harper's Monthly.* These essays ranged from Mark Twain to American verse, from drama to Barrett Wendell's "Notions of American Literature"; they touched on "an Italian view of Humor" and "a possible difference in English and American fiction." They presented to his generation, as well as to ours, important appraisals of such men as Lowell, Mark Twain, Zola, Tolstoy, Hawthorne, Ibsen, Longfellow, James—to mention only a few of the writers whose works Howells had read and reviewed over the years as they had appeared. We find also appraisals of the novelists such as Frank Norris, H. B. Fuller, Robert Herrick, Brand Whitlock, Leonard Merrick; of the plays of Henry Arthur Jones; and of the poetry of Madison Cawein. Since Harvey was primarily interested in politics and social questions, we find among these essays studies of "A Great New York Journalist" (E. L. Godkin), "Some Unpalatable Suggestions" on the treatment of criminals in this country, a consideration of "John Brown After Fifty Years," and others indicating that Howells' interest as a critic extended far beyond literature.

The year after Colonel Harvey purchased the House of Harper, he also took over the editorship of *Harper's Weekly* in order to make use of its columns as a mouthpiece for his political views, which were at that time liberal. Having accumulated a fortune early in life, Harvey, like John Brisben Walker of *The Cosmopolitan*, plunged into journalism in the interest both of personal power and the cause of liberalism. Harvey urged Howells to write for the *Weekly* with complete freedom. In a letter to Norton of April 6, 1902, Howells spoke with triumph "of the chance which has been most generously given me to say what I please of current events in *Harper's Weekly*":

> The result is that I have fairly given it an anti-imperialistic tone. The present head of the house trusts me so entirely that he said the other day when starting for England to 'write what I pleased' for the Weekly. He is young enough to be my son, and my relations with Harper and Brothers have never been so pleasant as now. Perhaps it is the chance of fighting for right things that gives me some hope of them. At any rate you will see that I am trying to say a good word for decency in various directions. I think my main use is in saying it ironically.[13]

Howells' letter to Norton was evidently written just after he had completed a contribution for *Harper's Weekly* called "The Limitations of Irony," in which he had found an opportunity to discuss the Boer War. Howells' irony continued to play upon such issues as "the Philippine matter," labor problems, the Negro question, "race-patriotism," and various aspects of imperialism in these unsigned articles which appeared in the *Weekly*, until Harvey resigned his editorship in 1913 after having fallen out with Woodrow Wilson and the whole cause of liberalism.

On the other hand, when Howells took his seat in the old, red

"Easy Chair" in December, 1900, his whole tone changed from that which marked the *Weekly* utterances. As he explained to his readers in his opening essay, the Chair itself had only recently been ordered up from a dusty corner of the storeroom where it had lain on its side for the eight years since the death of his honored predecessor, George William Curtis. Awakened from "a deep sleep," the Easy Chair wished to know at once "what is now 'the conversation of the town,'" to which Howells was forced to reply, "Well, you know, that is an embarrassing topic, for the Easy Chair is supposed to have no politics, and the 'conversation of the town' is so largely political, just now." Instead of discussing politics and other difficult matters, Howells explained to the dazed old Chair the various aspects of daily life in the new century, which had altogether changed.

Following immediately after Howells' opening essay is Alden's introduction to Harper readers of the new editor, so "highly esteemed and so welcome" by staff and public alike. Alden, no doubt, had not forgotten that it was he who first persuaded Howells to "let himself go" in "familiar and confidential communications with his readers" many years earlier, in spite of Howells' avowed objection. "We don't believe he disliked this sort of writing as much as he appeared to," wrote Alden when Howells again assumed the role of the familiar essayist. "It may be," added Alden, "that, after all, he has generally avoided it as one who denies himself an indulgence." The restraint put upon Howells as a novelist, said the editor, may now make him turn with renewed zest to "another kind of writing, in which he can more freely unbosom himself. The 'Easy Chair' gives him every desired opportunity for such expression."

For his generation, the editor was, no doubt, well advised thus to tone down the writer who had waged a battle for realism in the "Study" more than a decade earlier. But Alden's statement in this essay of the principles that were to govern the newly revived department explain, in a measure, the fact that Howells' essays for the "Chair" are, for the most part, less arresting than those he had written for the "Study." J. W. Harper had refrained from making use of the admonishing "little bell," as far as the editor of the "Study" was concerned; in fact, he had encouraged serious discussion of social questions. Alden, on the contrary, in the days when the House still retained a vivid memory of bankruptcy, announced at once that the "Easy Chair" would "avoid the discussion of what are known as 'burning questions,' and of themes that divide sects in religion, parties in politics, and classes in society." No periodical in the city puts more value, said Alden, on "the writer's individuality. In Mr. Howells' interpretation of life we shall know his heart as well as his thought."

In his essay of May, 1900, marking "Fifty Years of *Harper's Magazine*," Alden wrote, "The 'Easy Chair' will always be remembered as the most graceful and elegant *causerie* in American literature" (961). Howells' way, indeed for the next twenty years, of making the "Easy Chair" his own, only added to the "grace" and "elegance" of that department, and this Alden fully appreciated. In the *Book News Monthly* (June, 1908), Alden, as a "Fellow Worker," attempted to summon up his "impressions" of the quiet man who had worked in the office next to his for so many years. Howells "presents no mark for observation in physiognomy, gait, or gesture," Alden wrote, and then added: "From a meeting with him you do not carry away a picture of him, not even a subjective portraiture in distinct line. He has discussed nothing, insisted upon nothing, expressed no views of life—has not even told you an anecdote to remember him by, or served to point an anecdote for you to tell of him. Yet you have been impressed" (33).

Alden explained Howells' impressiveness by remarking that he was "the man of feeling in his whole complex nature." Those who know him, said Alden, are aware of this pervasive characteristic but are "baffled in their attempt to express their feeling of it," and fall back on the word "gentle." Howells "has the near sense of life, a glowing interest, a genial curiosity; and from this warmth is the light of his seeing—never a dry or cold light."

This "light," which played upon the familiar essays of the "Easy Chair" for the first two decades of our century, pleased many readers in country towns and great cities, who looked to the "Dean" for their ideas and opinions. But by the time Alden died in 1919 and Howells a year later, the virtues of the refined "man of feeling" had long since gone out of favor. Howells' essays for the "Easy Chair" are largely responsible for an exaggerated reputation for "gentility" which was fastened on Howells by H. L. Mencken and other journalists of the 1920's. They overlooked, as readers today also tend to do, the far more distinguished and vigorously critical essays Howells wrote for the *North American Review* and *Harper's Weekly*.

Needless to say, in the twenty years that Howells wrote for the "Easy Chair," he expressed himself on a wide range of "burning issues," such as war, poverty, imperialism, and New York architecture, as well as on a host of minor topics—"the whirl of life in our first circles," "the fickleness of age," "a day at Bronx Park." However, it was these chatty essays, rather than the more serious and at times controversial subjects, which were selected in 1910 for *Imaginary Interviews,* a Harper publication. Just as Howells' first "Easy Chair" essay had been couched in the form of an interview, so were the selections in this charming —but seldom read—collection of "imaginary interviews." Sometimes Howells conversed with a stranger on a bench in Central Park, sometimes with a niece who wondered why her uncle failed to put "love" in his novels, and sometimes with his hostess at a dinner party. So successfully had Howells' "individuality" made its way with the readers of the "Easy Chair," that he was emboldened in February of that year to write directly to Duneka to ask that his salary be raised from $833.33 to $1,000 a month; Howells at seventy-three was sufficiently appreciated at Franklin Square to know that his request would be granted.

Declared on all sides "our leading American novelist and critic," honored by degrees from Yale, Oxford, Columbia, Princeton, and other institutions, and elected the first president of the American Academy of Arts and Letters, he was considered by the House to be its most distinguished editor and contributor. In 1911, after many years of careful planning, the Library Edition of Howells' writing began to appear. Perhaps it was Alden who insisted, when an edition of the complete works of his colleague was under discussion in 1902, that this handsome thirty-two volume set should begin with Howells' non-fiction, rather than with his fiction. Of the six volumes which did appear in 1911, only two were novels, *The Landlord at Lion's Head* and *A Hazard of New Fortunes.* Perhaps the Library Edition was conceived on too grand a scale; perhaps the public taste for Howells had shifted even at the time when the edition was launched. In any case, when J. Henry Harper, in 1912, published *The House of Harper,* no hint of a misgiving was to be found in his proud announcement: "We are just on the eve of publishing a complete Library Edition of the works of W. D. Howells. For half a century Mr. Howells has been producing books which stand among the best in American Literature. Let us hope that he will continue through his writing to entertain and enlighten us for many a year to come" (330).

On March 2, 1912, Colonel Harvey invited President Taft and

four hundred other notables and near-notables to Sherry's Restaurant in New York to help celebrate Howells' seventy-fifth birthday. Whether to encourage the waning public interest in the Library Edition of Howells' works, or to announce Colonel Harvey's return to the Republican Party after his 1911 break with Woodrow Wilson—or, indeed, truly to celebrate the seventy-fifth anniversary of America's enthroned literary figure—would be impossible to say. Speeches were made, toasts were drunk, and then Howells arose to address the assembly. The affair, he said, was neither of his "wishing" nor of his "deserving"; it was "created solely by that genius for hospitality in our host." At the close of Howells' "graceful speech of response," one of the guests tells us, the lights were lowered and "an odd figure" stepped forth, Silas Lapham himself, to remind his creator "We'll live together" when the rest of Howells' books are forgotten. The prediction rings true, for we of a later generation know that *The Rise of Silas Lapham* is Howells' most read book, and that his reputation—as he himself knew—would have been more secure had he been able to withstand the comforts of the "Easy Chair."

II   *Heroines of Fiction*

A few months after Howells assumed the editorship of *Harper's* "Study," in January, 1886, a series entitled "Men of the Day," in a popular weekly presented a full-page cartoon of the new occupant. Scalpel in hand, Howells was pictured standing behind an operating table on which lay the unconscious form of a beautiful girl. Howells was looking not at his victim but at a distant point of space; on his countenance was the kindly but objective look of the pure scientist who wielded his knife in the interest of truth. Beneath the drawing was the caption, "W. D. Howells: Demonstrator of the American Girl," for it was as the coolly scientific and often ruthless analyzer of "feminine nature" that Howells was widely known in his own day.

From the beginning of his novel-writing career, Howells had, indeed, startled his readers by presenting them with careful studies of girls who failed to conform to conventional patterns of behavior. A reader might well have asked, in puzzled surprise, "Do brides and grooms actually quarrel so much of the time on the wedding journey? Would a simple girl from the Middle West refuse to marry a chance acquaintance from Boston merely because he had, on one occasion, snubbed her? Should Dr. Breen have had a profession at all, and if she insisted on having one, was she a fit heroine of fiction? Was Marcia Gaylord's divorce typical enough of the times to be called 'a modern instance'? Is it probable that the bookish daughter of Silas Lapham, rather than the beautiful one, would finally win the lover?" These questions and many more like them lingered in the minds of Howells' readers—most of them women—after they had pursued to the end his curiously detached studies of the "American girl." To the reviewer of "Books for Summer Readers" of *Life*, May 27, 1897, Howells seemed, in *The Landlord at Lion's Head*, almost to have upset "the balance of proprieties in a tale that several times threatened to be a little near the ragged edge." The reviewer points out that in this story of "Jays and Gentlemen," Jeff Durgin not only dropped "a damn or two," but also managed to kiss "a country girl and a city girl" in the same summer. Still more disturbing was the behavior of the heroine herself, who "at the very end," unromantically consented to marry the hero only after "thinking it over."

No doubt the more discerning readers perceived that Howells paid women the highest tribute of all by assuming in his novels and stories that his "heroines" were potentially rational creatures—and even quite as reasonable as his so-called "heros." Vain, foolish, and undisciplined they might be, but so also were men. As an important aspect of his theory of realism, Howells necessarily recognized the possibility of living according to the dictates of reason; the very purpose of his novels, which he insisted were moral in intent, was to remind both men and women that civilization itself depended on their ability to be guided by "reason" rather than by "passion" in their solution of the ordinary problems of existence. The novelist, therefore, should forget the "gaudy hero and heroine"; he should prefer to paint life in the unheroic terms of the average people whom he sees about him every day humbly attempting to do their duty. Then and then only, wrote Howells, could "the light of civilization"—the light of reason—shine through the novel; and if it failed to tell the truth about actual men and women, then fiction corrupted.

Howells felt, when he left the "Study" six years later, that he had not won acceptance for his concept of realism; he never, however, altered his beliefs in his later life, for he was essentially a rationalist. Though the terms in which he stated his views in his novels and essays after the turn of the century were somewhat softened and tempered, he remained the ironically objective

"Demonstrator of the American Girl." *In Heroines of Fiction* (1902) Howells became the demonstrator of the heroines of the novelists he had read and loved from his youth. Though his knife was not so sharp as it was in 1886, it was the same instrument, somewhat blunted from use, upon which he had always relied.

One of the two lectures which Howells' carried with him on his second speaking tour was entitled "Heroes and Heroines of Fiction" and from this lecture grew his two-volume study of "Heroines." Howells actually delivered the lecture only once, at Grinnell, Iowa, on October 28, 1899; on that occasion the reporter who wrote up the lecture remarked that "Mr. Howells' subject was 'Heroes and Heroines of Fiction,' but his theme was heroines."[15] The lecture was so coldly received (Howells wrote his wife the next day that he found himself addressing "450 refrigerators") that he never ventured to read it again but relied solely on his second lecture, "Novels and Novel-Writing." However, when he returned to New York late in December, he offered to Colonel Harvey the notes he had accumulated for his first lecture as a possible serial for one of the several publications of the House, *Harper's Bazar,* which was especially designed to suit the taste of women. From the vast amount of reading and re-reading of novels from Goldsmith to Mrs. Humphrey Ward which Howells had accomplished at Kittery Point the previous summer, he was now ready to write the essays. Handsomely illustrated, these entertaining studies were serialized in the *Bazar* between May, 1900, and January, 1902, when they were immediately published in a two-volume edition by Harpers.

"I began the *Heroines* for the *Bazar,* this morning, and I guess I shall have some fun out of it,"[16] he wrote his daughter on March 5, 1900. Undoubtedly Howells did enjoy reconsidering the novelists whom he had appreciated for many years and from whom he had constructed not only his views on novel-writing, but also many of his ideas on "feminine nature." He considered Defoe the actual founder of the modern novel, but, he wondered, could *Roxanna* be left on the living-room table? Fielding was a "blackguard" reflecting the crude manners of an earlier day; Richardson, though subtle, was too prolix for the modern reader. The sense of humor displayed by Fanny Burney in *Evelina* was, indeed, delicious; but what a bad old, dicing, drinking, brawling century it was! The "divine Jane" was, of course, supreme, for in the world of Miss Austen, common sense tinged with irony prevailed. The Brontë sisters were too personal, fascinatingly daring as their romances were; and Miss Edgeworth did not know when to stop moralizing. No writer had surpassed George Eliot, though she was often too serious and too confused. Trollop—whom, Howells tells us, enjoyed his moment of popular favor between 1860 and 1865—was a far greater novelist than contemporary readers realized; and Mrs. Humphrey Ward just missed being as impressive as George Eliot. Scott, Dickens, and Thackeray were reconsidered with more tolerance than Howells had shown ten years earlier. Hardy was the greatest English novelist of the modern world; his women were part of nature herself. It was Henry James, however, who actually pointed the way to the future novel in his sense of the true subtlety of feminine personality. Zola, Flaubert, and Tolstoy, Howells did not discuss, for he was tracing the Anglo-Saxon tradition and not the Continental. A product of mid-century positivism, Howells had from childhood felt himself at home in the English tradition of Goldsmith, Jane Austen, and Trollop; their quiet sense of a reasonable order of things matched his own. Though Howells had been immensely enlarged by his reading of Turgenev, Björnson, Flaubert, and many other Continental writers, in his own novels he remained true to the tradition into which he was born.

Howells in the summer of 1900, took a large, comfortable house near Annisquam, Massachusetts, and here he re-perused these familiar novels. He discovered again the basic beliefs on which he himself had built; namely, that only when "reason" guides the pen is the novelist able to avoid the false passion, the false heroism, the false sentiment which lies at the base of all evil, in actual life as well as in fiction. The novelist, who is always a moralist, must wield the dissecting knife in order to discover "truth," which is the source of the only "beauty" worth discussing. To be "modern," according to Howells, is to share the duties and responsibilities of the scientist and not to succumb to the essentially unscientific methods either of exaggerated naturalism or melodramatic romanticism. "Ugly realities" are not ugly if they are true; "passion" is a part of life but so is the family mortgage—both are to be considered and dealt with in a study of daily living.

Though Howells in the 1890's and later reviewed the startlingly new books of Stephen Crane, Henry B. Fuller, Frank Norris, and many others, he himself belonged in his insistence on the importance of rational behavior in life as in fiction to an earlier period. The essays in *Heroines of Fiction* were addressed to "the refined reader" of our "cultivated" age; they dealt with the "Nice Girl," who, Howells insisted, always had been the real "heroine" of fiction and always would be. A medallion of Howells reading his manuscript to his daughter, Mildred, done in 1897 by Augustus Saint-Gaudens is, perhaps, a perfect illustration of the "refined girl" of the period.

Since Howells continued to study the heroines about him, both real and imagined, we can properly consider his own ability as a novelist, after the turn of the century, by the measuring-stick which he offered us when he asserted in *Heroines of Fiction* that "a novelist's power is to be tested largely by his success in dealing with feminine nature." Committed as he was to the belief that to be moral is to be reasonable, Howells placed each of his heroines upon the operating table and attempted, with a deft incision, to restore his erring patient to "reason" and thus to health and happiness. From the beginning of his career as a novelist, Howells had consistently sustained this ironically detached attitude toward women; as he grew more conscious of his critical creed, he expressed his views on the false romantic (he called it "romanticistic"), first in *Criticism and Fiction* and, ten years later, in *Heroines of Fiction*.

In the novel Howells published in 1902, *The Kentons*, the serious, devoted daughter of a kindly Midwestern family has fallen fatuously in love with an unworthy lover. In *The Son of Royal Langbrith* (1904), a mother causes even more havoc by "sacrificing" herself first to a scoundrel of a husband and then to a selfish son. In *Miss Bellard's Inspiration* (1905), the heroine, after misunderstandings and confusions, is "inspired" to accept the appropriate suitor. In *The Vacation of the Kelwyns* (1920), a high-minded girl, suffering from a false sense of social superiority, almost fails to recognize the real nobility of her lover. Each of these heroines has to learn, through humbling experience, how to assume a more "realistic" attitude toward herself in the world in which she must live. Already familiar with Isabel March, the Lapham sisters, Mrs. Bowen, and many other Howells heroines, we are prepared to find a certain aura of "romance" playing over these charming girls and women in spite of the avowed "objectivity" of their creator. This poetic atmosphere Howells justified as "the romance of the real," and he carefully distinguished this quality of romance from artificial (hence unreal) romanticism.

WILLIAM DEAN HOWELLS

When we examine more closely the first of these novels of the
1900's, *The Kentons,* we find it remarkably similar in point of
view to Howells' earlier novels; we are either charmed, or
amused, or bored—according to our tastes—by this "commonplace" account of the Kenton's summer trip to Europe. Judge
Kenton, his wife, and four children have lived for a number of
years a quietly contented, normally quarrelsome domestic life
in a square, brick mansion, set in extensive grounds in the midst
of the thriving little town of Tuskingum, Ohio. Richard, the
elder son, now living with his wife in a somewhat smaller house
next door, had gradually taken over most of his aging father's
law practice. Ellen, the judge's favorite—and our "heroine"—
proved to be a pale, slender girl, inclined to spend her morning
strumming the piano and her afternoons at the town library. In
the evenings she either helped her father arrange his notes and
documents for his anecdotal history of his Civil War regiment,
or conversed with the "lecturers" who visited the town and
always stayed in the judge's handsome mansion. Lottie, aged
sixteen, scorned reading of any kind, laughed at "lecturers,"
and found chatting with boys on the vine-covered verandah more
rewarding than serious conversation. Boyne, two years younger
than Lottie, kept a stern eye on his sister's "carryings-on" at
picnics and church festivals and duly reported them to his in-
dulgent, anxious, loving parents.

Though Ellen was really more beautiful than Lottie, no one
seemed drawn to her "until a man came who was not one of the
most cultivated in Tuskingum." The intruder, whose name we
eventually learn was Clarence Bittridge, was a reporter on the
Tuskingum *Intelligencer* "which he was instinctively characteriz-
ing with the spirit of the new journalism" (8-9). Ellen, who had
never before attracted the romantic attention of any of the
visitors to the hospitable house, was immediately swept off her
feet by this flippant, mocking young man. As the judge observed,
one could tell how unworthy he was as a suitor by the very
fact that he brought "his cigarettes and banjo into the house at
his second visit." We recognize, of course, in this free and easy
character, the ghost of Bartley Hubbard, who was, in his turn—
as Howells admitted years later to Brander Matthews—the
shadow of his younger self when a gay reporter in Columbus,
Ohio.

The stages by which Howells traces the growth of Ellen's
"passion" to the point where our "heroine" becomes thin, pale,

and spiritless are as quietly inevitable as a study of the progress of a slowly developing disease, which, indeed, Ellen's infatuation proves to be. The Kenton family finally decides that action must be taken and unwillingly leaves the comfortable home for a stay in New York; here Bittridge, accompanied by his vulgar little mother, pursues Ellen. Neither snubs, kindness, nor stern glances can cope with the effrontery of Clarence, who outwits the parents' vigilance and manages to take Ellen, without a chaperone, to "a play" on Broadway. Bittridge's attempt to kiss the unwilling girl when he returns with her to the hotel at eleven o'clock makes her realize fully the dastardly character of her lover. Only a long sea-voyage, in the course of which she meets an attractive, cultivated and humorous young minister, brings her to the "reasonable" resolve to leave unworthy "passion" strictly alone. Restoration of health and spirits enables Ellen at last to find true "romance" as well. But before she places her slender hand into the firm grasp of Mr. Breckon, she has to come to the difficult conclusion that she has made something of a fool of herself and that, furthermore, she has brought trouble and confusion on her entire loving family.

Breckon, indeed, is as given to fun as "the scamp" from whom the Kenton family flees; the young minister's "levity" on all occasions offends even the frivolous Lottie, who thinks ministers should not joke; and it causes young Boyne, with whom Breckon shares a stateroom, to assume an added dignity. Ellen herself turns pale and leaves the dining salon when the minister's joking startles her into realization of her absurd seriousness. These very jokes, however—aided by the tossing ship which conveniently throws Ellen into the minister's arms—at last help Ellen to forget the agonies of her infatuation and restore her to as much "commonsense" as her character permits.

Breckon, like the unfortunate Bittridge, bears a temperamental relationship to Howells; for both lovers are clever and both attempt to deal humorously, as well as romantically, with an over-serious heroine. The first, however, is evil at heart, and the second is good—a distinction which Ellen recognizes with difficulty. To Howells, *evil* is closely associated with the "romanticistic," while *good* frequently leads by natural stages to the true "romance" found in ordinary experience. The novel which confuses these values is at once lacking in aesthetic, as well as in moral significance.

After her marriage, Ellen herself ponders "that hateful episode

of her psychological history," her passion for a light, untrust-
worthy suitor, and decides that she must have in her character an
"essential levity of nature," under her appearance of gravity (315).
Breckon, however, sees into the puzzle and suggests to her that
she was first drawn to her future husband by "a certain un-
seriousness which reminded her of Bittridge, in enabling him to
take her seriousness lightly." Breckon amuses himself by calling
Bittridge his *alter ego* (316), which indeed he is; both lovers
are "alter egos" of Howells himself who perfectly realized the
difficulty of bringing his heroine of the "gentle, dark eyes, a
little sunken," into reasonable relations with ordinary life. The
instrument he used to bring Ellen back to health was sharpened
by irony and humor; to operate at all on such a lovely girl seemed
to many readers of his day an example of "the wanton cruelty
of Mr. Howells."[17]

Other critics, however, in Howells' day as well as ours, complained that too much of life was left out of such novels as those
of Howells. According to a woman critic, addressing a group in
Chicago, contemporary American writers were "too strictly
patroled by the spirit of the young girl." Satiric fiction of wit
and delicacy was inadequate, for it never really touched on "the
great things of life, the problems of existence which are tearing
like wolves at your heart and mine." Such problems were hinted
at but "never grasped and handled firmly." Howells, in his column
for *Literature,* March 10, 1899, attempted to respond to this
attack, reported in the New York *Times,* first, by listing the
novelists who, he thought, were dealing successfully with "the
wolfish problems of existence," and then by proposing the question, "What, after all, are problems of existence?" For those
who have no money, mused Howells, there is the question of a
job and how much one is paid; for those who have money,
there is the question of losing it or "the secret remorse for wasting
it," not to mention "the corroding shame for spending it selfishly
while many hunger and freeze in sight of the riot." A mortgage,
Howells points out, is not a bad thing "for a real, wolfish, tearing
problem"—nor is a nagging wife, or a brutal husband, "or a
lingering, hopeless sickness." There are other "domestic problems," Howells remarks, "such as a daughter's wish in her innocent heart to marry a fool or a drunkard, and how to prevent it;
or a son's determination to bring a goose or a cat into the family
circle, and how to keep him from doing it." Such questions "rob
the nights of sleep, and turn the watcher's hair gray and age the

soul itself"; these are the problems worth the attention of the novelist.

Howells was broodingly turning these thoughts over in his mind in January of 1899 when he submitted to Colonel Harvey the first chapter of *The Kentons* and in the summer of 1901 when he actually settled down at York Harbor to complete his tale. On May 21, 1901, he wrote to T. B. Aldrich, "we are at York Harbor, where we were three years ago, and to-day I have resumed a story which I expect to finish there."[18] The following September, Howells and his wife took the Fall River boat from Boston to New York and settled into their "flat" on 59th Street. Here Howells started "drubbing away at the old typewriter" as soon as the books were arranged on their shelves.

By November, he wrote again to Aldrich concerning his progress on *The Kentons*: "I did most of a novel last summer, which Col. Harvey has high hopes of—so high, I can't reach them. I think the notion is pretty: how a love-affair is not merely the affair of the two young people, as we used to think, but the affair of the father and mother and brothers and sisters. H. and B. mean to issue it without serializing it, which will be a new thing for me."[19] Harper and Brothers brought the book out in April, 1902; T. B. Aldrich, Brander Matthews, and many other personal friends expressed their appreciation of his story at once. Howells himself, however, was quite aware of the fact that his novels were no longer popular; of the reception of *The Kentons* he wrote to Matthews on April 8, 1902, "the book has been fairly killed by the stupid and stupefying cry of 'commonplace people.' I shall not live long enough to live this down, but possibly my books may. I confess that I am disheartened."

Disheartened as Howells was by the reception of *The Kentons*, by the refusal of his readers to rejoice with him at the "apparently homely average of our common life," Howells continued to regard women with the objective detachment of the scientist. But his patient adherence to the "truth" pleased neither the conventional woman nor the romantic man among his readers, for both had "keen appetites for the false and impossible." Coating the pill of reason with humor, irony, and gentle flattery, Howells appealed in the "Easy Chair" to the latent reasonableness of his women readers with his comments on their treatment of servants, or their taste in interior decorating, or their respect for impoverished English aristocrats. He ruefully objected to public love-making in Central Park, wondered what Benjamin Franklin would think of the Colonial Dames, and expressed the hope that ladies might be taught to remove their enormous "theater hats" during the matinées. Suffused with irony, no doubt often missed by the readers of *Harper's*, these essays, like those of Joseph Addison or E. B. White, were frequently hardly more than amusing glimpses into "the times"; occasionally, however, they touched on a serious aspect of the "woman problem" of the early twentieth century.

Howells' "Easy Chair" of November, 1901, for instance, is devoted to a consideration of the views on women's education expressed by Dr. Stanley Hall, president of Clarke University. Dr. Hall believed, as did most men and women of his day—and many in our own—that women required a modified education, especially designed to prepare them for taking their place in society as wives and mothers. Howells, after years of contemplation of women, both old and young, was prepared to point out to Dr. Hall that he was wrong on more than one count. The first was that there are not enough husbands to go around, especially in New England; the second, that "the girls seem to know more, or at any rate to have read more, and are altogether brighter and quicker, than the young men they meet."

Howells tells his readers that for years at the summer resorts up and down the Atlantic coast he has studied this numerical and cultural disparity between the sexes. In "the sympathetic vacuity, the wide, generous inanity, in which the summer resort conditions all life," one may contemplate "the young girls, not to mention the old girls, who swarm in the ideal proportion of sixteen to one upon the undergraduate youth and the post-graduate age of the other sex." As gold was superior to silver in Bryan's famous "16 to 1" silver-gold ratio of the 1896 campaign, so the women prove to be "the hopeless superiors" of the men—"hopeless, in what a dark, double sense!" For, Howells points out, "the cold science of statistics" makes it quite clear that "only one out of three, or four, or five, educated or co-educated women marry, and of these as few again become mothers, or, if they do, survive the cares and duties of maternity."

Grotesque as it may seem, or amusing, or even tragic, the question, "palpitating in the thoughts of many," is what shall be done with the women, or what are they going to do with themselves? Since the chances of catching a husband are "dwindling to the vanishing point for so many of them," should the aim of a college education be wifehood and motherhood? Should college boys he educated chiefly for fatherhood? "The notion seems to be the same in both cases and in either form a little offensive." Since women, as well as men, must earn a living, let the girls be "fitted to teach school, or keep books, or study art, or journalism, or medicine, or law"—nor is the proposition changed, remarked Howells dryly, by the fact that there are "plenty of nice stupid young fellows for the girls to marry if they had not been educated over and above them." The part women play—"it is very like working"—has not been so much chosen by them as forced on them "by the brutal and entirely man-made conditions of the life which prevails throughout the world ironically calling itself Christendom." Howells says, in conclusion, "we now all know that A.D. 2000 is the true millennium"; meanwhile, he harbored the hope that, a hundred years before that happy time, women might share with men the blessings of an education which would assume equal distribution of the reasoning power.

Howells' interest in "the cold science of statistics" prompted him to welcome "the new woman," as she was thought of at that time, and to support her cause. When, in 1907, he took a second look at the women of Altruria, in *Through the Eye of The Needle*, he found them garbed in simple but charming clothes, attending civic meetings, and casting their votes like the rational creatures he had always supposed them to be. In the interest of women in the less enlightened American civilization of 1912, Howells, at the age of seventy-five, walked down Fifth Avenue in a suffrage parade, thus publicly declaring his allegiance to the "cause." As a "Demonstrator of the American Girl," however, he explored the shortcomings of women as well as their strengths, and avoided "heroines" of the romantic sort. "I find myself diffident of heroines in fiction because I have never known one in life, of the real faultless kind; and heaven forbid I should ever yet know one," Howells observed in 1903 in his essay on "Mr. Henry James's Later Work."[20]

III *A Traveler from America*

From *A Foregone Conclusion* to *The Kentons,* Howells had taken his characters traveling, for, in crossing the ocean, as Howells himself had discovered, confused ideas are often dispersed by fresh Atlantic breezes. Furthermore, contact with Italian beggars, German princes, patronizing Englishmen and a closer view of religious processions, wrangling parliaments, and complicated railroad lines gave the traveler a renewed sense of "the sincerity and reality of America."[21] From his early experiences as a consul in Venice to his last trip to England in 1913, Howells was drawn to Europe because of the refreshment, both physical and mental, he found in foreign lands; at the same time he always felt a simple American's disdain for outworn civilizations entangled in the cruelties, injustices, and depravities of a dying feudalism. "We are usually of two moods," Howells wrote in a paper for *Harper's Weekly*, May 25, 1895. "We either mock or blame them very much, or else we admire them with something very like a foolish face of praise."

Though Howells was in no sense a novelist, who, like Henry James, capitalized on "the international scene," he was a remarkably successful writer of books of travel, the charm of which depended in no small measure upon their narrative quality. While still writing for the *Ohio State Journal*, Howells discovered the trick of relieving his accounts of "Summer Travel" by "Glimpses" of the people he had met on excursion boats or in hotel lobbies; this same informality contributed to the effectiveness of *Venetian Life, Italian Journeys,* and *Tuscan Cities.* Surprised by his own success, Howells, at the beginning of his career, perceived how, by stressing the anecdotal aspect of these travel essays, he might launch himself into novel-writing. As we have noted, Basil and Isabel March set out on *Their Wedding Journey* in the early 1870's, traversing the same route taken a few months earlier by the Howellses; in 1899, they took *Their Silver Wedding Journey,* obediently following the itinerary through Germany of the actual couple whose shadows they, of course, were. In a sense, *A Chance Acquaintance, The Lady of the Aroostook, Indian Summer,* and many other Howells novels are skillfully elaborated accounts of his own travels.

As Howells advanced in age, the annual novel which had flowed so easily from his pen even when he was well along in his middle years became increasingly burdensome to him—especially "the love-business." Instead of a novel a year Howells prevailed upon the new managers of Harpers to accept a series of "fictionalized" travel books, mirroring the six trips he actually made between 1904 and 1913 to England, Italy, Germany, and Spain. "I was a traveler long before I was a noveler," he wrote in 1912.[22]

Though Howells persisted in his lifelong quarrel with the novels of Scott, Bulwer-Lytton, Thackeray, and, finally, Kipling,

and though he introduced designing Englishmen into several of
his novels, it was, nevertheless, to England that he traveled
most frequently as he grew older and that he commented upon
most interestingly for his American and English readers. Four
travel books and many letters to friends and family reflect the
mixture of pleasure and annoyance he felt whenever he found
himself again on the island from which all of his ancestors had
migrated hardly more than a hundred years earlier. The very
complexity of his feeling for England enhanced, therefore, the
charm of the essays Howells sent home to the various publications of Harper and Brothers.

But Howells had further reasons for making numerous trips to
England. He could, for instance, confer with his British publisher, David Douglas; he could also meet and talk with Henry
James, Edmund Gosse, James Barrie, and many other English
and American friends who welcomed him abroad. London dinner
parties, teas on the terrace of Parliament, excursions to Oxford,
luncheons on the Char—all these were heart-warming to the
aging, sociable, distinguished, international personality which
Howells had become; they also enlivened the packets of manuscripts which were sent, without fail, to his publisher.

It was, however, his health that moved Howells to leave for
England with his daughter Mildred in March, 1904. *The Son of
Royal Langbrith* had kept him writing "too hard"—"I'm rather
run down nervously," he admitted to Mark Twain, "and that's
why Pilla is taking me abroad."[23] The plan, outlined in a letter
of February 14, was that he should first drink the waters at Bath
to "get some radium into me out of them" and then travel about
for a few weeks before the arrival in England of Mrs. Howells
and John. The children would spend the summer, leaving the
elder Howellses in Europe for the remainder of the winter. During the weeks before the arrival of his wife, Howells wrote long
letters back to her; and these he used later as the basis for
London Films and *Certain Delightful English Towns*.

"Writing in the hotel parlor," on March 15, 1904, after the
hour and a half trip from Plymouth to Exeter, where he and his
daughter had found rooms in "a rickety old hotel" overlooking
the cathedral close, Howells hastily jotted down notes about what
he had seen from the train window—cowslips along the railroad
tracks, glimpses of the sea, grey-stone cottages opening into
bright little gardens, and finally, dull, overcast skies which
suddenly turned sunny and lit up their third-class compartment.

Everything interested Howells, for he and Mildred were merely
newly arrived American tourists, delighting alike in old Saxon
churches and crumpets for tea. Howells ended his letter to his
wife abruptly, promising to "stuff this with photos"; the two
travelers then no doubt strolled about the town, camera in hand,
before returning to dinner in the corner of their chilly British inn.
This letter and four others included in Howells' *Life in Letters*
can be read with the same indiscriminate pleasure Howells
must have felt in writing them. In one of them, for example, is
a glimpse of Henry James, who called upon father and daughter
after their arrival in London: "He is *very* stout, and all over,
filled out from head to foot, in a sort of chamfered squareness.
He made many tenderly awed inquiries about you and John."[24]
And in another letter London is seen from the top of an omnibus,
after a "glorious day, warm and bright" spent mostly at the
National Gallery: "The *stateliness* of the streets astounds me at
times, in their long stretches of massive architecture, unbroken
by blocks. . . . A massive *roar* that goes up from them is like
a lion's. . . . It's tremendous." The houses, however, are refrigerators; Howells shivers down to the parlor fire every morning
to warm up with coffee and eggs, bacon or fish. Instead of working on his essay by the blaze, however, Howells and Mildred
decide to go out and see something "every fine morning."[25]
Lunch at the Stracheys, a drive to Kew, a stroll among people
of fashion in Hyde Park, a glimpse of the king leaving Bucking-
ham Palace—every sight, sound, and smell interests and amuses
this Traveler from America bent on collecting "tentative impressions" for future essays.
In spite of "a sort of fuzzy-mindedness" which overtakes
everyone in England, himself included, Howells preserves enough
American "clear-thinking" to realize that the English seldom know
what they are doing things for: "That's why they're able to put
up with royalty and nobility; they've not thought it out." Moreover, "James says he has not known above two women who were
not snobs; but there are several more men, though they are
very rare, too. Monarchy is a fairy tale that grown people believe
in and pay for. They speak quite awedly of royalties and titles,
and won't join in the slightest smile about them."[26]
One of the most marked of the "superficial English characteristics," is indeed the "loyalty" called forth by "the mere mention of
the Royal Family" (193). Praised by the Prince of Wales as
"prime among the civic virtues and duties," this unreasoning

loyalty has become to the Englishman "a sort of religious principle," about which no one dares joke. A visitor of "good taste"
and "good sense" also accepts with circumspection the "aristo-
cratic forms of society" which naturally grow from this respectful,
not to say reverential, attitude toward monarchy. Though Howells
on this trip to England and several subsequent visits in 1909, 1910,
and 1913 grew increasingly fond of the English as individuals,
he remained outspokenly critical of all the social injustices of
the British social hierarchy.

And do the English like us, or understand us, Howells asks,
any more than we like or understand them? It is useless to suppose they do: "if we surprise them into a kind of respect, we
are still something to them like a cross between Canadians and
Anglo-Indians, and much like Australians." One of the lady-
pensioners with whom Howells had tea at Hampton Court
turned to him after a tour of the apartments and said, "You are
an author, I believe." Howells jokingly replied, "I'm a library,
I've written so many books." "Oh, how very nice!" said the lady,
lapsing into silence. Howells commented to his wife: "What a
book I *could* make about England."[27]

Though *London Films* charmed the readers of Howells' day, it
is certainly not the book which Howells *could* have written had
he fully expressed his thoughts. It is, indeed, not quite such
good reading as Howells' letters home to his wife. Though
London is described in Chapter XII, for example, James is left
out of the picture; and, though Hampton Court is fully discussed
in the next chapter, the lady-pensioner is omitted. The question
as to whether or not "the English like the Americans better than
formerly" is discussed in Chapter VI under the heading "Some
Misgivings as to the American Invasion," and in it Howells has
very sensible comments to make concerning the attitudes of the
traveling Americans and their hosts. A foible of Americans is
that they long to be loved; but, he notes, "they want to be taken
nationally," even more than personally, by foreigners (59). The
English, if they give the matter a thought, can hardly love us
nationally since they fought against us in the Revolution and
sided with the South in the Civil War. They are quite willing,
however, to welcome us personally, and even to become our
friends, though they are unable to embrace us "in the lump,"
as we would fain be loved. The English are very polite, but they
have not changed their political views; they would not "willingly
wound the American visitor, unless for just cause, like business, or

the truth" (59). That American fares best who allows himself to be "taken individually, rather than typically," and this is precisely how Howells allowed himself to be taken as he traveled about to the cities and towns of England.

The very opening sentence of "The Landing of a Pilgrim at Plymouth," the first "delightful English town" he visited, suggests why Howells moved so harmoniously among the English. To do so is hardly a problem, he implied, for surely "no American, complexly speaking, finds himself in England for the first time" —that is, if he is of English extraction. His English ancestors stir within him as soon as he steps on shore; and they, together with his American forefathers, "who were nourished on the history and literature of England," combine to create "an English consciousness" which makes him understand and even share his cousins' respect for kings and strong tea, for ancient manor houses and deer parks. He almost forgets that these estates are tended by tenants who have no concept of "equality" and no hope of becoming landowners. Except for the facts that the houses are uniformly chilly and that cabbage is served in its various forms at every meal, all is pleasant, decorous, and cheerful; the English have evolved a system which not only works but works "admirably."

Of course an alien American, "if he has a heart to which the ideal of human equality is dear," shrinks at the thought that those who till the fields and lumber and woods "have no ownership in severalty or in common" of the lovely landscape stretching before him. However, certain "withering doubts" are sure to accost the "pilgrim reverting from the new world," for he is sadly aware of the fact that class distinctions and social injustice have become as firmly established in America as in England. An after-dinner stroll on the promenade at Plymouth overlooking the sea, convinces this pilgrim that, "in what is done by the public for the public, we are hardly in the same running with England." This much, Howells says, he must confess to the reader if he is "ever to claim any American superiority in these 'trivial, fond records'" of his summer travels in the land of his ancestors.

Howells, who had for many years made England the butt of his jokes, witticisms, and serious criticism, was deeply affected by his "Fortnight in Bath." Having come to England expressly to "take the waters," he lingered for several weeks in this softly grey town, set among the rolling hills, where he drank in "tradition" as he imbibed the "waters." Bath was to him the most "delightful" of the English towns he visited because it was the richest in literary tradition. Though he passed his mornings, he says, duteously sipping the nauseating liquid offered him in the almost deserted old Pump Room, he actually hoped to encounter among the Roman pillars Catherine Morland, Mr. Tilney, and other characters made familiar by Jane Austen. Disregarding the few forlorn visitors of the day, Howells was aware of the shadows of Fanny Burney and Beau Nash, as well as that of Miss Austen. Guidebook in hand, Howells wandered with his daughter up and down the terraced city, reading every historical plaque attached to the decorous eighteenth-century dwellings in which literary folk had dwelt.

Like James's "Passionate Pilgrim," Howells was swept off his feet by tradition. "I remember," he wrote in this essay on Bath, "how once when I sat peacefully at dinner, a feeling of the long continuity of English things suddenly rose in a tidal wave and swept me from my chair, and bore me far away from the soup that would be so cold before I could get back" (55). Surely these English, "passing so serenely from fish to roast, from salad to sweets," and talking so blandly of the weather, had not changed for a thousand years and would not alter for another thousand. "In my American consciousness I felt myself so transient, so occasional, so merely provisional beside them." Generations hence, they would be, or believe themselves to be, "the first people in the world"; and, finally, as dwellers in the very last of the monarchies, they would look around with pity on "the class-less equalities of the rest of the world"(56). From his table in the dining room, Howells glanced about him with amusement and concluded that this country, where "the servant thanked the served for being served, and the served thanked the servant for serving," had realized "a social ideal unknown to any other civilization." In England no voices were raised above "the high chirpy level"; there was not only no display of passion (passion with the Englishmen is reserved for business) but also no sound of laughter, only the murmur of well-bred voices and the rustle of waiters moving softly in and out among the tables. How had these Englishmen come to be what they were? Their temperament, or the blend of temperaments contributing to the English character, had been formed through centuries of tradition. Americans knew nothing comparable.

Howells was more than once overtaken by similar "psychological seizures" as he traveled about the island which he, as an exiled son, both loved and criticized. In June, 1904, the University of Oxford bestowed upon him the degree of Doctor of Letters. After he had "got safely through all," Howells wrote to his sisters in Ohio that the nervous strain of the experience was only somewhat relieved by the sight of his wife and daughter looking down at him from the balcony of the auditorium. "A great roar of applause" went up from the undergraduates as he received his degree, he wrote, and "not a single jibe." The brief ceremony, during which he was eulogized in Latin, was followed by "all sorts of teas and dinners,"[28] and then by many callers.

The October, 1906, issue of the *North American Review* carried a long, melodious essay, simply entitled "Oxford," which was later included in *Certain Delightful English Towns*. It was, in fact, an elaborate expansion of the brief remarks written home to his sisters. If Harvard, Yale, Princeton, and Columbia, said Howells, could by some magic find themselves in the same small town, something of the beauty—if not the antiquity—of Oxford might be achieved. In his loving description of punting on the Char, of gazing down on college towers from the roof of the Radcliffe, in his delight at the "vivid green light of a grassy quadrangle," not a hint is given the reader as to the purpose of Howells' visit (627). When "the academical events of the Sheldonian Theatre" are described, we do not learn that Howells was a participant. No American university could emulate, he wrote, "the bravery of the scarlets and crimsons and violets and purples" worn by the scholars in the academic procession, "before which the iridescent fashions of the feminine spectators paled their ineffectual hues." In that procession, individual differences "of looks or statures" were forgotten; "all were clothed with the glory of the ancient university which honored them"(633). Though Howells basked in the glory, he did not acclaim publicly his own honored position.

Notes for this essay and many others were carried to St. Remo, Italy, in October, where Howells and his wife rented an apartment in "a pretty villa" amid palms, olives, roses, oleanders, and orange trees, and settled down for a busy, dull, lonely winter. Here Howells more than made good his commitment to Harpers to "get a book" out of his impressions of England; two books, *London Films* and *Certain Delightful English Towns*, were published in 1906 from the material which had already come out in *Harper's Monthly*, *Harper's Weekly*, and *The North American*

Review. No sooner had the first essay appeared in the December, 1904, issue of *Harper's* than the English journals reprinted Howells' comments, so great was public interest in the thoughts of this distinguished visitor from America. Howells wrote to Perry on January 9, 1905: "We're wearing the winter away, and I'm writing up a lot of my English material, which I expect to make a book of. Some of the London papers quote it from the magazine, picking out the plums which are sugared, but leaving the bitter almonds which flavor the whole. It is droll."[29]

Doubtless the English did not catch the flavor of these "bitter almonds" which Howells thought seasoned the whole simply because it was lost in the fragrance of sugar plums. "I am old, and I like to be thought kindlier than I am,"[30] he observed. Much of the "bitterness" of his feelings for England remained locked in his own heart, except that which is to be found in several letters to C. E. Norton. From the Villa Lamberti he wrote him on November 4, 1904:

> She [my wife] is openly and I secretly homesick, as in fact we have been all summer in spite of the intense interest of our English sojourn. At times we enjoyed it greatly, and at other times not, but it was interesting always. I quite long to tell you of it, sunk in some deep arm chair by your study fire, but it is physically and spiritually impossible to write it. I think the intimacies of it would amuse you, and it is a pity that such things must not be put into print, for they ought. What you say of the Oxford episode revives all the pleasure of it, and some of the pain. If the elderly man I am could set it all down, it would be a unique, if not a precious gift to literature, and what a 'character' I would create out of myself![31]

In April, 1905, the Howellses returned to a New York hotel. There they remained until late in May, poised "for flight to our rugged little nest on the Maine coast," Kittery Point, where, Howells wrote to an English friend, "I have a big library which was once a stable, with the stalls turned into book-shelves; and I hope to add a volume this summer to the superfluity of my own literature."[32]

The copy for the last essay of *London Films* had already been sent to Franklin Square and the introductory installment of *English Towns* had begun to appear when Howells arrived at his summer home. Howells felt now for the first time "sensibly tired." He found that he and his wife, after a year abroad and a few restless weeks in New York, only wished to "sit and stare at the sea." During this period when, as Howells admitted, "I *could* not use my head," he was moodily brooding over his impressions of England revisited, which he despaired of expressing fully in the promised essays. "I wish I could see you and talk long, long with you about England, and of course about myself," he wrote to Norton on June 11, 1905, during the month when he found it impossible to work:

> The impression of England on me was so great as to be almost pulverising, but out of the dust I am too old to be made a new man of. I shall never be able, in what I write, to impart the sense of this, and I see much pity in my having gone out of my American way to be crushed. I was fitted to my groove, and contentedly slipping on in it to the end. Now, I find myself so much at odds with what I used to be that I do not know what sort of re-beginning to make; this quite irrespective of the rightness of England or the wrongness of America for each is in fact inevitably right in its way.[33]

Three months later, on September 10, Howells, still at Kittery, wrote again to Norton, this time to report that "the mind-weariness" he experienced earlier in the summer had quite passed away and that he was writing now as "furiously" as ever and "mainly about England." To save himself from "disgrace," he had been reading English history morning, noon, and night and discovering "what an amazing people they have been."[34] Only the fact that we, too, are English by blood made it possible for us boldly to "stand up against them" at the time of the Revolution. Howells recalled what Norton had said to him "of the thinness of the soil we work in here, and the depth of theirs." Emerson caught their character "surpassingly" in *English Traits*, Howells observed, nor have they really changed significantly since his essays were written.

During the year when Howells was traveling through England and meditating on his impressions at leisure at St. Remo, Henry James was revisiting his native land and gathering together his final impressions for *The American Scene* (1907). "H. James" stopped at Kittery, one terribly hot day before he sailed for England, Howells wrote to Norton, their mutual friend, adding that he was glad his guest had left as early as he did, for any more of such weather "would have branded him with too deep a hate of our poor hemisphere."[35] James's visit brought back to

Howells the lively discussions of thirty years earlier, before James had decided to make England his home. In 1904-5, then, the two old friends exchanged hemispheres, perhaps to vindicate, to check, to reconsider their earlier decisions; both men were shaken by their experiences. Howells remarked to Norton that, after James's visit, he awoke the next morning "thinking of the folly of nationalities, and the stupid hypocrisy of patriotism." No doubt, he said, he would have changed his mind by the time Norton should have received his letter; "but now I ask why J. or I, even, should not live forever out of America without self-reproach?" James would, perhaps, "grow lonelier with age." But age brings loneliness anywhere, added Howells, who, like his fellow novelist, was a lifelong traveler in his own country or abroad, and never fully content with either.

In the autumn of 1905, the Howellses left their home in Maine and returned to New York, this time to the Hotel Regent at 70th Street and Broadway. Though Howells' days, and nights as well, were crowded with a round of engagements—a visit with Norton at Shady Hill; a dinner party at Delmonico's marking Clemens' seventieth birthday; a trip to Cambridge to see a Greek play; a journey to Washington in the interest of a copyright bill—he faithfully worked in hotel room or country barn on an essay for the *North American Review,* or on a revision of a play, or on a new novel. Early in January, 1906, Howells and his wife left for Atlantic City where they stayed in a comfortable hotel near "a pretty little theater and a vaudeville show." Though in quest of health and distraction, Howells never paused in his work: "of course I'm writing all the time; trying to get the better of my English material,"[36] he signaled to Norton in February.

A year after the appearance of *London Films* and *Certain Delightful English Towns,* Howells was busily engaged in revising and enlarging *Venetian Life,* the travel book which had brought him early and lasting fame. In working over the familiar material, "the old wine got into my brain," Howells wrote Norton on October 13, 1907. "I began to dream of Italy once more, with such effect that I babbled in my sleep to Harpers of it. They agreed so joyously and instantly that we are now all but booked for Naples on the *Republic,* sailing Nov. 30."[37]

The trip, which resulted in *Roman Holidays and Others,* was prolonged until late the following spring. From Kittery, in July, 1908, Howells wrote to Norton at Shady Hill, "Now at last I am here, with some doubt whether or not I was not in a better place before." In this long letter, Howells described some of the experiences of his stay abroad—his drives through the Bois in Paris with "my dear old Perry," and his walks in the parks of London with James. He added that, though he and his daughter were "intolerably well," his wife returned from Europe "very much broken down."[38]

In November, 1908, Howells was elected the first president of the American Academy of Arts and Letters, an office which he held until his death. By the following August, Howells himself suffering from his "old liver complaint," was ordered abroad for a rest. But his wife, who had accompanied him on so many journeys, was unable to go with him to England in the summer of 1909. Soon after his return to this country, word reached him that he had been elected—after the appearance of *Seven English Cities* (1909)—Honorary Fellow of the Royal Society of Literature of the United Kingdom. Howells hardly savored this honor, for the condition of his wife was worsening month by month. Elinor Mead Howells died on May 6, 1910, and Howells was left again with the sense that death, which "has been happening since the world began," is "incredible . . . Nothing helps, or begins to."[39] Early in June, Howells sailed to England again with his daughter; for travel, especially to the British Isles, remained to him one of the solaces of life even in the midst of loss and change.

Four years later, Howells wrote three reminiscent essays entitled "In an Old-Time State Capital" for *Harper's Monthly*, September to November, 1914. Always in need of a feminine reader and critic, he asked a cousin of his wife and a friend of the Howellses since the old days in Columbus, Mrs. J. G. Mitchell, to read and criticize the manuscript for him. After he had finished his "Columbus history," he wrote to her in consternation, "but I have not been able to say anything about meeting Elinor, the vastly most important thing in my whole life. I haven't brought myself even to mention her, or so much as to say that here I met the one who became my wife. What shall I do?" If he should indulge his own feelings, he wrote, "I should not say anything; that part of me is inexpressible."[40]

Two years later, when these papers became a part of *Years of My Youth*, Howells inserted a single paragraph about his meeting during the winter of 1860-61 with Elinor Mead, and about their long and devoted married life.

CHAPTER 6

Final Appraisal

I *Western Retrospect*

STIRRED by his renewed contact with Clemens, who returned to this country in October, 1900, Howells attempted, in an essay for the *North American Review*, to search out the western origins of the genius of his friend. In doing so, Howells began a quest for his own western roots, a quest which led him at last to his final autobiographical account of his Ohio boyhood, *Years of My Youth* (1916). Howells' "western retrospect" also inspired two autobiographical novels and a biography of Twain, all of which were interwoven with the circumstances of his life in the early twentieth century.

On their return to New York, the Clemenses rented a house, 14 West 10th Street, just off Fifth Avenue, and not far from the Howellses' apartment at 115 East 16th Street. Soon the old association, which had never really lapsed, was resumed. Clemens looks "younger and jollier than I've seen him for ten years,"[1] Howells wrote to their mutual friend, T. B. Aldrich.

Having lived through a tragic decade marked by bankruptcy, the loss of his daughter, and an exhausting lecture tour around the world, Clemens returned to find himself almost a national hero. Howells, having suffered a personal tragedy several years earlier, had enjoyed in the 1890's perhaps his most productive period and was now at the very height of his prestige both as a critic and as a novelist. Though they had seen one another whenever possible during this busy period and had never ceased to exchange letters as full of the gaiety as of the sadness of old friends, it was a solace to this "pair of old derelicts"—to borrow Clemens' phrase—to cease "drifting around" for a while and to find themselves near neighbors in New York.

Two events, Howells wrote in the *North American Review* of February, 1901, had given him "a fresh excuse" for examining

again the literary output of Samuel Clemens: first, the publication of a uniform edition of his work; second, his return to his
own country "after an absence so long as to form a psychological
perspective in which his characteristics make a new appeal." In
"Mark Twain: An Inquiry,"[2] Howells analyzed what he felt to be
the "new appeal" of Clemens' unique genius; it was, indeed, the
old appeal of the western writer to which Howells had responded
many years earlier. What is the source, origin and meaning of
Mark Twain's humor, often marked by "tragical seriousness"?
From the first, Twain's humor was felt to be a permanent part
of "the breadth of vision with which he compassed the whole
world, and tried for the reason of things." In searching for the
answer to the question that has puzzled all critics of Mark Twain,
Howells went back to his own memories of Ohio woods and
streams in order to grasp imaginatively Clemens' Missouri.

"The Western boy of forty or fifty years ago," said Howells in
his essay, Mark Twain "grew up so close to the primeval woods or
fields" that their poetry became a part of him; when he, in his
own good time, became aware of literature, he dealt with that
simply and directly too. Glancing through the handsome volumes
of the Uniform Edition of *The Writings of Mark Twain* (1899),
Howells observed that he did not see any indication that Twain
had ever set about consciously to produce literature or to reproduce life. "When filled up with an experience that deeply
interested him, or when provoked by some injustice or absurdity
that intensely moved him, he burst forth, and the outbreak might
be altogether humorous, but it was more likely to be humorous
with a groundswell of seriousness carrying it profoundly forward."
In all of these outbursts there seemed to Howells something
"elemental" which was at the same time "indefinably Western."
Now that Mark Twain has achieved a world-wide fame, Howells
pointed out in "Mark Twain: An Inquiry," we are in danger of
forgetting not only how American he is but also how "truly
Western." Nor is it "alone in its generous humor" that his work
is Western. "Any one who has really known the West (and really
to know it one must have lived it) is aware of the profoundly
serious, the almost tragical strain which is the fundamental tone
in the movement of such music as it has" (170).

But the Missouri which Clemens knew was not only Western,
it was also Southern, for it partook of "the peculiar social civilization of the older South from which his native State was settled,"
Howells observed (171). His humor, therefore, was quite capable

of seeing the "sardonic comi-tragedy of the squalid little river town" where Huck Finn grew up, especially after Clemens' return from "the vaster Far West" and his sojourn in the East. It is possible, wrote Howells, that Mark Twain's early insight into the absurdity and the injustice of slavery made him for the rest of his life less "purblind" than most humorists; "if the knowledge and vision of slavery did not tinge all life with potential tragedy, perhaps it was this which lighted in the future humorist the indignation at injustice which glows in his pages. His indignation relieves itself as often as not in a laugh" (180).

This shared western background gave Howells and Clemens a way of regarding the political and social scene with both indignation and laughter; Howells in his "Inquiry" into Mark Twain reveals as much of himself as he does of his friend. Soon after his review he wrote Aurelia, on February 24, 1901: "I see a great deal of Mark Twain nowadays, and we have high good times denouncing everything. We agree perfectly about the Boer War and the Filipino war, and war generally. Then, we are old fellows, and it is pleasant to find the world so much worse than when we were young."[3]

In May, 1901, Howells moved uptown once more. "We lived in the same city," Howells wrote sadly in *My Mark Twain*, "but for old men rather far apart, he at Tenth Street and I at Seventieth, and with our colds and other disabilities we did not see each other often." The noise and the dirt of lower New York proved too much for Mrs. Clemens, however, and before many months had elapsed, the Clemenses had rented a spacious mansion at Riverdale, overlooking the Hudson and the Palisades. Here, Howells remembered, "I began to see them again on something like the sweet old terms . . . the good talk, the rich talk, the talk that could never suffer poverty of mind or soul, was there, and we jubilantly found ourselves again in our middle youth." The "good talk" was soon interrupted by an actual journey to the "frontier" of Howells' boyhood (82-83).

Early in the spring of 1902, at a time when he had "pretty much stopped sleeping" because of the burden of his social life and that of his writing, Howells, with his brother Joseph, took "a voyage on the Ohio river" similar to the trips they had made together in their boyhood when they had drifted down the river in boats piloted by their Dean uncles. Far from being a restoring experience, the excursion left on Howells a melancholy impression of a scarred and industrialized West; and this vision became an essential part of his retrospective view of the frontier life which he had more than once in his writing been tempted to romanticize.

On March 19, 1902, he wrote of the experience to his old confidant, C. E. Norton, an Easterner who knew little of the beauties of the western world of Clemens and Howells: "I am just returned from a voyage on the Ohio River, from Pittsburg to Cincinnati and back—a thousand miles of turbid, Tiber-colored torrent, flowing between the loveliest hills and richest levels in the world." But the idealized countryside of his boyhood was becoming industrialized; the midwestern frontier—the source of his belief in democracy, brotherhood, and the natural goodness of man—was changing. What did it mean? Howells continued:

Through veils of coal smoke I saw the little ugly house, in the little ugly town, where I was born, the steamboat not staying for me to visit it. The boat did, however, let me visit a vanished epoch in the life of the shores, where the type of Americanism, for good and for bad, of fifty years ago, still prevails. It is all, where man could make it so, a scene of hideous industrialism, with topless chimneys belching the fumes of the bottomless pit; but thousands of comfortable farmsteads line the banks which the river is always eating away (to its own hurt,) and the diabolical contrasts of riches and poverty are almost effaced. I should like to write a book about it.[4]

Soon after his return to New York, Howells learned of the death of Bret Harte in London, a man whom he had loved and befriended but never really admired. News of this break in the old fellowship of friends from the West set him dreaming of the Bret Harte "who had lately come East in his princely progress from California" and of a "lurid lunch" at Ober's Restaurant, attended by Fields, Aldrich, Keeler, Harte, and Clemens. Memories of Bret Harte, shared by Aldrich and Clemens, brought an exchange of letters between Kittery Point and Saranac Lake, where Aldrich was spending the summer, and of visits made possible by a little coastwise trolley between Kittery and York Harbor, where the Clemenses had rented a house.

Youthful aspirations, the approaching old age, the elusive quest for identity—these were the thoughts much on the minds of the three aging friends. Howells expresses this complex of thought and feeling in a letter of July 3, 1902, written to Aldrich, in which he admitted,

I should not mind being old, so much, if I always had the young, sure grip of myself. What I hate is this dreamy fumbling about my own identity, in which I detect myself at odd times. It seems sometimes as if it were somebody else, and I sometimes wish it were. But it will have to go on, and I must get what help I can out of the fact that it always *has* gone on. I think I could deal with the present, bad and bothering as it is, if it were not for visions of the past in which I appear to be mostly running about, full of sound and fury signifying nothing. Once I thought that I meant something by everything I did; but now I don't know.[5]

Clemens, Howells added, "has written a very acrid allegory, in the last number of *Harper's Weekly*, about this subject of old age. How every fellow thinks he has discovered it!" Meanwhile, Clemens was living "in very tolerable comfort at York Harbor," where Howells expected to visit him soon. Howells, no doubt, derived a certain consolation from these summer visits, where, sitting in wicker chairs with cooling drinks beside them, they could happily inveigh against "this d---- human race." In order to insure the continuance of these choice meetings, Clemens at this time organized a Human Race Luncheon Club, confined to four members, of which Howells was one.

But Howells found even more comfort at Kittery Point in the hours of quiet reading in his made-over barn of the books he had known and loved in his youth; such reading was always a necessary part not only of the digestion of his own past but also of the inception of new ideas for books he might write. During the summer in which he was cheerfully condemning the human race with Clemens, he was also rereading the metrical tales of George Crabbe, a complete edition of whose works he had recently purchased. Crabbe's studies of eighteenth-century village life brought into focus Howells' own meditations on his early experience in Jefferson, which still lingered in his mind after his "voyage on the Ohio River." Early in October, Howells wrote to Norton at Shady Hill from his library at Kittery:

You will be amused to learn that [Crabbe] has shaken into form a vague purpose I have lately had to study in verse the life of the Ohio village where the most wretched years of my later boyhood were passed. I used to hate it, so that for many years after my escape from it I troubled to think my dead body might be brought back prisoner and buried there. But I have long since forgiven it; and I now see it in tender retrospect which seems friendly to a treatment in heroic couplets, with the overtone

Pre-popian poets. I should like to show you my beginning, but for the present I spare you.[6]

The "beginning" of the poem to which Howells referred never developed beyond the early stages; he was soon back in New York immersed in his usual round of dinners and meetings of all sorts, which, somehow, he sustained while producing his steady flow of "Easy Chair" contributions, novels, plays, and essays. One of the saddest—though no doubt one of the gayest— of the many dinners attended by both Howells and Clemens was that given in October, 1903, by Harpers. The occasion was Mark Twain's departure for Italy, where the Clemenses hoped to restore Mrs. Clemens' health by moving permanently to Florence.

In a long and reflective letter from Howells to Clemens in Italy, Howells thanked his friend for his commendation of his December, 1903, "Easy Chair" about Bret Harte; commented on Twain's own contribution, "A Dog's Tale"; and recommended to him a book by Russell Wallace, *Man's Place in the Universe*, which had somewhat restored Howells' faith in the human race. "You ought to read that book; then you would not swear so much at your own species."[7] The two tragedies in store for Twain—the death of his wife in 1904 and of his daughter Jean in 1909—focused his thoughts on "man's place in the universe," in such a way, however, as to reinforce his most atheistical convictions.

Like Howells, Twain, too, sought to find himself by a backward glance at his own beginnings; in his home on Fifth Avenue and Tenth Street, where he moved after the death of his wife, he set to work in 1906 on his *Autobiography* with the assistance of Albert Bigelow Paine. Howells often visited him, resuming his talks of a lifetime in "an upper room" overlooking several New York backyards; and he frequently helped Twain to recall for his dictated memoirs episodes in which they had shared. But soon again the talks were interrupted, for early in 1908 the Howellses left for Italy and Clemens moved into "Stormfield," the mansion at Redding, Connecticut, designed for him by Howells' son John.

The association of these two friends of many years was drawing rapidly to a close. On Howells' return from abroad, he visited Clemens for one joyous weekend which proved to be their last together. Howells found a telegram from Paine, when he reached his own apartment very late on the night of Clemens' death. Next morning, April 22, he wrote to Twain's daughter that "suddenly your father was set apart from all other men in a strange majesty. Death has touched his familiar image, into historic grandeur." Howells realized that in losing Clemens he had lost much of his own western world. "You have lost a father," he added in his note to Clara. "Shall I dare tell you of the desolation of an old man who has lost a friend, and finds himself alone in the great world which has now wholly perished around [him]?"[8]

Though his wife was at this time in her final illness, Howells at once began writing the story of his friendship with Twain from the time in 1869 when Twain had stepped into the *Atlantic Monthly* office to their last weekend visit at "Stormfield" in March, 1909. In a little over a month after Twain's death, he wrote to Paine: "I have finished the 'memories,' and now that they are done they do not record Clemens as I had hoped. But they record my affection for him."[9]

"My Memories of Mark Twain" appeared in three installments between July and September, 1910, in *Harper's Monthly* and were immediately published as *My Mark Twain*, which also included Howells' reviews of Twain's work from 1869 to 1901. Written during a period of great personal grief—his wife had died two weeks after he had lost Clemens—these clear, calm, often humorous, always realistic descriptions of Howells' contacts with Mark Twain remain today the most varied and vivid glimpses of Twain's mercurial personality. In the last paragraph of *My Mark Twain*, Howells describes his old friend "lying in his coffin amid those flowers with which we garland our despair in that pitiless hour." He looked a moment at the face he knew so well and observed that "it was patient with the patience I had so often seen in it: something of puzzle, a great silent dignity, an assent to what must be from the depths of a nature whose tragical seriousness broke in the laughter which the unwise took for the whole of him" (100-1).

Not only the rapid composition of *My Mark Twain*—which is, indeed, also an autobiography of Howells—but the preparation of his own Library Edition, which he had begun in earnest in 1909, turned Howells' thoughts back to earlier scenes in Ohio, endowing them with a "retrospective vision" and a new perspective. To accompany the Library Edition, he wrote his brother Joseph on July 4, 1909, "I am going to write a literary autobiography, which will treat of the where, when and how of them all [his books]." He had already asked Aurelia to send him the weekly letters, covering a period of fifty years, which, he estimated, came to over 2,500 missives. When they arrived, Howells took a week to arrange them chronologically. "It is cruel hard looking over them, and like delving in the tombs. I wish I was young enough to make material, literary material, out of the experience, but I recognize every day this part of my life is over. Things suggest themselves, but they don't grip me, and hold me to them as they used."[10]

Though the Library Edition was discontinued after six volumes and the autobiographical prefaces Howells wrote for these are of minor interest, it is to be observed that all of the important books Howells wrote after this reliving of his literary past, were auto-biographical in nature, though several, such as *New Leaf Mills* and *The Leatherwood God,* were narrative in form. Both of these are clearly seen visions of an earlier Ohio, modified by his later view from the deck of a boat and perhaps by his talks with Mark Twain. *New Leaf Mills* is transparently autobiographical; Howells, after a summer of writing, calls it, indeed, "my Eureka story" in a letter to Joseph in which he urges his brother to recall "the smallest and most unimportant incidents" he could remember concerning "the *raising of our new house.*" Who was there? What did they say and do? "I believe father decided not to offer whiskey as a refreshment, and mother gave coffee instead."[11]

In *New Leaf Mills,* Ann and Owen Powell do not serve whiskey to their neighbors when they gather in the spring to help raise the roof of the new house, for this gentle, deeply cultivated, Swedenborgian pair mistrust the manners of the backwoodsmen among whom they have come to live. The day, however, is very jolly; and, after the beams are hoisted aloft, long tables of "victuals" are served to the sweating men by their sunbonneted womenfolk. Suddenly Owen observes that one of the beams has slipped its pin; a neighbor shouts laughingly that he would gladly climb up and secure the beam—"But I couldn't do it on no coffee." "Hain't you got a jug of corn juice around somewhere, Mrs. Powell?" At that moment the surly miller who, all through the year had resented the presence of the Powells in the neighbor-hood, comes reeling across the road carrying a black jug. Already half-drunk, he climbs to the roof, unmindful of the shouts below; he crazily clambers higher and higher until he reaches the dan-gling stud, which he fixes into place by repeated blows from the jug until it shatters and the miller comes lunging through the air.

On this episode, real or fictitious, turns the little tale of the

Powells' attempt to lead a quiet, laborious, but decent life among the "barbarians" of the Ohio frontier. The miller recovers but troubles accumulate, just as they did when the Howells family attempted to establish a paper-mill in the little settlement of Eureka when William Dean was a small boy. Though Powell, like Howells' father, dreamed of an ideal community where he might work as hard as his neighbors while reading Pope, Tom Paine, and Swedenborg aloud to his barefoot boys and girls around the fire in the evening, he was forced at last to retreat to the near-by town where his elder son had succeeded in renting a store. Here Powell held fast to his "fundamental principles of justice in politics," but confined his expression of them to aiding the escape of fugitive slaves. In spite of his wife's dislike of pigs grunting close to the chimney-piece, of winter winds whistling through the chinks of the cabin, of ignorant neighbors unmodified by school or church, Powell dreamed of Robert Owen's coopera- tive communities. Powell, like the elder Howells and William Dean himself, argued, though less strenuously than formerly, that "if some such conception of society could possess the entire State, a higher type of civilization would undoubtedly even- tuate" (154).

Though Clemens and Howells were familiar with similar pre- Civil War frontier conditions in country towns and woodland clearings, the former grew after the turn of the century increas- ingly scathing in his views of "the d---- human race"; Howells, however, never relinquished his dream of a society built on the Christian, socialistic principles instilled into him as a boy. When Howells was embodying these notions in *Through the Eye of the Needle*, Clemens was working on his fantasy, *The Mysterious Stranger*; both tales reflect the western boyhood experiences of two elderly members of the Human Race Luncheon Club. Over a very good dinner, served to the club on Howells' last visit at "Stormfield," these two old philosophers (the only members present) were able to enjoy "a roaring good time" together as they discussed the nature of man. Twain's atheistic views of God's relationship to man, he considered too strong for publication; no doubt they contributed to Howells' most searching study of the frontier, *The Leatherwood God* (1916).

Leatherwood Creek—a small community of tall corn, swampy creeks and primeval forest—is quietly pursuing its simple ways when it is visited around the first quarter of the nineteenth century by a tall stranger with an evangelical message, Joseph

Dylkes. Conceiving of himself first as a preacher, then as Christ, and finally as God himself, this miserable, long-haired, black-garbed scoundrel is finally able to divide the community into two warring factions, the Little Flock and the Herd of the Lost. The "Hounds," the community "Vigilantes," almost succeed in lynching the "God" who is reduced to cowering in the swamps before he is finally driven out of town.

Except for the fact that the figure of Dylkes is appalling in its gaunt fanaticism and cowardice, and the figure of the King in *Huckleberry Finn* is hilariously funny to the point of ribaldry, one might think the adventure at Leatherwood Creek was merely another chapter in Twain's tale of a backwoods community somewhere along the Mississippi. The character of Matthew Braile, a country lawyer locally known as "Squire," is Howells' own invention, however, and has no counterpart in Clemens' story. The Squire is a reader of Tom Paine, a sceptic, a humorist, and a believer in the right of every man to the protection of the law. Genially smoking his corncob pipe on the porch of his two-room cabin, Braile watches the world pass by on the dirt road beyond his white fence and makes up his own mind about the "Divinity" who has brought so much trouble to his simple neighbors. With jokes, common sense, courage, and a set of Blackstone, Braile manages to avert the miscarriage of justice and, at the same time, to rid the community of an impostor. In so doing, Braile reflects Howells' horror of religious frenzy, sexual aberrations, frontier lawlessness, and fanaticism of all kinds.

Though *The Leatherwood God* did not appear until 1916, Howells was at work on it as early as 1906 and before the appearance either of *Through the Eye of the Needle* or of *New Leaf Mills*. The story itself was based on Judge Taneyhill's account in the *Ohio Valley Series* of an actual occurrence in a frontier village; the vision of Ohio Howells had caught from the boat in 1902 gave substance to the tale. This story was still in his mind when he wrote again to his brother Joseph, February 24, 1907, suggesting another such trip in order to renew his sense of the backwoods. "Yes, I still hope to do *The Leatherwood God*," he wrote. "Perhaps by the time I get at it you will be settled near Salesville on the Ohio River, and we will visit the scene together. It is a great scheme, and I should like the notion of making it my last great novel."

In a sense, Howells succeeded in his hope, for into this novel, which one is tempted to call "great," he poured the homely feeling for the log cabin, the beauty of the night wind through ancient trees, the sounds of frogs and birds in swampy wilderness —and his fully matured belief in reason, human dignity, and the rights of man. Howells was, as he wrote his brother in this same letter, also at work on "a sequel to the Altrurian business," *The Eye of the Needle,* in which he expressed, in the form of a fantasy, his dream of the good society. While Altruria reflected the simplicity of rural America before the industrial era, it embodied the true spirit of a civilized culture, so lacking not only in nineteenth-century Leatherwood Creek, but in the country as a whole in the first quarter of the twentieth.

Though Howells never made his second trip down the Ohio River with Joseph, he did interrupt a busy summer at Kittery, a few months after writing to his brother, to take a hurried journey West with his wife and son. Back at Kittery once more Howells wrote on August 22 to Norton:

> Ten days ago my wife and I took up our fardels and went out by lake to Duluth, with John, who started there for his outing in Yellowstone Park. It has been a prodigious, a continental experience, from which we scantly escaped poisoning by the filthy water on the steamer; but having got home alive, we look back on the Northwest with wonder. It was as if we had never seen the world before. But it was the primitive world, with all the geologic agencies at work for the wine-owners and ship-owners. The *scale* was impressively vast. A carfull of coal was picked up, as if it might have been a cup, emptied into a ship, and set back on the rails as if nothing had happened. The beauty of the region is as great as its strength; but it is a savage beauty yet, with a sort of lust for civilization.[12]

The "savage beauty" of the area in which they were born and reared and what happened to it during the rapid industrialization of the post-Civil War days moved both Clemens and Howells to look retrospectively to the West that they had known. Their visions, reflected in their later writing, were widely different, but they drew them together so closely as friends that, after the death of Mark Twain, Howells was chosen as the one who should preside at the commemoration for Twain. Though it was "a terrible trial" to him, Carnegie Hall was crowded "from floor to roof with 3000 people, and a thousand left on the sidewalk, who didn't get in."[13]

Several years later, at his own seventy-fifth Anniversary Dinner in 1912, Howells referred to "a humorist," who, when he died, gave us a sense of "Shakespearean loss"; the soul of Mark Twain, he said, both humorous and tragic, had "divined and uttered the inmost and most immanent American mood" and had passed "lastingly into the American consciousness." Howells' own western-looking books—*New Leaf Mills* and *The Leatherwood God*—are also a part of "the American consciousness" in their recognition of the harshness, the crassness, and the fanaticism which have always marked the frontiersman. Association with Mark Twain during the last ten years of his life drew this complex of thought and feeling to the fore again, and it finally resulted in the clear-spirited interpretation of a westerner by a westerner, *My Mark Twain.* Howells' "western retrospect" was further sharpened by several journeys through the country he had known as a boy; and the ugly marks of industrialization along the familiar waterways caused him to question his own Altrurian dream of the 1890's and to remind him that the frontiersman's rapaciousness still characterized the twentieth-century industrialist. *New Leaf Mills* and *The Leatherwood God,* though retrospective, are also a comment upon American civilization as Howells saw it in his later years.

II "The American Howells"

Early in April, 1903, Charles Eliot Norton wrote to Howells asking permission to place his letters to Lowell in the Harvard library. Howells promptly consented: "Since Lowell thought them worth keeping, they may as well cumber those archives." Howells added that he could well imagine his "poor ghost flittering about the alcoves and taking a diaphanous, thin pride in the serious student's acceptance of them as proof that Lowell cared for me."[14]

Since the time Howells wrote this letter, his "poor ghost" has seen the arrival at this library of many packets of his letters to Norton, to James, and to hundreds of other friends and acquaintances. And the "serious student" is all too prone to find "proof," in Howells' correspondence of attitudes, ideas, and feelings which, though partially valid, require qualifications. An example of the ambiguity that surrounds all of Howells' important relationships may be found in his extensive correspondence with Henry James, only a small portion of which has been studied.

Because Howells and James were fellow craftsmen as well as devoted friends, their exchanges of views not only in letters but also in essays, conversations, comments in letters to others, and even in their prefaces and novels are of peculiar interest in defining their literary positions. James's judgment of Howells' power and his older friend's comments both on James and himself may be considered a guide to an appraisal of Howells' permanent "place" in American literature.

Perhaps because Norton was old and forgetful, perhaps because the letters themselves were written over thirty years earlier, he at this time sent Howells the James letters to himself, written in the early seventies, and containing a number of allusions to his younger friend. The letter of James which Howells singled out for comment in his reply to Norton is dated August 9, 1871, and reads:

> Howells is now monarch absolute of the Atlantic to the increase of his profit and comfort. His talent grows constantly in fineness but hardly, I think, in range of application. I remember your saying some time ago that in a couple of years when he had read Ste-Beuve etc. he would come to his best. But the trouble is he never will read Ste-Beuve, nor care to. He has little intellectual curiosity, so here he stands with his admirable organ of style, like a poor man holding a diamond wondering how he can wear it. It's rather sad I think. . . .[15]

When Howells read this yellowing letter in 1903, he was at the height of his own fame both in this country and abroad—and far more widely read than either Norton or James; he could, therefore, afford to survey the intervening years and pause to brood over the words of his younger colleague whose more brilliant gifts he had seized every opportunity to praise. Since Howells' comment to Norton gives us his most extensive self-appraisal of his own writing and also opens up the essential difference between Howells and James, we will quote the paragraph in full. "It was kind of you," wrote Howells, "to include James's early letter to yourself among those Miss Grace is sending me, and I won't pretend I have read them with less interest because of certain allusions to me in them." He continued, "In a way I think their criticism very just";

> I have often thought my intellectual raiment was more than my intellectual body, and that I might finally be convicted, not of having nothing *on*, but of that worse nakedness of having nothing

in. He speaks of me with my style, and such mean application as I was making of it, as seeming to him like a poor man with a diamond which he does not know what to do with; and mostly I suppose I *have* cut rather inferior window glass with it. But I am not sorry for having wrought in common, crude material so much; that is the right American stuff; and perhaps hereafter, when my din is done, if any one is curious to know what that noise was, it will be found to have proceeded from a small insect which was scraping about on the surface of our life and trying to get into its meaning for the sake of the other insects larger or smaller. That is, such has been my unconscious work; consciously, I was always, as I still am, trying to fashion a piece of literature out of the life next at hand.[16]

With this modest, but assertive, statement in mind, we turn to the essay by Howells entitled "Mr. Henry James's Later Work," which appeared in the *North American Review* of January, 1903. Norton himself, as former editor of that magazine, no doubt had read Howells' appraisal with interest and curiosity, for he had already expressed to Howells his serious misgivings as to the tendency of these "later works" of James.

The novel which Howells considers at length in this essay, *The Wings of a Dove,* brings him at once face to face with the fact that "it has been Mr. James's lot from the beginning to be matter of unusually lively dispute among his readers." This is especially true of his women readers, who, though fascinated by his presentation of themselves, have nevertheless always repudiated his insinuations. This "feminine enmity" Howells deals with by insisting that Milly Theale, like Daisy Miller, represents all that is "charming and honorable" in the American girl and that the surrounding corruption hinted at by James rather than described, is distinctly European. Milly is "New Yorkish" in the old, patrician, Knickerbocker sense; her "masses of money" were made for her by others, leaving her "the intellectual refinement" which comes from being "born and bred in conditions of illimitable ease."

Why, then, asks Howells, do American readers feel for James a certain "fascinated repugnance?" Is it because his later novels are placed before the reader as unresolved "conundrums?" But that is the very nature of life itself, says Howells, and hence of the best modern literature. Is it that James is insisting upon an inner corruption, a lurking evil which he never defines? That, too, is true to life itself, Howells insists; and James's novels are distinctly for "the mature reader" who has rights of his own. Why does James place his heroines in London, Paris, and Rome rather than in New York or Boston? Perhaps, writes Howells, the true reading of the riddle of James's use of the international scene is that such a character as Milly Theale "is most appreciable in that relief from the background which Europe gives all American character." Howells himself, one slowly realizes, was as baffled as his readers by the problem posed by his friend's expatriation.

James, for his part, continued to ponder the "limitations" of his prolific and successful fellow novelist. At the very time when Howells' appraisal of his later fiction was published in the *North American Review*, James's novel, *The Ambassadors*, was also appearing; and it was Howells himself, James tells us in his *Notebooks*, October 31, 1895,[17] who supplied him with "the germ" of his study of Strether. Through Jonathan Sturges, a mutual friend, James heard what Howells had said to him as he placed his hand on his shoulder and glanced about a lovely old garden in Paris: "Oh, you are young, you are young—be glad of it: be glad of it and *live*. Live all you can: it's a mistake not to. It doesn't so much matter what you do—but live. This place makes it all come over me. I see it now. I haven't done so—and now I'm old. It's too late. It has gone past me—I've lost it. You have time. You are young. Live!"

After completing *The Ambassadors* in the summer of 1901, James wrote to tell Howells of Sturges' report (*Notebook*, 228) of the "five words you said to him one day on his meeting you during a call at Whistler's." James had found the words "charming," he wrote; no doubt Howells himself had long since forgotten them, but they had "sprung" out of the *Notebook* four or five years after they had been spoken and had become "the faint, vague germ, the mere point of the start of a subject." Since the initials "W.D.H." were inscribed by the notation, James wished to assure his friend that the Strether in his novel had "got away from you or from anything like you!" Though the character of Strether as it is developed in two long volumes bears no relation to that of Howells, James's original notes on "the elderly man who hasn't 'lived,' hasn't at all, in the sense of sensations, passions, impulses, pleasures," gives the reader an insight into James's sense of Howells' narrow range which he had felt since his early letter to Norton. Here is a man, notes James, who has "never really enjoyed," who has lived "for pure appearances and daily tasks," who has never "battled with his passions" or been "harassed by his temperament"—or suspected, until too late, "what he was losing."[18]

James sent the "The Project" of *The Ambassadors* to *Harper's* just before the turn of the century and the reorganization of the magazine. Here the novel remained for several years until, with the urging of Howells, it was serialized in the *North American Review* early in 1903. If Howells recognized himself in the "American, distinguished and mature, who had been in Europe before, but comparatively little and very 'quietly,'" (*Notebook*, 373), he was at least not displeased by the picture. "I wonder if you are looking at James's *Ambassadors*?" he wrote to Norton in April of that year. "It is very good work."[19]

James's description through the character of Strether, of his "rather fatigued and alien compatriot, whose wholly, exclusively professional career had been a long, hard strain" was not unlike, indeed, the picture which Howells had drawn, many years earlier, of the hero of *Indian Summer*, Colville, who, in his turn, had glimpsed in Florence the refreshment of spirit which Europe offers the elderly, rather austere man of letters who has somehow failed to "live." James had, on more than one occasion, found that a novel by Howells offered him a suggestion for one of his own.

Conscious, through many years of intercourse, of a certain kinship—and difference—in their approach to the international theme, Howells in 1885 playfully inserted in Chapter XIV of *Indian Summer* a passing allusion to his younger colleague. Seated at the end of a summer afternoon in a beautiful Florentine garden, one of the "characters" suggests that they might seem to a passerby to be people in a novel. Colville takes up the idea at once. " 'Oh, call us a passage from a modern novel, if you're in the romantic mood. One of Mr. James's.' " A member of the group objects: " 'Don't you think we ought to be rather more of the great world for that? I hardly feel up to Mr. James. I should have said Howells. Only nothing happens in that case!' " Colville responds, seizing the opportunity to escape from the others with the charming young heroine: " 'Oh, very well; that's the most comfortable way. If it's only Howells, there's no reason why I shouldn't go with Miss Graham to show her the view of Florence from the cypress grove up yonder.' " The elderly chaperon, Mrs. Amsden, gives her consent: " 'No; he's very particular when he's on Italian ground.' " Then rising from the bench, she leaves Colville and Miss Graham to their own devices since they had decided that they were not in a "romantic" James novel but only in a "comfortable" one by Howells. With ample opportunity to succumb not only to the lures of Miss Graham but to the more seductive charms of Europe, Colville— like his author—soon discovered (90) that, as a matter of fact, "it was the problems of the vast, tumultuous American life, which he had turned his back on, that really concerned him," rather than a love affair with Miss Graham. Howells and James, as novelists and friends, played in and out of each others' minds.

The long and appreciative letter which James wrote to Howells on the occasion of his seventy-fifth Birthday Dinner, subtly sustains the unresolved argument between the two as to the American versus the international novel. "Having myself to practice meaner economies," writes James, "I have admired, from period to period, your so ample and liberal flow; wondered at your secret for doing positively a little—what do I say a little? I mean a magnificent deal!—of Everything."[20] James's seeming hesitation as to whether Howells, in over fifty years of writing, had only succeeded in doing "a little of everything," reflected the reservation he had always felt for his less far-ranging friend, who had, nevertheless, captured public approval as James had not. "Just by remaining at your post," he continued, hastily making amends, "you have piled up your monument."

"The monument" James admires is that remarked upon many years earlier by T. S. Perry, James Russell Lowell, Henry Adams, and others. It is built by Howells' "documentary" novels which reflect the minutest detail of American life in the late nineteenth and the early twentieth centuries—the very color of the bonnet-ribbons and hats, as well as every shade of feeling and thought of changing eras. Howells had the advantage over James, the latter admits, of "breathing an air that has suited and nourished" him. Lured though he was from time to time by the European scene, Howells remained faithful to the American setting. "The *real* affair of the American case and character, as it met your view and brushed your sensibility, that was what inspired and attached you, and, heedless of foolish flurries from other quarters, of all wild or weak slashings of the air and wavings in the void, you gave yourself to it with an incorruptible faith." While James himself roamed further afield in quest of larger prizes, Howells settled for the "home-grown humanity" under his eyes. "You saw your field with a rare lucidity," notes James with perhaps a touch of irony; "you saw all it had to give in the way of the romance of the real and the interest and the thrill and the charm of the common."[21] As evidence of Howells' "lighter-fingered prelude," James lists *A Foregone Conclusion, The Undiscovered Country, The Lady of the Aroostook,* and *The Minister's Charge*; these novels paved the way for *A Modern Instance, The Rise of Silas Lapham, A Hazard of New Fortunes, The Landlord at Lion's Head,* and *The Kentons,* "that perfectly classic illustration of your spirit and form." Thus, "stroke by stroke and book by book," Howells built up his own "monument" which, to James, in his generous summation, appears to be an "exquisite notation of our whole democratic light and shade and give and take, in the highest degree *documentary*."[22] No other writer can approach Howells in "value and amplitude" nor in "essential distinction."

Howells wrote to James, as soon as the "divine madness" of the Birthday Dinner had subsided, to thank him for the letter "so fully, so beautifully kind," which he says, would help mitigate "those dreadful moments of self-blame"[23] haunting his sleepless nights. The tribute was not read at the banquet but was, instead, published first in *Harper's Weekly* and then reprinted in the *North American Review.* James, for his part, was disappointed that the letter was not read aloud: "I confess," James wrote to Howells, "I am sorry that the letter I contributed was not read out—as it was particularly and altogether 'built' to be; I wanted to testify publicly to you and to be thereby present or participant."[24]

Howells and James seldom actually met again after this final public acclaim of Howells' position in American literature. Howells himself bought a house at York Harbor during the summer of 1912, not caring to stay at Kittery Point after the death of his wife. Here he read aloud to his daughter, James's essay, "Mr. and Mrs. J. T. Fields," and wrote at once to thank the author for the "kind mentions" he made of him. Not only did James's paper rekindle "so many old faded fires," but it also prompted Howells to comment sadly upon the fact that "a change has passed upon things," with the result that "I could not 'serialize' a story of mine now in any American magazine, thousands of them as they are." Howells added, "I am comparatively a dead cult with my statues cut down and the grass growing over them in the pale moonlight."[25]

"Dead cult" though Howells, half humorously, felt himself to be when he wrote to James on June 29, 1915, it was to the editor of the "Easy Chair" that *Harper's* turned for comment when James died in England eight months later. Because Howells had found the right words to say of Mark Twain in 1910, *Harper's* hoped he might from the depth of his memories summarize his personal and critical views of the other—and opposite—great figure of our literature. However, *Harper's* failed to meet Howells' terms, and the plan was abandoned—to Howells' relief, his daughter reports, "as he was old and tired, and dwelling on the past was painful to him."[26]

That James continued to haunt Howells' mind is attested by the fact that he wrote the introduction to an edition of *Daisy Miller* in 1918; that he included him in his compilation of *The Great American Short Stories*, which appeared with "A Reminiscent Introduction," several months after Howells' own death; that one of the last "Easy Chair" contributions he ever wrote was a review of Percy Lubbock's edition of *The Letters of Henry James* (1920); and that he left unfinished at his death an essay entitled "The American James." Though Howells lamented that James had become "The English James" when he gave up his American citizenship in 1915, he nevertheless staunchly defended his right to do so: "I am just thinking of becoming a citizen of Maine,"[27] Howells joked to Brander Matthews at the time; and he insisted that "in the course of his long life in England [James] did not grow less American."[28] Perhaps Howells suggested the inscription one finds carved over the grave of Henry James: "Henry James, O.M./Novelist, Citizen/of Two Countries/Interpreter of His/Generation on Both/Sides of the Sea."

Glancing backward to the old Cambridge days, to his early meeting with Henry James, and to the time when he himself was "beginning to study our American life," reminded Howells, perhaps, of the "idyl of the middle eighteen seventies," *The Vacation of the Kelwyns*, which he had begun to write more than ten years earlier, calling it, at that time, *The Children of the Summer*. It was just the sort of reminiscent picture that James and Norton particularly enjoyed. "I have worked at odd times during the winter," Howells wrote Norton April 15, 1907, "on a longish, slowish sort of New England idyl which I call *The Children of the Summer*. Since I left off working at it the thing has taken reasoned shape in my mind, and I fancy your liking it."

Howells was less sure that his aging confidant would like

the second manuscript on which he was working at the same time, *Through the Eye of the Needle*. While *The Children of the Summer* was taking "reasoned shape" in his mind, he casually remarked to Norton, "in the midst of all, I have given my own dream of Utopia, which I fancy your not liking . . . I call the thing *Through the Eye of the Needle*, and it is to be published soon."[29] The book, made up in large part of essays which had appeared in various publications during the 1890's, came out only three days after Howells' letter was written; and he was in no doubt as to Norton's views of his "socialistic" tendencies, for he and Norton had clashed over their social ideas during their many years of friendly communication. The "New England idyl," in which Howells tests out these same social concepts—this time in a New Hampshire hotel instead of in Altruria—Norton could never have seen; *The Vacation of the Kelwyns* only appeared after the death of its author and of Norton.

James found Howells' early novels "the more attaching . . . for their referring themselves to a time and an order when we knew together what American life *was*—or thought we did, deluded though we may have been!" In his last "languid idyl," *The Vacation of the Kelwyns*, Howells returned to the time and place of these first ventures into fiction—to the New England he knew in the 1870's. With the brooding insight of his later years, however, he sees in the Kelwyn's quest for rural rest and peace an illustration of his own mistrust of achieving an earthly paradise, based on "altruism." The very opening sentence of this perfectly paced tale takes us into the ironic realism of Howells at his best, and at the same time reminds us of Jane Austen's introduction of the Bennett family in *Pride and Prejudice*. In calmly judicious words, Howells begins: "Kelwyn's salary as a lecturer in the post graduate courses would not have been enough for his family to live on; but his wife had some money of her own, and this with his salary enabled them to maintain themselves upon the scale of refined frugality which was the rule in the university town, and to indulge, now and then, a guarded hospitality."

When the Kelwyns, with their two little boys, were at last uncomfortably established in a large Shaker farmhouse in New Hampshire, various problems of human society unexpectedly presented themselves to this lecturer in Historical Sociology, who had never before thought of "applying his science to his own life or conduct." The Shaker community itself represented an "ideal community"; however, it was obviously too ideal to survive, and only a few elderly Shakers now occupied the empty houses. The Kites, engaged by the Shakers to clean and cook, garden and drive the old carriage for the Kelwyns, proved to be lazy, ignorant, somewhat arrogant, and yet, in their way, happy with each other. Should the Kelwyns, who suffered from Mrs. Kite's strong tea and heavy biscuits, turn out their inefficient helpers? And, indeed, *could* they? On what terms were the helplessly stranded pair to accept the visiting school teacher who called himself a "workman," but seemed, in speech and bearing, to be a "gentleman?" Should one permit the teacher, Emerance (*Emerson and eminence* combined, perhaps), to instruct Mrs. Kite in cooking, and then should one finally admit this obviously superior-inferior human being into the family and sanction his proposal of marriage to Mrs. Kelwyn's own niece? All these questions involving class, work, property, manners, education, religion, are "resolved" in the half-humorously, half-ironically conceived sylvan love scenes with which the novel ends.

Through the Eye of the Needle, the "romance" on which Howells was working in the spring of 1907 when he began the novel, *The Children of the Summer,* gives us, in rather abstract terms, Howells' philosophical convictions on the questions raised by the novel. Both books are studies of the problems presented to "human nature" by an attempt to live in ideal communities; both express Howells' hope, mingled with his misgivings, that "altruism" might eventually prove stronger than "selfishness." *The Vacation of the Kelwyns* (as the novel was finally named when it was published after Howells' death) would certainly have proved more acceptable both to Norton and to James, for in this "summer idyl" Howells returned in his imagination to the scenes of the 1870's, well remembered by these three friends. He viewed these familiar settings with the wisdom and the humorous sadness of his latter days.

Though Howells and James continued to correspond until the death of the latter in 1916, the very last account we have of their meeting is to be found in a long, unpublished letter which Howells addressed to Norton on July 16, 1908. Howells wrote from Kittery Point and attempted to touch on the high points of the year in Rome, Naples, Paris, and London. "We had three weeks in Paris, where I drove every day in the Bois with my dear old Perry, and talked and talked. H. James was there visiting our sister-novelist, Mrs. Wharton, and again he was in London during our four weeks, and I saw him never too often. He is older and sadder and sweeter, and we conversed of many things of the past, with one long, dear walk through the Park well into Kensington."[30] Thus these friends parted; Howells and James ended where they had begun, walking the streets and strolling through parks, endlessly searching for "the key to our rich and inexhaustible mystery," the writing of fiction "in the modern vein."

Howells survived James by four years. Old and tired though he was, he remained to the end remarkably productive. Living for a part of the year at York Harbor, returning in the autumn to New York, and journeying to the South to seek warmth in the spring, Howells wrote stories, sketches, letters to the newspapers; more important still, he retained among the younger writers his host of friends, who continued to seek him out for counsel. He died in his New York apartment a little after midnight on the morning of May 11, 1920.

Howells' funeral took place on May 12, 1920, from the Church of the Ascension, New York; Hamlin Garland sat with some eight or ten members of the Academy of which Howells was still president at the time of his death. "The pews were filled with those who knew and loved Howells; and as I stood looking down at the casket, I found it difficult to believe that it contained his body. It was so small—and his fame so great." Garland voiced the experience of hosts of young writers of his day when he noted in his *Literary Log*: "When I went to him for advice he gave it in a few lines, sometimes in a single sentence. He never talked at random, never felt about for a word. Often he aided my decisions by two words—'Why not?' . . . For several years after his death I often dreamed of sitting with him in his library, discussing books and men just as we used to do in life."[31]

Howells was cremated and his ashes buried in the Cambridge Cemetery, Cambridge, Massachusetts, on a ridge overlooking the Charles River, between the graves of his wife and his daughter Winifred, and not far from the grave of Henry James.

James remained essentially romantic, drawing his sustenance from the soil of Europe; Howells, also romantic, or, at least, poetic at heart, was at the same time more of a classicist, with "a feeling for the human relation, as the social climate of our country qualifies, intensifies, generally conditions and colours it."

For him, the material close at hand, "the American stuff," was sufficient for a lifetime of novel-writing.

Howells, in his belief in America, "common" and "crude" though it was, as the setting for his "realistic" novels, believed that this country supplied a bountiful sufficiency for younger writers as well. From Henry James to Mark Twain, from Hamlin Garland to the youthful Theodore Dreiser, Howells listened to, encouraged, and admonished writers for over fifty years. At the same time, he maintained the perfect integrity of his own lucid, ironic, casual prose. This "diamond," his "admirable organ of style," which James had thought he might never learn to wear, Howells had made excellent use of in the course of his long and varied career. The "poor man" became a rich man by remaining sensitively aware of the American character and the American condition before World War I. By recording his observations in stories, novels, plays, and essays, Howells formed a library of suggestive material for later writers such as Theodore Dreiser, Sinclair Lewis, J. P. Marquand, and even Ernest Hemingway. As late as 1916, Howells was engaged in writing his "next novel," to be called *The Home-Towners*. It is these same "home-towners" whom writers after Howells have continued to discuss in novels which in their turn have now become "classics"—*Main Street, An American Tragedy, The Late George Apley,* and *In Our Time.* They, too, belong to the great tradition of American writers who tried to "tell the truth" about ordinary people in the language and circumstances of their times. Howells, during his life and after his death, has been misunderstood all too frequently by writers seeking to define their "new" creeds of realism. But, as James reminds us, "The critical intelligence . . . has not at all begun to render you its tribute."[32]

The "tribute" which the "critical intelligence" of today renders Howells must be based on an understanding of what the term "realism" meant in the last quarter of the nineteenth century, and on Howells' individual expression of this "new way of writing" in over forty novels. Like Turgenev, Howells fell heir to the scientific thought of the mid-century which found that the microscope and the camera suggested a range of material beyond the horizon of the older novelists. Like the impressionistic painters of the same period, Howells perceived that "reality" is not limited to the accumulation of photographic detail, but varies according to the light in which it is seen. Hence, Howells felt the psychological implication of realism, and depended for his effects not on intricate plots, but rather on establishing the "point of view" of the beholder, usually through dialogue. Tolstoy awakened Howells to the possible depth of experience into which a novelist might reach; by temperament and by literary tradition, however, Howells belonged to the objective, the classical school of Goldsmith and Jane Austen. To this more detached, more lucid critical realism he constantly returned in his own writing after experiments on "broader" canvases. Subscribing, as he did, to the realism which implies choice in material, Howells withstood the naturalism of Zola, to which many younger writers succumbed, for, as he frequently noted in the "Editor's Study," Zola was merely "romantic" in his use of crowded pictures of human misery. True "romance," Howells felt, was to be found in the tales of Hawthorne, where fantasy was combined with psychological insight into character.

Fortunately, Howells was a critic as well as a novelist, and was able to justify his own habits as a writer of fiction by discerning statements of his literary "creed." To Howells, ordinary men and women, caught in the "complicity" of their human relationships, and pursuing their apparently dull ways, were in "the light of democracy" the real heroes and heroines who should be the concern of the novelist. Romance, humor, a sense of poetry, and idealism, seemed to Howells as much a part of the experience of these "commonplace" people as tragedy, disease, ignorance, and selfishness. Since the novelist is essentially the moralist, he must keep his values clear, Howells thought, though the means by which he elucidates them should never be dogmatic; plot, character, and dialogue speak without the help of further words from the author. Howells clearly saw before him his literary program when, in 1872, he published his first novel, *Their Wedding Journey,* and he decided at that time to make use of the "common, crude" material of his own experience. From this simple beginning Howells' novels developed in range and complexity, from *A Chance Acquaintance* to *A Hazard of New Fortunes.* He became, according to Hippolyte Taine, "a precious painter and sovereign witness" of his age.

One of the ironies of our literary evolution in this country is that since World War I, and even earlier, the term "realism" has become associated with violence, crime, and ruthlessness. Howells himself at the turn of the century saw the movement coming; he called it "sensationalism" and considered it merely another form of the old, beaten-up rag-baby, "romanticism."

Notes and References

Chapter One

1. *Years of My Youth*, pp. 124-39.
2. *Ibid.*, p. 141.
3. *Ibid.*, pp. 142-44.
4. *Ibid.*, pp. 161-62.
5. *Ibid.*, p. 148.
6. *Ibid.*, pp. 154-59.
7. *Ibid.*, p. 227.
8. *Life of Abraham Lincoln* (1860), pp. 51-52.
9. *Years of My Youth*, p. 202.
10. *Ibid.*, pp. 193-94.
11. *Literary Friends and Acquaintance*, p. 15.
12. *Ibid.*, p. 24.
13. *Ibid.*, pp. 26-27.
14. *Ibid.*, p. 28.
15. *Ibid.*, pp. 37-38.
16. *Ibid.*, pp. 39-40.
17. *Ibid.*, pp. 44-45.
18. *Ibid.*, p. 48.
19. *Ibid.*, pp. 51-57.
20. *Ibid.*, pp. 59-60.
21. *Ibid.*, pp. 60-65.
22. *Ibid.*, pp. 65-66.
23. *Years of My Youth*, pp. 212-15.
24. I, 309.
25. *Years of My Youth*, pp. 232-34.
26. *Ibid.*, p. 234.
27. *Literary Friends and Acquaintance*, p. 81.
28. *The Life in Letters of William Dean Howells* (2 vols,), ed. by Mildred Howells (1928), I, 70.
29. *Ibid.*, I, 85.

Chapter Two

1. *Literary Friends and Acquaintance*, pp. 103-4.
2. *Ibid.*, p. 111.
3. *Ibid.*, p. 112.
4. *Ibid.*, p. 182.
5. *Ibid.*, p. 184.
6. *Life in Letters*, I, 112.
7. *Literary Friends and Acquaintance*, pp. 212-27.

8. *Life in Letters,* II, 397.

9. *Ibid.,* I, 144.

10. *Literary Friends and Acquaintance,* p. 117.

11. *Life in Letters,* I, 146-47.

12. *Ibid.,* p. 150.

13. *Literary Friends and Acquaintance,* pp. 138-39.

14. *Life in Letters,* I, 139.

15. Manuscript letter, Ohio State Historical Society, Columbus, Ohio.

16. *Life in Letters,* I, 160-61.

17. *The Letters of John Fiske* (1940), ed. by Ethel F. Fiske, p. 200.

18. *Life in Letters,* I, 159.

19. "Recollections of an Atlantic Editorship," *Atlantic Monthly,* C (Nov., 1907), 594-606.

20. *Life in Letters,* I, 294.

21. *The Letters of Henry James* (1920), ed. by Percy Lubbeck, I, 30.

22. Manuscript letter, Ohio State Historical Society, Columbus, Ohio, March 31, 1871.

23. Quoted by Dorothy Dudley, *Forgotten Frontiers* (1932), p. 197.

24. *Life in Letters,* I, 162.

25. Written on the back of a photograph of Howells. Unsigned and undated. Print Room, New York Public Library.

26. *Life in Letters,* I, 171.

27. *Ibid.,* I, 180.

28. *Ibid.,* pp. 174-75.

29. Virginia Harlow, "William Dean Howells and Thomas Sergeant Perry," *The Boston Public Library Quarterly,* October, 1949, p. 135.

30. *Life in Letters,* I, 175.

31. *Letters of Henry James,* I, 34.

32. *Life in Letters,* I, 181.

33. *Letters of Henry James,* I, 30-31.

34. Manuscript letter, Houghton Library, Harvard. Quoted by Leon Edel, *Henry James: The Untried Years* (1953), p. 273.

35. *Life in Letters,* I, 170.

36. *My Literary Passions,* p. 229.

37. *Ibid.,* p. 230.

38. *North American Review,* CXCVI (July, 1912), 101.

39. *Life in Letters,* I, 192.

40. *Dimitri Roudine* (1873), p. 87.

41. *Harper's Weekly,* XXX (June 19, 1886), 394-95.

42. *Life in Letters,* I, 232.

43. *My Literary Passions,* pp. 231-32.

44. Letters from Howells to James R. Osgood, February 18, 1881. Cited in Introduction to *A Modern Instance* (1957), p. vii.

45. Abraham Cahan, *Bletter Fun Mein Leben* (1926), Vol. IV, Ch. I, Pt. 4.

Chapter Three

1. *My Mark Twain,* p. 15.
2. *Ibid.,* pp. 6-7.
3. Howells to Thomas Bailey Aldrich, December 8, 1901. Quoted by Henry Nash Smith and William M. Gibson, *Mark Twain-Howells Letters* (1960), I, 3.
4. *My Mark Twain,* pp. 9-10.
5. *Ibid.,* p. 19.
6. *Harper's Monthly,* CXXI (July-September, 1910).
7. *Life in Letters,* I, 191.
8. *Ibid.,* I, 194-95.
9. *Atlantic Monthly,* XXXVI (December, 1875), 750.
10. *My Mark Twain,* p. 124.
11. *Life in Letters,* I, p. 207.
12. *My Mark Twain,* p. 48.
13. *Life in Letters,* I, 212.
14. *Mark Twain-Howells Letters, op. cit.,* I, 112.
15. *Ibid.,* p. 121.
16. *Life in Letters,* pp. 208-9.
17. *Mark Twain-Howells Letters,* I, 113.
18. *The Complete Plays of W. D. Howells,* ed. by Walter J. Meserve (1960), p. 70.
19. *Life in Letters,* I, 294.
20. *Ibid.,* pp. 295-96.
21. *My Literary Passions,* p. 241.
22. *Life in Letters,* I, 315-16.
23. Manuscript note, Houghton Library, Harvard.
24. *Life in Letters,* I, 318.
25. *Ibid.,* p. 325.
26. Meserve, *op. cit.,* p. 207.
27. Albert Biglow Paine, *Mark Twain: A Biography* (1912), II, 762.
28. *Life in Letters,* I, 363-64.
29. Paine, *op. cit.,* II, 98.
30. *Life in Letters,* I, 366.
31. *Life in Letters,* I, 361.
32. *Ibid.,* p. 387.
33. "Mr. Howells's Paper," *The House of Harper,* J. Henry Harper, 1912, p. 320.
34. *The Diary and Letters of Rutherford B. Hayes,* ed. by Charles Richard Williams (1924), IV, 435.
35. *Life in Letters,* I, 419.
36. For a full account of Howells' letter to F. F. Brown, see John

W. Ward, "Another Howells Anarchist Letter," *American Literature,* XXII (January, 1951) 489-90.

37. *Life in Letters,* I, 402-4. See Joseph E. Gary, "The Chicago Anarchists of 1886: The Crime, the Trial, and the Punishment," *Century Magazine* XLV (April, 1893), 803-37.

38. *Ibid.,* p. 404-5.

39. *Ibid.,* p. 404.

40. *Ibid.,* p. 416.

41. *Ibid.,* p. 372.

42. *Ibid.,* p. 408.

43. *Harper's Magazine,* LXXV (July, 1887), 316.

44. *Life in Letters,* I, 417.

45. *Ibid.,* I, 413.

46. "Bibliographical," Library Edition (1907), p. vi.

47. *Ibid.,* pp. vii-ix.

48. "Mr. Howells's Paper," *op. cit.,* p. 321.

49. *Criticism and Fiction and Other Essays by W. D. Howells,* ed. by Clara M. Kirk and Rudolf Kirk (1959), pp. 47-48.

50. *Letters of an Altrurian Traveller,* ed. by Clara M. Kirk and Rudolf Kirk (1961). "Traveler" was spelled with a single "l" when used in the title of the book; it was spelled with a double "l" when the essays appeared in the magazine.

Chapter Four

1. *Life in Letters,* I, 371.

2. For an account of Howells' relation to this movement, see "Howells and the Church of the Carpenter," Clara and Rudolf Kirk. *The New England Quarterly,* XXXII (June, 1959), 185-206.

3. *My Literary Passions,* p. 251.

4. *Life in Letters,* II, 25.

5. *Ibid.,* p. 26.

6. *Ibid.,* II, 27.

7. *Ibid.,* II, 57.

8. "A Posthumous Pilgrimage," *The Boston Evening Transcript* (May 22, 1920), pp. 4-5.

9. *The Spectator* (January 2, 1904), pp. 16-17.

10. Manuscript letter, Houghton Library, Harvard.

11. *The Life and Letters of Sir Edmund Gosse,* by Evan Charteris (1931), p. 155.

12. *Life in Letters,* I, 230.

13. *Ibid.,* pp. 232-33.

14. *Literature* N.S., No. 12 (March 31, 1899), p. 266.

15. *Harper's Weekly* (April 27, 1895), p. 390.

16. "Henrik Ibsen," *North American Review,* CLXXXIII (July, 1906), 10.

17. *Life in Letters*, II, 94.
18. *Ibid.*, p. 96.
19. *Ibid.*, pp. 82-83.
20. *Life in Letters*, II, 97.
21. "Mr. Howells's Paper," *op. cit.*, p. 324.
22. *Life in Letters*, II, 119-21.

Chapter Five

1. *Life in Letters*, II, 117.
2. *Ibid.*, p. 127.
3. "Mr. Howells's Paper," *op. cit.*, p. 324.
4. *Life in Letters*, II, 121.
5. *Ibid.*
6. *Ibid.*, p. 117.
7. *Ibid.*, p. 137.
8. *Ibid.*, p. 129.
9. "Howells's Paper," *op. cit.*, p. 324.
10. *Ibid.*, pp. 324-25.
11. *Life in Letters*, II, 137-38.
12. *Ibid.*, p. 144.
13. Manuscript letter, Houghton Library, Harvard.
14. *Tit-bits*, May 1, 1886. Copied from a portrait of Howells painted by L. P. Vinton in 1881.
15. Quoted from the *Grinnell Herald*, by Harrison T. Meserole, "The Dean in Person: Howells' Lecture Tour," *The Western Humanities Review* (Autumn, 1956), p. 342.
16. *Life in Letters*, II, 127.
17. Hunt Cook, "The Wanton Cruelty of Mr. Howells," *Chap-book*, Jan. 1, 1898.
18. *Life in Letters*, II, 144.
19. *Ibid.*, p. 151.
20. *North American Review*, CLVI (January, 1903), pp. 126-27.
21. *Life in Letters*, II, 79.
22. "Mr. Howells's Paper," *op. cit.*, p. 326.
23. *Life in Letters*, II, 186.
24. *Ibid.*, p. 190.
25. *Ibid.*, p. 192.
26. *Ibid.*, p. 193.
27. *Ibid.*, pp. 197-98.
28. *Ibid.*, p. 201.
29. *Ibid.*, p. 205.
30. *Ibid.*, p. 213.
31. Manuscript letter, Houghton Library, Harvard.
32. *Life in Letters*, II, 208.
33. Manuscript letter, Houghton Library, Harvard.

34. *Life in Letters*, II, 210-11.
35. *Ibid.*, p. 211.
36. Manuscript letter, Houghton Library, Harvard.
37. *Life in Letters*, II, 245.
38. Manuscript letter, Houghton Library, Harvard.
39. *Life in Letters*, II, 285.
40. *Ibid.*, p. 333.

Chapter Six

1. *Life in Letters*, II, 138.
2. Included in *My Mark Twain* (1910).
3. *Life in Letters*, II, 142.
4. *Ibid.*, p. 154.
5. *Ibid.*, pp. 158-59.
6. Manuscript letter, Houghton Library, Harvard.
7. *Life in Letters*, II, 179.
8. Clara Clemens, *My Father: Mark Twain* (1931) p. 291.
9. *Ibid.*, pp. 283-84.
10. *Ibid.*, pp. 267-68.
11. *Ibid.*, p. 290.
12. Manuscript letter, Houghton Library, Harvard.
13. *Life in Letters*, II, 290.
14. *Ibid.*, II, 172.
15. Manuscript letter, Houghton Library, Harvard. Quoted by Edel, *op. cit.*, p. 276. Permission to quote kindly granted by Professor Edel.
16. *Life in Letters*, II, 172-73.
17. *The Notebooks of Henry James*, ed. by F. O. Mattheissen and Kenneth Murdock (1927).
18. *Ibid.*, p. 228.
19. *Life in Letters*, II, 171.
20. *The Letters of Henry James*, II, 223.
21. *Ibid.*, p. 224.
22. *Ibid.*, p. 225.
23. *Life in Letters*, II, 316.
24. *Ibid.*, p. 319.
25. *Ibid.*, pp. 349-50.
26. *Ibid.*, p. 355.
27. *Ibid.*, p. 352.
28. *Ibid.*, p. 396.
29. *Ibid.*, p. 242.
30. Manuscript letter, Houghton Library, Harvard.
31. *My Friendly Contemporaries; A Literary Log* (1932), pp. 295-96.
32. *The Letters of Henry James*, II, 226.

Selected Bibliography

PRIMARY SOURCES

1. *Critical Texts*

Complete Plays. Ed. by Walter J. Meserve. New York: New York University Press, 1960.

Criticism and Fiction and Other Essays by W. D. Howells. Ed., by Clara Marburg Kirk and Rudolf Kirk. New York, 1959.

Discovery of a Genius: William Dean Howells and Henry James. Ed. by Albert Mordell. Introduction by Sylvia E. Bowman. New York, 1961.

A Hazard of New Fortunes. New Introduction by George Warren Arms. New York and London: E. P. Dutton and Co., 1952.

"Howells's Unpublished Prefaces." Ed. George Arms. *New England Quarterly,* XVII (December, 1944), 580-91.

Indian Summer. Ed., introduction and notes by William M. Gibson. New York: Houghton Mifflin Co., 1957.

Letters of An Altrurian Traveller (1893-94). Introduction by Clara and Rudolf Kirk. Gainesville, Florida, 1961.

Life in Letters. Ed. Mildred Howells. Garden City, New York: Doubleday, Doran, and Co., 1928.

Life of Abraham Lincoln. Indiana University Press, 1960.

Mark Twain-Howells Letters. Eds. Henry Nash Smith and William M. Gibson. 2 vols. Cambridge, Massachusetts: Belknap Press of Harvard University Press, 1960.

A Modern Instance. Ed., introduction and notes by William M. Gibson. Boston: Houghton Mifflin Co., 1957.

Prefaces to Contemporaries (1882-1920). Ed. by George Arms, William M. Gibson, Frederic C. Marston, Jr. Gainesville, Florida: Scholars Facsimiles and Reprints, 1957.

Representative Selections. Introduction, bibliography, and notes by Clara Marburg Kirk and Rudolf Kirk. New York, 1950. Reprinted. New York: Hill and Wang, 1961.

The Rise of Silas Lapham. Ed., introduction by George Arms. New York: Rinehart and Co., 1949.

————. Ed., introduction by Edwin H. Cady. Boston, 1957.

————. Introduction by Clara and Rudolf Kirk. New York, 1962.

The Shadow of a Dream and *An Imperative Duty.* Ed., introduction by Edwin Cady. Twayne's United States Classics Series, ed. S. E. Bowman. New York: Twayne Publishers, Inc., 1961.

A Traveler From Altruria. Introduction by Howard Mumford Jones. New York: Sagamore Press, 1957.

2. *Bibliographies*

GIBSON, WILLIAM M. and ARMS, GEORGE. *A Bibliography of William Dean Howells.* New York: New York Public Library, 1948.

KIRK, CLARA M., and KIRK, RUDOLF. *William Dean Howells, Representative Selections, with Introduction, Bibliography, and Notes.* New York: American Book Company, 1950. George Arms and William M. Gibson prepared the "Selected Bibliography" for this book, which was reprinted in 1961 with a revised bibliography.

————. *The Howells Sentinel,* published from time to time since 1951; five numbers have appeared. George Arms and William M. Gibson have prepared current bibliographies.

REEVES, JOHN K. "The Literary Manuscripts of W. D. Howells, A Descriptive Finding List." *Bulletin of the New York Public Library,* LXII (June and July, 1958), 267-78, 350-63.

SECONDARY SOURCES

BENNETT, GEORGE N. *William Dean Howells, The Development of a Novelist.* University of Oklahoma Press, 1959.

CADY, EDWIN H. *The Road to Realism.* Syracuse Univ. Press, 1956.

————. *The Realist at War.* Syracuse University Press, 1958.

CARTER, EVERETT. *Howells and the Age of Realism.* Philadelphia and New York: J. B. Lippincott Co., 1954.

CLARK, HARRY HAYDEN. "The Role of Science in the Thought of W. D. Howells," *Transactions of the Wisconsin Academy of Sciences, Arts and Letters,* XLII (1953), 263-303.

COOKE, DELMAR GROSS. *William Dean Howells, A Critical Study.* New York: E. P. Dutton and Co., 1922.

FIRKINS, OSCAR W. *William Dean Howells, A Study.* Cambridge: Harvard University Press, 1924.

FRYCKSTEDT, OLOV W. *In Quest of America, A Study of Howells' Early Development as a Novelist.* Harvard Univ. Press, 1958.

HARVEY, ALEXANDER. *William Dean Howells, A Study of the Achievement of a Literary Artist.* New York: B. W. Huebsch, 1917.

HOUGH, ROBERT L. *The Quiet Rebel, William Dean Howells as Social Commentater.* University of Nebraska Press, 1959.

KIRK, CLARA M. *W. D. Howells, Traveler From Altruria.* New Brunswick, N.J.: Rutgers University Press, 1962.

WOODRESS, JAMES L. JR. *Howells & Italy.* Durham, North Carolina: Duke University Press, 1952.

Index